THE FACE
OF GOD
AMONG US

for my dear friend Eddie

much love,

John

THE FACE OF GOD AMONG US

How The Creator Educates Humanity

By John S. Hatcher

Bahá'í
PUBLISHING
Wilmette, Illinois

*He Who is everlastingly hidden from the eyes of men
can never be known except through His Manifestation,
and His Manifestation can adduce no greater proof of the
truth of His Mission than the proof of His own Person.*

—Bahá'u'lláh

FOR TERRY CASSIDAY

Bahá'í Publishing
415 Linden Avenue, Wilmette, Illinois 60091-2844

13   12   11   10   4   3   2   1

Library of Congress Cataloging-in-Publication Data

Hatcher, John, Dr.
  The face of God among us : how the creator educates
humanity / by John S. Hatcher.
     p. cm.
  ISBN 978-1-931847-70-4 (alk. paper)
  1. Bahai Faith—Doctrines. 2. Revelation—Bahai Faith. 3.
Revelation. 4. God—Knowableness. I. Title.
  BP370.H374 2010
  297.9'32117—dc22
                                        2009054203

Cover design by Robert A. Reddy
Book design by Patrick Falso

CONTENTS

CONTENTS

CONTENTS

CONTENTS

CONTENTS

ACKNOWLEDGMENTS

I would first like to acknowledge the loving assistance of Senior Editor Terry Cassiday, to whom this work is dedicated. Before her passing, Terry contributed such a great deal to the work of the Publishing Trust during her tenure there. She made my association with the Trust and with those who worked under her totally enjoyable and effortless. She is sincerely missed by all whose hearts she touched with her special blend of competency and kindness.

I would also like to express my appreciation to General Manager Tim Moore, who possesses so many gifts and has developed such a wonderful creative vision for the important work of this vital institution. On a personal level, he has managed to convince me that what I attempt to do has merit and, most important of all to me, insists that my work renders service to this precious Faith. Whether or not he is right, his persistent assurance inspires me as I continue with my writing, and I consider him a dear friend.

I would like to express my sincere appreciation to the fine work done by Bahhaj Taherzadeh who bore the lion's share of the editing duties on this lengthy and complex project. His attention to detail and his suggested changes are always well-considered and almost always just what is needed. The result is that we have developed a great working relationship, the benefits of which I look forward to sharing for books to come.

Finally, I would like to acknowledge the thoughtful and careful assistance of my wife, Lucia, whose judgment is always reliable, whose intellectual capacity never ceases to amaze me, and whose love and support is absolutely essential in everything I do.

INTRODUCTION

THEME

It is the purpose of this book to study the strategy by which God educates humanity. The principal point of view for this discourse will be the teachings of the Bahá'í Faith, but we will also discuss and consider the theories and theology of various religions and belief traditions.

The focus of our discussion will be an attempt to assess two overarching theories. The first of these is the premise that God has devised creation to educate us so that we might enter an enduring love relationship with the Creator. The second premise is allied to the first. It is the idea that the fundamental strategy at the heart of this divine plan involves Teachers sent by God to accomplish this objective.

Religions may refer to these Beings with a variety of appellations, such as avatars, prophets, or messengers. The Bahá'í writings often refer to Them as "Manifestations" to designate the belief that in addition to revealing spiritual guidance, these Teachers also perfectly model or "manifest" Godliness in terms of human character and behavior, the very paradigm They admonish us to emulate.

STRUCTURE

In approaching the subject of what these Beings are like and how They teach us, we will examine four main subjects, each of which constitutes one of the four parts of this study.

The first part discusses the purpose of the Manifestations. The premise we will examine regarding this purpose is the way in which They seem to be charged with assessing the needs of humanity at a particular stage of our continuing advancement. Then, like a divine physician, They devise a remedial course of action to correct what has gone awry and to introduce new and more advanced methods for fostering our development.

The second part discusses the nature or ontology of these divine Beings. The primary focus of this part is an attempt to resolve once and for all the question that has plagued so much of religious history. Are the Prophets or Manifestations enlightened and inspired human beings? Are they God incarnate? Are they neither ordinary human beings nor God, but another order of being altogether?

The third part examines the powers of the Prophets, what these divine emissaries are capable of doing that is beyond the capacity of ordinary human beings. Specifically, we will study Their capacity to reveal the "Word of God" or the "Book," Their teaching techniques, what seems to be an inherent superhuman knowledge, and Their professed power to do whatever They feel would be appropriate and efficacious in educating humanity.

In the final part we attempt to discover the rationale behind the consistently indirect methodology in everything They do: in Their humble appearance among us, in the incredible poetry of the language They employ, in the creative nature of the laws They reveal, and in Their apparent willingness to endure every ordeal or humiliation to which They are subjected.

SOME BACKGROUND ABOUT THE BAHÁ'Í FAITH

Since we will be examining these subjects from the theoretical perspective of the Bahá'í teachings, it would be helpful for the reader to know a little about this world religion.

Succinctly stated, the Bahá'í teachings affirm that all the religions through human history are really one religion revealed in successive and progressive stages by Manifestations or Prophets. These divine

Educators are sent by God approximately every 500 to 1,000 years to advance the spiritual and social progress of humanity.

Though equal in capacity, completely aware of each other, and fully coordinated in Their unified purpose, each Manifestation brings a new revelation from God containing revised laws and more advanced spiritual guidance. This new revelation suffices until such time as humanity is ready for the appearance of the subsequent Manifestation who will pick up where the previous one left off by ushering in another stage in the enlightenment of humanity.

Begun in the middle of the nineteenth century in Persia (now Iran) by Mírzá Ḥusayn-'Alí, whose title is "Bahá'u'lláh" ("the Glory of God"), the Bahá'í Faith is now the second most widespread religion in the world, second only to Christianity.

In over a hundred volumes, Bahá'u'lláh explains that all the Manifestations of God have the same station and powers, but each gears His teachings to the needs and capacities of humanity for a particular stage in our collective spiritual evolution as a global community.

Underlying this view of human history is the belief that the ultimate purpose of humankind is the establishment of a global commonwealth organized according to spiritual principles of collective justice and a secure and enduring peace. It is in this sense that Bahá'u'lláh proclaims that all previous religions helped prepare us for this critical turning point in human history—to realize that the time has at last arrived to begin the construction of a global infrastructure to accommodate our newly emerged identity as citizens of a single world community.

AUTHORITATIVE TEXTS OF THE BAHÁ'Í FAITH

A word should be said about the terms employed in this study alluding to the "authoritative texts" of the Bahá'í Faith and to the four central figures who established the Bahá'í institutions. Inasmuch as

Bahá'ís accept as Manifestations both Bahá'u'lláh and the Báb—the herald and forerunner of Bahá'u'lláh—the works of both are regarded as the revealed Word of God and thus as authoritative and infallible guidance.

Bahá'u'lláh also revealed a binding covenant with His followers in which He designed the blueprint for an administrative order and designated 'Abdu'l-Bahá, His eldest son, as the authoritative and infallible interpreter of Bahá'u'lláh's revelation and as the head of the Bahá'í Faith, the Center of His Covenant.

In his own detailed Will and Testament, 'Abdu'l-Bahá elucidated and fleshed out Bahá'u'lláh's administrative order by establishing the institution of the Guardianship; by appointing Shoghi Effendi as the first Guardian; and by defining the authority of the Universal House of Justice, the body that Bahá'u'lláh designated to be the supreme institution of the World Order He envisioned.

Because of this binding covenant, the writings of Bahá'u'lláh, 'Abdu'l-Bahá, Shoghi Effendi, and the Universal House of Justice are regarded by Bahá'ís as being "authoritative," and as having the "same effect as the Text itself" ('Abdu'l-Bahá, Will and Testament, p. 20).

PART 1

THE PURPOSE OF
THE PROPHETS OF GOD

The Prophets and Messengers of God have been sent down for the sole purpose of guiding mankind to the straight Path of Truth. The purpose underlying Their revelation hath been to educate all men, that they may, at the hour of death, ascend, in the utmost purity and sanctity and with absolute detachment, to the throne of the Most High.

—Bahá'u'lláh

1

WHY THE CREATOR CREATES

I was a Hidden Treasure.
I wished to be made known,
and thus I called creation into being
in order that I might be known.
— the *ḥadíth* of the Hidden Treasure

Before we can begin to understand how the Prophets of God function as divine Educators, we first need to understand God's purpose in bringing about creation and, even more particularly, His purpose in fashioning humankind as the fruit or culmination of that project. Only by comprehending that purpose can we begin to appreciate the Creator's method in employing an indirect method of instruction involving Prophets or Manifestations Who act on His behalf. More particularly, only in light of understanding that purpose can we appreciate why these specialized Beings are essential to our progress, what distinctive nature enables Them to fulfill this function, what special powers and capacities are at Their disposal, and why it seems inevitable that They seem destined to suffer at the hands of the very same beings on whom They wish to bestow love, enlightenment, and guidance.

If we were to start this discussion at its true beginning, we would start by proving the existence of God, and, having done that, prove

7

that the nature of this Being is such that He would find it desirable to bestow love, learning, and guidance to His creation. Fortunately, this task has already been accomplished quite well elsewhere.[1] For our present purposes, therefore, let us assume that there is a God Who is responsible for our creation and Who, for some reason, wishes to make us better than we are, both as individuals and collectively as an evolving global civilization on planet Earth. However, even if these aforementioned proofs seem to indicate that the Creator is essentially benign, let us discover more exactly what rationale underlies His desire to bring about creation in the first place. As a corollary quest, let us then try to understand why discerning His rationale is essential to appreciating the methodology He has employed in accomplishing these outcomes.

SOME MONOTHEISTIC IMAGES OF GOD

Since our only consistent and accepted authoritative portrayals of God derive from the utterances of those Prophets Who established the major religions, let us begin by briefly examining some of the images of the Creator that have emerged from some of the more familiar faith traditions. This is a particularly useful beginning because the historically anthropomorphic images of God we may have inherited from clerics and followers of so many religions may not always accord with what the Prophet-Founders of the religions intended.

For example, we may think the jealous, vengeful, wrathful tribal chieftain image we might derive from parts of the Old Testament more terrifying than comforting. Sometimes His actions seem over the top or capricious. Certainly His direct "hands-on" intervention in human

---

1. See the proof presented by my brother, William S. Hatcher, in his philosophical treatise *Minimalism: The Bridge between Classical Philosophy and the Bahá'í Revelation* and, less minimally and less rigidly, from a scientific perspective, by me in *Close Connection: The Bridge between Spiritual and Physical Reality*.

history seems a bit hard to accept—parting seas for the righteous while destroying the entire army of Pharaoh, some of whom may have been very decent young men. Certainly we might wonder why this God of miracles and wonders no longer seems interested in intervening in human affairs to punish the wicked or assist the downtrodden.

Indeed, we might opt for a more loving and forgiving God, like the image of a loving and caring shepherd that David portrays in his Psalms. Or we might prefer the image presented in exacting detail by Christ, a heavenly Father who would sacrifice His only son to bring about the forgiveness and redemption of humankind.

Of course, Christ's image of God became a bit mangled or confusing after the Council of Nicaea (AD 325) when Christian clerics determined that God and Christ are, in fact, one and the same Being. This image of a God who could quite literally take on human form and appear among us, is not unlike the Greek gods and goddesses who, according to mythological accounts, frequently became incarnate and became thoroughly involved in human affairs.

Almost exactly three hundred years after the Council of Nicea, Muḥammad hardly condemned this image of God depicted in the literalist interpretation of the Trinitarian doctrine that prevailed in most of Western Christendom. And while Muḥammad upholds the miracle of the virgin birth of Christ, as well as Christ's station as the Messiah, He found it blasphemous that the Catholic church had also determined that Mary, as mother of Christ (and therefore, logically, the mother of God as well), might be a better image of authority than the abstract notion of a heavenly Father image. At the Council of Ephesus in 431 it was determined that Mary was not only the Mother of God, and therefore to be venerated, but also Mother of the Church, and therefore the most effective intermediary between the believer and God. After all, if you're in trouble, from whom would you prefer to seek assistance, from God the Father, or God's Mother?

9

MUHAMMAD'S IMAGE OF GOD

According to the Prophet Muḥammad, Whose ministry began in 622, the Trinitarian doctrine, along with the image of God on which it is based, is completely flawed and quite blasphemous. In addition, if the first premise established at the Nicaean Council was erroneous, and Christ was not of the same essence or station as God, then every doctrine based on or derived from that syllogism was likely to be equally flawed.

This is not to say that Muḥammad was in any sense disdainful of Christ or Christianity. Muḥammad acknowledges that Christ was a Manifestation or Messenger of God, that He was the Messiah, that He was indeed born of a virgin, and that Mary was the foremost woman of the Christian dispensation. But at the forefront of Muḥammad's image of God are His statements in the Qur'án emphasizing the singleness and uniqueness of God. From the point of view of Islamic belief, the Deity is exalted far beyond the limitations of language or human conception. Furthermore, Muḥammad asserts that God is an indivisible spiritual essence that cannot be divided up or portioned out to any other being, not even to a Prophet or Manifestation of God.

In this sense, there are three abiding themes in the Qur'án that are especially relevant to our study: the assertion that there is only one God and those who add gods to God are committing the grossest sort of blasphemy; that God has always had in place an established, enduring, and systematic plan by which He has nurtured and guided humankind through a sequence of Messengers who bring new "Books" or revelations; and that Muḥammad, whose "Book" is the Qur'án itself, is the most recent of these Messengers. Most other doctrinal discussions in the Qur'án are subordinated to one of these three central themes. The laws, of course, are scattered throughout the Qur'án.

Muḥammad expands and clarifies the image of God significantly by talking at length about the various "names" of God, those attributes that allude to the inherent nature or qualities of God. For example, God is described as just, loving, forgiving, beneficent, and benevolent. A second category of the "names" of God alluded to in the Qur'án are the references to the powers of God. For example, He is also described as ever-forgiving, omnipotent, omniscient, and omnipresent. Inseparable from this theme of the "names" or attributes and powers of God are Muḥammad's often repeated allusions to the educational system by which God has covenanted to be always in the "presence" of humankind. The means by which God accomplishes this is to send Messengers Who function at His behest and Who perfectly exemplify or manifest His attributes, in spite of being persistently rejected, disdained, and persecuted by the very people whom They are sent to educate and assist.

These two themes are inseparable and reciprocal aspects of a single thesis. God as an essentially metaphysical Being does not need to intervene personally in human events—His metaphysical hands do not reach down to direct human affairs, as implied in the Old Testament or as portrayed in Michelangelo's masterpiece on the ceiling of the Sistine Chapel. That telling gap depicted in the painting between the fingers of God and Adam becomes bridged by those Messengers Whom God empowers to carry out His bidding.

Muḥammad calls these Beings "Messengers" (*Rasul*), and in numerous súrih (chapters) of the Qur'án, He catalogues, often in chronological order, some of the Prophets of God that have appeared in history. One of the more familiar of these recitations occurs in the Súrih of Húd, where Muḥammad remarks that each Prophet came with clear proof of His station and yet was rejected by the very people to whom He appeared.

While Muḥammad emphasizes the stories of those Prophets in what is sometimes called the "Abrahamic" line of prophets (those who are descended from Abraham as opposed to the "Dharmic" line consisting

11

of Prophets such as Krishna, Buddha, and Zoroaster), He also makes it plain that this process is not confined to a particular period of time or a particular place. In súrih 10:47, Muḥammad states, "To every people (was sent) a Messenger: when their Messenger comes (before them), the matter will be judged between them with justice, and they will not be wronged."[2]

We can presume, in other words, that the opportunity to receive guidance and the responsibility of the people (nation or tribe) to recognize the Messenger and accept His guidance is universally applicable to all regions of the earth, even as remnants of past great civilizations are still being unearthed along with their laws, traditions, and beliefs.

THE BAHÁ'Í CONCEPT OF GOD

Like the image we infer from the Qur'án, the concept of God in the Bábí and Bahá'í religions is likewise a Being beyond any exact or complete comprehension, an essentially unknowable Creator of infinite love and logic. He is purposeful, absolutely benign, and fully in control of His creation and the educational system He has established as the purpose of reality.

The Bahá'í texts assert that knowledge of the character of the Prophets is tantamount to knowledge of God. Therefore a study of the authoritative accounts of the lives of the Báb and Bahá'u'lláh contributes greatly to our understanding of the Creator, His purposes, and His methodology.

TWO CATEGORIES OF PROPHETS

The Bahá'í texts distinguish between Major Prophets (also called Universal Manifestations)—Those who bring a new "Book" and start

---

2. All citations to the Qur'án are from Abdullah Yusuf Alí, *The Qur'án: Text, Translation, and Commentary* (New York: Tahrike Tarsile Qur'án, Inc., 2001), though I have eliminated the line breaks and, in cases where the translation is awkward or misleading, substituted my own translation.

a new religion—and minor prophets—those who assist, reinforce, or reinvigorate an existing religion. In discussing this distinction, 'Abdu'l-Bahá contrasts the "independent" Prophets or the Manifestations of God with the minor prophets who are themselves "followers" of the Manifestation in Whose dispensation they live:

> [T]he Prophets are of two kinds. One are the independent Prophets Who are followed; the other kind are not independent and are themselves followers. The independent Prophets are the lawgivers and the founders of a new cycle. Through Their appearance the world puts on a new garment, the foundations of religion are established, and a new book is revealed. Without an intermediary They receive bounty from the Reality of the Divinity, and Their illumination is an essential illumination. They are like the sun which is luminous in itself: the light is its essential necessity; it does not receive light from any other star. These Dawning-places of the morn of Unity are the sources of bounty and the mirrors of the Essence of Reality.
>
> The other Prophets are followers and promoters, for they are branches and not independent; they receive the bounty of the independent Prophets, and they profit by the light of the Guidance of the universal Prophets. They are like the moon, which is not luminous and radiant in itself, but receives its light from the sun. (*Some Answered Questions*, p. 164)

He goes on to give examples of this distinction by classifying Abraham, Moses, Christ, Muḥammad, the Báb, and Bahá'u'lláh as independent Manifestations. He classifies Solomon, David, Isaiah, Jeremiah, and Ezekiel as minor prophets.

In addition to elucidating the explanation of how the Creator has established a logical and progressive educational system for humankind, the Bahá'í texts also provide a greatly enhanced understanding of God's motive by explaining in detail the educational process that Muḥammad sketches in very general terms. For where Muḥammad is responding to the anthropomorphic image of God derived from Christianity by making absolutely clear the distinction between the station of the Prophets and the station of the Creator, the Bahá'í writings are able to build on that foundation by giving a much more exacting description of human history as a dynamic, logical, comprehensible, and divinely guided process.

Therefore while there still remain a variety of concepts of a Supreme Deity in extant systems of belief, the most abiding image has emerged from the more recent Abrahamic line of Prophets during which time the world has gradually become a global community "contracted and transformed into a single highly complex organism" (Shoghi Effendi, *World Order of Bahá'u'lláh,* p. 47). Therefore, while we can draw from features of this portrait as it emerged in Judaism, Christianity, and Islam, let us begin with the assumption of the fundamental parameters of the definition of God as delineated in the most recent in this line of religions—the Bahá'í Faith—as the basis for examining the next obvious step in a systematic study of the Prophets.

WHY THE CREATOR CREATES

Let us first consider why the Creator would think it a good idea to create anything at all, let alone a being as perplexing and troublesome as we human beings on planet Earth seem to be. More particularly, let us attempt to discover why the authoritative texts of the Bahá'í religion would affirm that human beings are the "fruit" of creation. These are, after all, the very same beings who seem presently incapable of self-governance and appear to be bent on the contamination of the minimal resources necessary for their own survival.

Possibly the best place to begin this process of examining the rationale behind the creation of human beings is to understand what Bahá'u'lláh interprets the term "húrí" to mean, because it is through appreciation of the symbolic sense of this term that we encounter one of the most cogent statements about the divine purpose for our creation.

HÚRÍS

Húrí is an Arabic term employed by Muḥammad to designate the "pure ones" or "white ones," the heavenly maidens that will be the reward of those who enter paradise. If taken literally, the term would seem to designate virginal maidens who become literally unveiled in a physical "heaven." However, as explained by Bahá'u'lláh, the term *húrí* is intended by Muḥammad as a symbolic allusion to spiritual and intellectual mysteries that become "unveiled" or unconcealed as a reward for the faithful. Accordingly, 'Abdu'l-Bahá observes that "mysteries of which man is heedless in this earthly world, those he will discover in the heavenly world, and there will he be informed of the secret of truth. . . ." (*Bahá'u'lláh and the New Era,* p. 209).

This explanation about the concept of "mysteries" as concealed wisdom is extremely important. It has become customary among the followers of some religions to regard "mysteries" as matters of faith, as concepts that, because they are "spiritual," defy or transcend logical explanation or the laws of cause and effect. The Bahá'í writings, on the other hand, state that the laws applicable to one aspect of reality are also applicable to the other. In other words, there is nothing in creation, whether an existent being or a sequence of events, that is without logical explanation or comprehension.

Consequently, instead of adoring "mysteries" or considering them beyond logical reflection and study, the Bahá'í writings exhort us to employ our mental and spiritual faculties, together with the assistance provided by the techniques for study taught and demonstrated to us by the Manifestations, to *solve* these húrís rather than worship them. We are encouraged, in other words, to remove the "veiled" meaning, instead of becoming entranced by the veil itself.

TWO CRITICAL HÚRÍS

Two useful examples of scriptural húrís can be found in two common allusions that have been the source of grievous consternation and conflict. One is a statement by Christ, the other a statement by Muḥammad. Christ called Himself the "Son of God," and Muḥammad referred to Himself as the "Seal" of the Prophets. The inability of the clerics and ordinary believers to understand the underlying poetic or symbolic meaning of these epithets has been the cause of untold conflict and confusion among followers of both religions.

Similarly, there are mysteries or húrís associated with the lives of all the Manifestations that seem beyond logic or reason. Christ mysteriously healed the sick and, according to Christian belief as inferred from biblical accounts, physically arose from the dead. Muḥammad, though an unlearned camel caravan leader, became suddenly endowed with astounding eloquence after He mysteriously received a revelation directly from God. Similarly, the circumstances surrounding the execution of the Báb in the barracks square in Tabríz were no less astounding and mysterious, as was the appearance of the veiled maiden to Bahá'u'lláh in the Síyáh-Chál.

And yet what Bahá'u'lláh makes clear, in his discussion of "mysteries" in His principal doctrinal treatise the Book of Certitude, is that the húrís that have the most profound and often the most deleterious effect on the divine system of human education are misunderstandings about particular statements in the language of the Manifestations. He further explains that these mysteries are not meant to remain veiled or concealed, nor is their meaning available only to some esoteric class of learned clerics. Like the parables of Christ, these passages are often symbolic or metaphorical expressions that have the intended effect of causing seekers or believers to think for themselves. In fact, Bahá'u'lláh states in the opening of this same discourse that the supposedly learned clerics and religious leaders are most often the least capable of penetrating the literal surfaces of poetic scripture to discern the spiritual meaning. They are the greatest sources of literalism and orthodoxy.

Bahá'u'lláh states pointedly that the ability to decipher or "unveil" these húrís is dependent on purity of heart and sincerity of motive, not so much on academic prowess or learning that can be acquired from or imparted through the formal training possessed by clerics and divines. One of the most obvious and weighty examples of the distinctive nature of this capacity occurs when Christ's analogical explanations of spiritual concepts are easily understood by his unlearned disciples but totally baffling to the learned Pharisees and Sadducees who ply Him with theological questions. Likewise, it is the supposedly learned bishops who at the Council of Nicaea apply a literalist interpretation to Christ's explanations of His relationship to God—"he that hath seen me hath seen the Father" (John 14:9)—and create the specious doctrine of literal Trinitarianism. This doctrine in which Christ is portrayed as God incarnate effectively undermines the entire notion of sequential and progressive revelations, a point that Muhammad repeatedly notes in the Qur'án in His discussion of the station of Messengers versus the exclusive status of God.

And yet, ironically, the same sort of literalist interpretation of a single Qur'ánic verse by later Muslim clerics would result in an equally flawed and perilous misunderstanding of the relationship of Muhammad and Islam to both past and future revelations. By interpreting Muhammad's statement that He is the "Seal" of the Prophets as meaning that He was the final Messenger from God and, further, that His revelation thus completes the revelatory process of the divine education of humankind on planet Earth, Muslim divines effectively duplicated the error of the Nicaean doctrine so hardily condemned by Muḥammad. Instead of believing Muḥammad to be the culmination of previous Prophets, but coequal with them in station, they portrayed Him as having a superior station, and Islam became perceived to be the final revelation from God intended to become spread throughout the world.

HOW HÚRÍS WORK

If Christ does not mean He is God, what does He intend by His statement that to know Him is to know God? Likewise, if Muḥammad does not mean that He has effectively sealed up or completed the process of enlightening humankind, what meaning does that verse have?

To a certain extent, I have explicated this process in detail in *The Ocean of His Words: A Reader's Guide to the Art of Bahá'u'lláh* in which I demonstrate how to apply some of the fundamental tools of hermeneutics (interpretation theory) to the artistry of Bahá'u'lláh's revealed works. But Bahá'u'lláh Himself devotes virtually the first half of the Book of Certitude to explaining this same subject—how to interpret or "unveil" the symbolic and metaphorical language of scripture. For as He explains at the outset of this discourse, the inability of clerics and divines to comprehend the poetic or symbolic nature of scripture has been a major cause of much of the misunderstanding and conflict that has plagued religious history.

As a demonstration of how to unveil the symbolic and metaphorical meaning of scripture, Bahá'u'lláh explains how Muslims could have converted Christians to Islam had they understood how to explicate the symbolic meaning of Christ's prophetic passages regarding His return. Bahá'u'lláh devotes approximately 100 pages of the Book of Certitude to demonstrating this point further. He focuses on Christ's allusion to His return in Matthew 24:29–31 and "unveils" the húrís in these three verses, though He humbly characterizes this explication to be but "a dewdrop out of the fathomless ocean of the truths treasured in these holy words":

This servant will now share with thee a dewdrop out of the fathomless ocean of the truths treasured in these holy words, that haply discerning hearts may comprehend all the allusions and the implications of the utterances of the Manifestations of Holiness, so that the overpowering majesty of the Word of God may not prevent them from attaining unto the ocean of His names and attributes, nor deprive them of recognizing the Lamp of God which is the seat of the revelation of His glorified Essence. (Kitáb-i-Íqán, ¶27)

During the course of His examination of these verses, Bahá'u'lláh observes that He is uncovering the "inner meaning" of just one of a myriad such passages of scripture and other types of concealed wisdom: "How many the húrís of inner meaning that are as yet concealed within the chambers of divine wisdom! None hath yet approached them;—húrís, 'whom no man nor spirit hath touched before'" (Kitáb-i-Íqán, ¶78).

This is an allusion to Muḥammad's verse in the Qur'án (55:54–56) where the Prophet describes those bounties that await those who ascend to paradise: "They will recline on Carpets, whose inner linings will be of rich brocade: the Fruit of the Gardens will be Near (and easy of reach). Then which of the favors of your Lord will ye deny? In them will be (Maidens), Chaste, restraining their glances, whom no man or Jinn before them has touched."

It is important to observe that Bahá'u'lláh here is not using the verse from the Qur'án to explain His own idea. Quite the reverse is true. He is actually demonstrating the inner meaning of the húrí of an often cited Qur'ánic verse to prove the very nature of a húrí itself. He explains the inner meaning of a verse that is commonly assumed by many Muslims to describe a physical reward in a physical afterlife—a verse that, according to Bahá'u'lláh, is actually stating symbolically that those who are faithful will be given insight to the inner significance of scripture and other verities that were veiled from them during their physical lives.

In short, Muḥammad's verse about húrís is itself a húrí. It is a passage that anticipates the concept explained by 'Abdu'l-Bahá that "When the human soul soareth out of this transient heap of dust and riseth into the world of God, then veils will fall away, and verities will come to light, and all things unknown before will be made clear, and hidden truths be understood" (*Selections from the Writings of 'Abdu'l-Bahá*, no. 149.3).

But perhaps the single most weighty statement about the importance of understanding the inner meaning of the revealed word, or the "Book," as scripture is often called in the Qur'án, is Bahá'u'lláh's observation that the reading or recitation of scripture without understanding has "no abiding" value or merit, because the purpose of the revealed word is to teach us about reality. If we are to be meaningfully informed, then obviously we must first understand what is being said to us.

Commenting explicitly about those Muslims who recite and memorize the Qur'án without understanding it, Bahá'u'lláh makes the following observation about the purpose of the scripture that constitutes the Qur'án:

Twelve hundred and eighty years have passed since the dawn of the Muḥammadan Dispensation, and with every break of day, these blind and ignoble people have recited their Qur'án, and yet have failed to grasp one letter of that Book! Again and again they read those verses which clearly testify to the reality of these holy themes, and bear witness to the truth of the Manifestations of eternal Glory, and still apprehend not their purpose. They have even failed to realize, all this time, that, in every age, the reading of the scriptures and holy books is for no other purpose except to enable the reader to apprehend their meaning and unravel their innermost mysteries. Otherwise reading, without understanding, is of no abiding profit unto man. (Kitáb-i-Íqán, ¶185)

During the course of the first 116 pages of the Book of Certitude, in which Bahá'u'lláh "unveils"" the prophetic verses of Matthew 24:29–31 regarding the signs of the coming of the Son of Man, Bahá'u'lláh also presents the reader with an exceedingly useful series of exercises in hermeneutics. Using these tools, Bahá'u'lláh explicates various levels of symbolism associated with Christ's prophecies and demonstrates how Christ was preparing His followers for the advent of Muḥammad.

In these exercises, Bahá'u'lláh again employs passages from the Qur'án at every turn to support His "argument" and to underscore His explication of particular points. We should again be careful to note, however, that far from assuming that His elucidation of these Qur'ánic passages are clear or obvious to His Muslim audience, Bahá'u'lláh is well aware that these explanations are demonstrating the meaning of húrís that would be equally veiled to literalist Muslim believers and clerics alike.

By placing these verses in the context of His argument about proofs of Muḥammad as foretold in the New Testament, Bahá'u'lláh is, conversely, using the Qur'án as a means for justifying to Muslims the validity of the Christian scripture and, as Bahá'u'lláh demonstrates later, as a means of showing how the Qur'án and certain hadíth prophesize the advent of the Báb.

Bahá'u'lláh is thus providing a cross reference for these critical passages for Christians, for Muslims, and, toward the final section, for

Bábís (people of the Bayán). For it is the followers of the Báb who will a year later, in 1863, be tested or "judged" as to whether or not they can recognize Mustagháth ("He Who is Invoked"), a reference in the writings of the Báb to "Him Whom God will make manifest" (Bahá'u'lláh) and to the "Latter Resurrection," the second part of the "Day of Resurrection" signaled by the twin revelations of the Báb and Bahá'u'lláh.

THE HADÍTH OF THE HIDDEN TREASURE

There is a strategic purpose in our digression about húrís. At the heart of every húrí is a spiritual or poetic explanation that provides us with clues to the entirety of the discourses of Christ and of Muḥammad. And among the most pivotal húrís discussed by both Bahá'u'lláh and 'Abdu'l-Bahá is the Islamic ḥadíth (tradition)[3] of the Hidden Treasure. In fact, once we come to appreciate the full implications of this single verse, we can discern concealed within it everything else there is to understand about the Creator and His purpose in bringing about human beings as the fruit of His creation.

The ḥadíth of the Hidden Treasure consists of three statements that, when their relationship to each other is fully appreciated, constitute a weighty and expansive syllogism:

> *I was a Hidden Treasure.*
> I wished to be made known,
> and thus I called creation into being
> *in order that I might be known.*

---

3. In Islam, a ḥadíth is an oral tradition derived from statements or actions of Muḥammad not recorded in the Qur'án. Some ḥadíth also derive from the actions and statements attributed to the Twelve Imáms. The source of this well-known tradition of the Hidden Treasure is unknown.

The speaker in this ḥadít̲h̲ is God, the Creator. Presumably God is stating why He brought creation into being—that He might be known. Without everything else we are given to understand about God, this passage could have a variety of interpretations and implications. But when we include into this syllogism those propositions that are already understood about the Creator in the Christian, Islamic, Bábí, and Bahá'í teachings, then this húrí begins to assume its full stature as a succinct explanation and emblematic representation of the entire process of creation.

One of the key inferences in this verse is the indirection with which the Creator has chosen to bring to fruition the education of human souls. This is not to say that the human being is separate from or independent of the rest of creation. Rather, as 'Abdu'l-Bahá notes, creation might be likened to a fruit tree, and "man is like the fruit; without fruit the tree would be useless" (*Some Answered Questions,* p. 201). Thus while clearly the human being is superior in capacity to the rest of creation, we cannot consider ourselves separate from or independent of the tree of creation any more than an apple might disdain the tree that produces it.

'Abdu'l-Bahá articulates this same proposition in an analogy where he observes that without human beings, the world of creation would be like a body without a soul:

> So, for example, the rays of the sun must shine upon the earth, and the solar heat develop the earthly beings; if the rays and heat of the sun did not shine upon the earth, the earth would be uninhabited, without meaning; and its development would be retarded. In the same way, if the perfections of the spirit did not appear in this world, this world would be unenlightened and absolutely brutal. By the appearance of the spirit in the physical form, this world is enlightened. As the spirit of man is the cause

of the life of the body, so the world is in the condition of the body, and man is in the condition of the spirit. If there were no man, the perfections of the spirit would not appear, and the light of the mind would not be resplendent in this world. This world would be like a body without a soul. (*Some Answered Questions,* pp. 200–201)

Therefore, for us as human beings to believe that we are the focus of creation is not sheer hubris—in a sense we are. At the same time, we are also an integral part of the rest of creation. And if we are wise, the last thing we should want to do is allow damage to the tree of our existence.

WHY US?

Environmentalists and animal rights advocates alike might understandably but incorrectly infer from these passages that human beings have hardly demonstrated the right to be regarded as the fruit of creation or of anything else. Concerned citizens of our planet might well regard us and the civilization we have brought forth as veritable assassins of creation. Consequently, we might find it useful to return to this simple ḥadíth to discover why we humans should be regarded as being worthy of primacy in the Creator's design of this educational program that is physical reality. What capacity or potentiality do we possess that would cause Him to think of us as strategic to His desire to be known?

Because He is omnipotent, the Creator could create whatever He wishes in whatever form He wishes. Therefore, if it were His purpose solely to create a being that knows Him, He could do so instantaneously with a single command: "*Kun fa Yakúnu*" ("Be!" and "It is"). Suddenly we would instantly exist in a condition of knowing the Creator. Instead of having us proceed through a lengthy historical process of gradually coming to understand who we are and what our purpose is, the Creator could have made His presence and His nature immediately apparent to us.

But the method by which the Creator wishes to be known—this protracted and sometimes arduous process we undergo, whether as a body politic or as individual aspirants to spiritual ascent—is dictated by another proposition implicit in this same ḥadíth of the Hidden Treasure. It is the proposition concealed within the explanation of exactly *why* the Creator wishes to be known in the first place.

In the ḥadíth the Creator says He was alone, and yet because by definition God is self-sufficient and independent of all else besides Himself, we can hardly conclude that the Creator is lonely or inadequate or in need of affection or worship. To assert anything like this would be totally illogical and contrary to the very definition of the Creator. The Creator does not need to create us any more than we feel some logical need to have children. If God is truly independent of all else besides Himself, if He is truly self-sufficient, then He can hardly be said to need anything. As all scripture in every religion makes clear, God will forever be singular and incompletely understood.

Therefore, we totally misunderstand the nature of this Being if we ascribe to him human frailty or longing or need. As scripture time and again makes clear, and as this ḥadíth states succinctly, the Creator desires to be known for an entirely selfless or altruistic motive—to bestow His love and other gifts upon a being capable of comprehending the value of such illusive and ineffable powers as knowledge and love, such virtues as justice and forgiveness, or such attributes as beauty and kindness.

Stated in terms of the logical relationship between the Creator and the created, the motive underlying this process is exclusively concerned with how best to bestow bounties that will redound to the benefit of that which is created. And, fully aware of the gifts He is capable of bestowing, the Creator has devised a process best suited to enable creation to know and benefit from a relationship with the Creator, for this is the greatest gift that can be given. And yet, for a being to appreciate fully and meaningfully this gift, its value must be understood and freely desired and accepted. Otherwise, that which is created would necessarily endure in a static condition. We would not possess the tools necessary to progress in that knowledge.

This necessity of free will as a part of our enlightenment is a key to every other feature of the educational process the Creator has devised. For the Creator to be known in any significant manner, that knowledge must be acquired by effort because true learning, like authentic love, is not a relationship that can be coerced or imposed, nor can it remain changeless. Hence in Arabic Hidden Word number five we find this profound axiomatic statement about this divine relationship: "Love Me, that I may love thee. If thou lovest Me not, My love can in no wise reach thee. Know this, O servant."

In this description of the sort of love that the Creator wishes for us to attain, we discern a relationship that surpasses mere affection. This mutuality of appreciation derives from a mutual recognition of the worth of the beloved. Like a perfect parent, the Creator loves us unconditionally. But like a wise parent, the Creator is trying to assist us in developing the capacity to perceive the nature of the Creator, to become aware of the worthiness of the nature of the Creator, and subsequently to desire nearness to the Creator. Obviously this "nearness" is not a physical presence but a realization of the endless gifts of knowledge and love the Creator wishes to bestow, and a progressively more intense and encompassing desire on our part to emulate those qualities and develop those faculties with which the Creator has endowed us. In this manner we can become trained in the art of expressing spirituality in daily actions and dramatic forms.

Without a doubt, the best analogous human motive capable of providing us with some glimpse into the Creator's love and altruistic desire to be known is, as we have noted, the human desire to have children. For while there can most certainly be any number of selfish motives for having children, there is also underlying this inherent urge a more lofty aspiration largely beyond our conscious knowledge. If for some reason a couple is unable to have children, they will sometimes spend incalculable amounts of time and money on medical procedures. If these do not work, a couple may then resort to adoption. And for what purpose? What are the less obvious sources of this drive within us?

Clearly we have some inherent need to bring forth progeny, and this need transcends the more mundane urges of perpetuating ourselves or our family name. Clearly no single answer to this húrí will suffice. But certainly among the most potent urges compelling this desire is the wish to bestow unconditional love on other beings capable, in time, of understanding, appreciating, and returning that love of their own free will. Another motive at work may be our desire to participate in the amazing process of bringing into existence a being capable of self-consciousness and autonomous development, of becoming a noble creation—a being that can benefit from all that we find inherently joyous to bestow, whether it is pure affection, education and enlightenment, or a thousand other little-noticed gifts we may never fully understand.

Lurking in the recesses of our thoughts may also be an unconscious awareness that the life we are setting in motion, together with the love we bestow to foster the development and progress of that life, will help sustain an ongoing chain of love that will reach far beyond the present moment and far beyond one or two souls.

But we don't really need to understand this desire. We accede to it. We enjoy it for what it is, possibly because we are, as the scriptures assert, made in God's image. And yet what other task or undertaking is more time-consuming, more arduous, more subtle and difficult to do well, than trying to be a good parent? We read books about how to do it. We listen to lectures and classes about it. We become frustrated, frightened, and vulnerable. As the saying goes, we have given a ransom to fate.

Our lives can be going along swimmingly in every other respect—we may have a good job, some leisure time, fulfilling relationships, the necessities of life—but let one thing happen to a child of ours, and our hearts are at the mercy of the outcome. Or stated in terms of a larger perspective, we may find it difficult to be much happier than our unhappiest child (or grandchild).

Perhaps my favorite line of all about parenting comes from the movie *Parenthood*, an essential source of solace and wisdom for all parents living in the postmodern world. Frank Buckman, the father/grandfather figure played by the late Jason Robards, consults with his grown son (Steve Martin) about what to do with his prodigal son who, once again, has returned home in financial and legal trouble. Trying to explain why he still feels obliged to try yet again to help this recalcitrant one, he says to his older and ostensibly well-adjusted son, "You don't understand. It's never over. You don't get to dive into the end zone, spike the ball, and do your little victory dance. It never stops!" In a well-known poem by Robert E. Hayden called "Those Winter Sundays," a grown son, reflecting on his own father now that he himself is going through the love-pain of parenting, says plaintively about his own lack of appreciation for all his father went through in trying to bestow love on him, "What did I know? What did I know of love's austere and lonely offices?" And indeed, parental love is so often austere, so often a lonely and thankless outpost, and so often filled with grief or regret or ingratitude.

Yet we persist in striving to participate in this most serious of all jobs—to bring forth new life and to attend to that life as if our own life depends on doing it well, because somehow it does. Yes, we do have a choice in this. We are never *forced* to be parents. There is no longer much social pressure to be a parent. But in spite of the pain and the responsibility and the vulnerability it imposes on us, this one act links us more closely to the motive in the mind of God the Creator than possibly anything else we can do or experience.

In short, the Creator creates that He might bestow His gifts of love, education, enlightenment, and advancement on a being capable of understanding and utilizing these gifts. But the "clincher" in this process of love and enlightenment, as it is with human parental love, is that to accomplish this task, the gift of unconditional love and assistance must be freely recognized and received because, as we have noted, an authentic love relationship, by definition, must be reciprocal.

This is not to say that love cannot be unilateral. Certainly we may dearly love another who does not love us in return. But for the power of our love to be unleashed and an authentic love relationship to be established, a bilateral or reciprocal process must begin. Only then can the power of this primal force grow and develop and become refined, whether this love is between two human beings or between the Creator and us, the created.

RECIPROCITY REQUIRES RESPONSE

Certainly our love relationship with God does not make us coequal with God, but it is still a relationship in which there is reciprocity. In the passage we previously cited from Arabic Hidden Word number five, in which the Creator states, "If thou lovest Me not, My love can in no wise reach thee," God is by no means implying that He will withhold His love from us unless we love Him in return. His love is unconditional, unvarying, relentless, constant. Bahá'u'lláh is affirming in this revealed axiom that a love relationship is not possible unless we willingly participate. And participation implies not merely our recognizing God's love for us but also our demonstrating that recognition by acting accordingly. That action may take the form of thanking God for bringing us into being and for enabling us to recognize His love for us, or in praising the infinite powers and attributes that He has potentially bestowed on us—"potentially" because we must employ them in our lives before they become actualized.

A simple analogy for this relationship with God can be understood in terms of a telephone call. God may be calling us and we may hear the ringing in the form of all sorts of reminders, whether in the love of others or in the beauty of nature. But God's love cannot "reach" us unless we pick up the phone, unless we receive His call. That reception is instigated when we take part in a dialogue, when we speak to Him in return so that there is reciprocal communion.

It is in this sense, no doubt, that prayer is prescribed and exhorted as part of a daily regimen in every religion, because this flow of communication is an essential ingredient in maintaining the health of this love relationship.

KNOWLEDGE PRECEDES RESPONSE

For God's love to reach us, to affect us, to uplift us, we must be aware of it. Only then can we become receptive to it and respond to it. Consequently, the knowledge or awareness of God's existence and desire—that we "pick up the phone"—must precede our response. And in order to be aware of God's love, we need to be guided to understand that to which we are attracted and what underlies that attraction. We need to be made aware of what distinguishes that ringing noise from the distracting din of all the other sounds that solicit our attention.

Again, the Creator is capable of fashioning a recipient in whatever way He wishes. If we accept this concept as a given, then we necessarily must conclude that we have been created precisely the correct way to accomplish the goals of the Creator. In other words, the gradualness with which we learn who and what we are and then proceed by degrees to discern the love of God as the motive force behind this educative process constitutes a perfect design for bringing about the desired result implicit in the ḥadíth of the Hidden Treasure.

The obviousness of this theme becomes apparent once we begin seriously to examine the axiomatic statement in the Bahá'í texts that we are inherently created to be desirous of understanding reality: "Science is the first emanation from God toward man. All created beings embody the potentiality of material perfection, but the power of intellectual investigation and scientific acquisition is a higher virtue specialized to man alone. Other beings and organisms are deprived of this potentiality and attainment. God has created or deposited this love of reality in man" ('Abdu'l-Bahá, *Foundations of World Unity*, p. 80).

2

THE HÚRÍ OF LOVE

And if, confirmed by the Creator, the lover escapes from the claws
of the eagle of love, he will enter the Valley of Knowledge and
come out of doubt into certitude, and turn from the darkness of
illusion to the guiding light of the fear of God. His inner eyes will
open and he will privily converse with his Beloved; he will set ajar
the gate of truth and piety, and shut the doors of vain imaginings.
—Bahá'u'lláh

The húrí lurking behind the force of love is extremely important. Within
it lies the key to the Creator's indirection in teaching us. Since everything
in creation manifests the attributes of the Creator, our inherent attraction to creation ultimately informs us—perhaps initially on a purely
intuitive or subliminal level—of the nature of the Creator Himself.

We may be attracted to the beauty of a polished stone, a fragrant
flower, a butterfly, a king snake, a greyhound, a gazelle, a porpoise,
because "All things, in their inmost reality, testify to the revelation of
the names and attributes of God within them. Each according to its
capacity, indicateth, and is expressive of, the knowledge of God. So
potent and universal is this revelation, that it hath encompassed all
things visible and invisible" (Bahá'u'lláh, *Gleanings*, no. 90.2).

That's why we love stuff! Not because we are inherently moribund
and materialistic. Everything, especially ourselves, reminds us of that
sacred source of our creation. That is why we are especially attracted
so intensely to other people, because love is an operant law of our creation, even as gravity is an extant law of relationships among physical

objects. And, whereas all things in creation manifest some attributes of God, only the human being is capable of manifesting *all* the attributes of God.

There is another useful lesson in this analogy of love and gravity. While the force of gravity depends on the proximity and the mass of the two objects involved, the force of spiritual attraction depends on the completeness and the complexity with which divine attributes become manifest in the two beings involved. In this sense, what we call infatuation or romantic love is not merely an invention or an illusion, as some philosophers have theorized. Indeed, love is a universal spiritual law and thus has an effect on us whether we wish it to or not: "Love is the cause of God's revelation unto man, the vital bond inherent, in accordance with the divine creation, in the realities of things. . . . Love is the most great law that ruleth this mighty and heavenly cycle, the unique power that bindeth together the divers elements of this material world, the supreme magnetic force that directeth the movements of the spheres in the celestial realms" ('Abdu'l-Bahá, *Selections*, no. 12.1).

MODERN LOVE

One of the unfortunate characteristics of contemporary society is that we lack any shared notions of morality, of family, or of community. As a result, we have also adopted a rather pitiful and unfortunate notion of love. For as we have already noted, underlying the Creator's desire to be known is His altruistic desire to share the bounty of His love with a being capable of becoming consciously aware of that love and a being also capable of understanding how to benefit from and respond to that love. And yet, without appropriate guidance, we may very well not recognize the actual source of what attracts us to someone else. As a result, the inherent urge within us can become diverted, deflected, or perverted. If we become entangled in attraction to something that possesses some attributes of the Creator, we may come to believe that the person or object itself is the source of the emanation of those attributes, rather than the Creator.

LOVE AS AN EVENT

Before we can appreciate the appropriate response on our part to this love relationship with our Creator, we must first realize the fundamental húrí of love, the profound "mystery" of love, because we have lost touch with the fullest implications of this force that binds us to the Creator and binds us to every other part of creation. We may marvel at the wonders of nature and the various forms of beauty emanating from one another, yet we may simultaneously be totally unaware of how these inherent attractions relate to our essential nature as divine creations.

Unveiling the húrí of love is no easy task for us. It is hard to be intellectual or objective about this unseen and indescribable magnetic force we all feel at one time or another in one form or another. We have equal difficulty in trying to discover language capable of accurately describing this ineffable sensation, though artists of every sort have tried. In addition, love seems to have so many varied forms and levels that we sometimes apply the term equally to all manner of feelings and affections we have—the love of a parent for a child, the love in a marital relationship, sexual attraction, the affection we feel for pets, the affinity we may have for noble ideas, or the attraction we may have for Chinese food, tennis bracelets, or a sports car.

So it is that while we can never hope to comprehend in any complete form the essential nature of this metaphysical force, we are obliged to learn as much as we can about how it operates within us, especially as it becomes capable of leading us to the more lofty expressions of our human nature. Of course, staunch materialists will attempt to explain this force in terms of biochemical processes. We can, however, find a wealth of helpful information about the more sublime attributes of this inner aspect of our "self" by examining some of the qualities of love as portrayed in informative passages in the Baháʼí texts.

We have already acknowledged that some degree of free will is involved in an authentic love relationship when it occurs between two cognitive beings. For though we may not be able to choose whether or not we are attracted to someone, we can determine how we respond to that attraction. For as we noted, unlike unilateral affection, such as our "love" of pistachio nuts, marzipan, or baklava, human love requires mutuality of attraction followed by a willful response.

FALLING IN LOVE

One of the more important attributes of love we need to comprehend if we are to unveil this húrí is that love is an organic process, not an event. For while this characteristic of love might seem patently obvious on an intellectual level, our contemporary perspective about love manifests "love" as a moment of orgasmic delight rather than as a sophisticated organic process. According to some scholars, we inherited this misapprehension from romantic notions about love that evolved during the medieval era in the courtly literature of Provençal France.

The concept of love as an event, as an impulse that strikes us down beyond our willful control is not entirely ridiculous. The fact is that the initial stages of attraction or infatuation do occur—we don't make this stuff up. We become smitten, whether we want to or not. We "fall" in love, and that's that.

We could at this point meander into a rather lengthy and tedious discourse on the origins of this attitude about love and how its pernicious influence on us individually and as a society has distracted us from achieving our full potential as human beings. But as I have already done much of this in a published article titled "Unveiling the

Húrí of Love," I think it sufficient here to note two major outcomes this assumption about the nature of love inflicts on us.

The first unfortunate outcome is that we have come to believe that once we "fall" in love, we are powerless to resist its hold on us. After all, we did not pursue this attraction. We did not seek it out. Love just happened to us! How, then, can we be held accountable or responsible for whatever course of action we take as a result? Being enthralled in the throes of love and love-longing was referred to in medieval romances and lyric poetry as "the malady of love." Military imagery was also often employed to describe being "conquered" by the victorious beloved. Love, in such a context, is a battle, and the opposing forces are the lover and the beloved.

When society as a whole concurs with this rather naive and juvenile understanding of love, then all sorts of actions that would otherwise be perceived as sinful or at the very least inappropriate or unwise are then considered acceptable and, in some cases, admirable and courageous. The husband or wife be damned! The children too! Even the dog! It could not be helped! Someone "fell" in love, so more power to them! Divide up the family, the children, the furniture, and the dog!

FALLING OUT OF LOVE

The second unfortunate outcome of this "take" on love as an accident, as an event beyond human control, is that if we can "fall" in love, we can just as unpredictably and unintentionally "fall out" of love. It matters not how much love he or she once had for the spouse or the children or the dogs and cats—when love fades, it's really nobody's fault, right? It could not be helped! One person "fell out of love" with the other, and it is clearly inappropriate and "unnatural" to stay in a "loveless" relationship.

In short, the lack of love is likewise considered a matter of fate, even if it results merely from weariness with the sameness of a relationship, regardless of how long it may have endured or how many are made to suffer as a result of its destruction. After all, it's nobody's fault. The relationship simply lost its zing, its zest, like a car when the smell of newness wears off or the transmission goes.

And naturally, when love is gone, there is no reason to consider the vows, the promises, the covenants and conventions of social, civil, or religious authority as binding, is there? After all, how can anyone be held accountable for forces beyond control?

CYCLICAL RELATIONSHIPS

If we allow ourselves to fall victim to the erroneous notion of love as a changeless emotional state of being, then our relationships are doomed to falter, and we are doomed to pursue the foxfire of cyclical relationships. Once the initial aura, perfect chemistry, and magnetic attraction wear off, we think we have fallen out of love. Consequently, we think it appropriate that we venture out again in a perilous but adventurous quest for "new love" which, we are led to believe, may be the "real thing" this time—it will not wear out or lose the glow and charm and delight of emotional fulfillment.

Of course, if we are driven by an erroneous notion of what love is or is meant to be, our quest will inevitably render our life as a pitiful trail of failed relationships, all of which end up the same way because that for which we crave, however much it may seem confirmed by tradition and romantic fiction, is but a chimera without any basis in reality. Here an oft cited axiom comes into play: Insanity is doing the same thing, over and over again, but expecting different results.

It is because we have been trained to accept as factual this mythic love that is instantly perfect and requires no effort or fine tuning that we are perfectly content to continue exposing ourselves and our progeny to various television series where a variety of central characters have really profound love relationships that endure one episode, or possibly two or three. Were these same characters our family or friends, we might consider characterizing such behavior as promiscuous or immoral. But if we accept these portrayals as anything bordering on reality, then on some level we must be as insane as the fictional characters themselves, hoping that the intense passion will last, yet knowing that if there are no more quests for love, the series must end with the boring sameness of everyday life. There could be no more quests, no more anticipation of that magic moment when the character has the first thrill of a new encounter, followed by a few successive encounters until, at last, the two give way to their passion for one another.

Fortunately, they will take a shower, go to their separate abodes, find something they don't like about each other, and start the process over again next week with someone else. But after all, this is not reality. This is just fiction, a bunch of fun, a bit of fluff, a diversion for us after a hard day of doing the not-so-glamorous work of earning a living and raising a family—things that, for some never-explained-reason, these characters never seem required to do.

It is so far off the mark—this formula for love—so hyperbolic that we might not think about what it is teaching us subliminally. If the same sort of tease successfully coaxes us to buy some medicinal or beauty product that we are told will bring us lasting youth and joy, should we not worry about trying to prevent our children or even ourselves from being exposed to such mindlessness? Surely such relentless mantras are as dangerous to our health as cigarettes, and yet we don't allow tobacco products to be advertised.

For some reason we are convinced our little ones will not absorb these lessons or emulate this behavior, even if their best friends might. We are confident that through some sort of osmosis our kids will absorb a more mature example of felicity that we model for them (unless they happen to watch us watching this stuff, laughing at it, intent on discovering if, at long last, the solitary detective or the emotionally maimed doctor will find solace in a lasting love relationship).

The obvious logical flaw in responding to the attraction a religious belief might have for us applies equally well to love in all its manifestations. Love relationships are doomed once the affective stage of the relationship ceases if the foundation of the relationship is emotional or sensual attraction. But if love is an organic process, rather than an event, it will be in a constant state of change, growth, and development, just like every other organic enterprise. Furthermore because we ourselves are organic, both physically and metaphysically, we are also constantly changing. Consequently, any relationships in which we are involved must necessarily evolve and develop and adapt to befit our continually changing condition.

If we think ourselves incapable of accepting this inherent attribute of love and of striving to deal with what these changes require from us, then we would be better off simply avoiding love relationships from the start. However, if love is an inherent force within us, this decision to ignore or deny love might require more stress and more free will and discipline on our part than it would to recognize the organic nature of love, to study and understand it, and then to attempt to become sufficiently self-aware so that we are capable of allowing change to be seen as a sign of growth and a cause for rejoicing, not a sign of "falling out of love."

LOVE AS PROCESS

When we step beyond the limitations of the traditional but obviously inaccurate and flawed concept of love, we can come to appreciate that an authentic love relationship is capable of enduring and of establishing a bulwark against the changes and chances of life. This is not to say that the initial emotional indices of attraction or infatuation are not powerful, real, and important. But if we begin to consider love as an organic process rather than a static condition of ecstatic attraction and adoration, then we realize exactly why the common understanding of love and the love relationship is inadequate and misguided.

Unfortunately, as it turns out, this fiction imitates reality. Or maybe we have become trained to imitate fiction. We have come to accept a moral perspective—or rather an amoral perspective—that real people, such as our own family or the family of virtually all the friends of our children, live with every day. It is precisely about such a cyclical paradigm that ʿAbduʾl-Bahá comments when he says that such "love" relationships as these are not really love at all, regardless of however much society may deem them so: "But the love which sometimes exists between friends is not (true) love, because it is subject to transmutation; this is merely fascination. As the breeze blows, the slender trees yield. If the wind is in the East the tree leans to the West, and if the wind turns to the West the tree leans to the East. This kind of love is originated by the accidental conditions of life. This is not love, it is merely acquaintanceship; it is subject to change" (*Paris Talks,* no. 58.8).

"Susie [or Sam], I'm afraid our relationship has changed." How often have we heard that line or some similar line in fiction as the death knell of a once prospering marriage? And though clearly some relationships are best ended, ordinarily the logical response to such an observation should be, "Yes, Susie [or Sam], isn't that great that we aren't the naive and immature people we were ten [or twenty] years ago when we were so full of immature expectations? Isn't it wonderful that we now know each other so much more deeply and have come to establish a truly collaborative and complementary relationship?"

When ʿAbduʾl-Bahá speaks of a relationship that is subject to "transmutation," he should not be understood to be denigrating just any sort of relationship or all manner of change or development. He is clearly alluding to a relationship predicated on blind affection, on fleeting infatuation, or on the illusion that true love should never experience any sort of variation. Change as part of development and growth is an inevitable and healthy part of any successful relationship. What we hope remains the same is that underpinning, the intellectual and spiritual basis for the relationship, even as Shakespeare's famous Sonnet 116 seems to speak of love as an "ever fixéd mark":

> Let me not to the marriage of true minds
> Admit impediments. Love is not love
> Which alters when it alteration finds,
> Or bends with the remover to remove:
> O no! it is an ever-fixéd mark
> That looks on tempests and is never shaken;
> It is the star to every wandering bark,
> Whose worth's unknown, although his height be taken.
> Love's not Time's fool, though rosy lips and cheeks
> Within his bending sickle's compass come:
> Love alters not with his brief hours and weeks,
> But bears it out even to the edge of doom.
> If this be error and upon me proved,
> I never writ, nor no man ever loved.

Both this poem and the comment by 'Abdu'l-Bahá might be inferred to confirm the contemporary view that if the emotional signs, the affective indices of love falter or fade—if we "fall out" of love—then it's not our fault because this was obviously not real love, not the right person, the proof of which is the fact that our emotions did not remain at the same constant level. After all, true love is forever! It does not change! It is "an ever fixéd mark."

THE TRUE COURSE OF LOVE

To respond to this common misconception, we first need to distinguish between change that is haphazard, and thus indicative of instability, and change that is the predictable and natural process of the healthy growth and development of any organic system. A second valuable distinction in assessing change has to do with whether we are examining the paradigm appropriate to a physical system or that which is appropriate to a metaphysical system.

True, some of the most common indices of a relationship may become manifest in outward physical actions and patterns of behaviors, the heart of a love relationship is the metaphysical or spiritual foundation upon which all other parts of a love are based. Obviously we are aware that we will change physically over time and that however much we might wish that the physical expression of our love might remain constant and changeless, the outward expression of our love will likewise become altered, regardless of what a plethora of ads for emollients and medications might have us believe.

The fact is that a love relationship not only must endure change, it should welcome and embrace change as the sole hope for its survival. Even if it were possible to have a relationship maintain stasis, we would soon find that it would no longer accommodate our changed self. Likewise, a love relationship, whether with another human being or with our Creator, though manifested by physical indices during our physical existence, must over the course of time relate ever more acutely to the spiritual or metaphysical basis for that relationship. Otherwise, the relationship is doomed to subside and decease. The solace in this realization is that because the authentic love relationship has a spiritual or metaphysical foundation, it is not subject to the physical laws of decay and decomposition. Of course, like all organic life, the love relationship is subject to a parallel law of affirmative change.

This parallel with physical organic beings can be stated in the following manner: In the same way that composite or physical beings are either composing or decomposing, so metaphysical organic realities are either ascending (developing or evolving) or descending (receding or deteriorating).

In other words, there is no such thing as stasis for any form of life: "Know that nothing which exists remains in a state of repose—that is to say, all things are in motion. Everything is either growing or declining; all things are either coming from nonexistence into being, or going from existence into nonexistence. So this flower, this hyacinth, during a certain period of time was coming from the world of nonexistence into being, and now it is going from being into nonexistence" ('Abdu'l-Bahá, *Some Answered Questions*, p. 233).

As 'Abdu'l-Bahá further notes in this same context, a metaphysical essence, such as the human soul, is likewise subject to the same law of change, though it is not subject to the law of decomposition. It is constantly changing its condition even though it never changes its essential reality: "Now, as the spirit continues to exist after death, it necessarily progresses or declines; and in the other world to cease to progress is the same as to decline; but it never leaves its own condition, in which it continues to develop" (*Some Answered Questions*, p. 233).

Obviously when we speak of growth, as opposed to the more ambiguous notion of change, we are speaking of positive change. Likewise, when we speak of growth in a metaphysical relationship or system as opposed to a physical system, we are speaking of a type of growth that does not necessarily involve a downside, some form of descent.

This conclusion can help us comprehend how love or a love relationship can be an "ever-fixéd mark," and yet still evolve or change. For even as 'Abdu'l-Bahá notes that the essential human reality, the conscious rational human soul, can evolve infinitely within the category of its existence (it never changes state—it will always be a human soul) so a relationship based on the laws of metaphysics, rather than on the laws of physics, likewise has the capacity for infinite growth or change while still remaining the same essential love relationship.

LOVE AND BELIEF

Interestingly, even though we may think of love between human beings, and other types of love, as being largely unrelated, the same attributes and processes apply in any love relationship. All loves are inherently organic processes, not events. Therefore, the same forces and "accidents"—the changes and chances of life—can be equally applicable to that affection we experience in our religious life. We may love God or love God's representative—Moses, Christ, Muḥammad, the Báb, or Bahá'u'lláh. We may come to love a member of the clergy or priesthood who helps sustain our relationship with God.

But if that relationship is also contingent primarily on our affective response (an emotional bond without any intellectual component), we may fall out of love with a church, a synagogue, a cleric, with a Prophet of God, or with the concept of God itself. We are especially susceptible to such a "falling out" during those times in our lives when unjust and inappropriate things befall us or those whom we hold dear. It is precisely for this reason that many churches among Protestant Christian denominations hold frequent "revivals"—meetings during which emotionally charged sermons are delivered, testimonials of faith are called forth, and all are summoned to the altar to be blessed, to rededicate their pledge of faith, and to have their "love" emotions recharged.

Another result of this attitude about love as it applies to religious faith and affiliation is that many consider it an appropriate practice to wander from church to church, temple to temple, mosque to mosque, or religion to religion if they should happen to grow weary of the emotional sameness of their present religious experience and want to discover some faith tradition that is more inspiring or exhilarating. Clearly the underlying assumption for this "love" relationship is that belief is primarily an emotional condition or a matter of "blind faith," not a logically based integrative force that provides constant guidance and a point of reference.

Akin to this process of falling out of love with a belief or a faith, and more lamentable from a strictly logical point of view, is the contemporary attitude that prompts "seekers" to wander about in search of the right "fit"—a religion or faith tradition that feels most comfortable, that best describes who we think we are and what we consider to be our goals and aspirations. The unspoken assumption in this approach is that we are in good shape spiritually and that we are exactly where we want to be. From such a perspective, we might not care to have someone with spiritual authority tell us that we should reform or reconsider our values to strive to become other than what we already are. After all, if we intend for our religion to make us feel good about ourselves, the last thing we want is for it to make us feel guilty or sinful. We want support, something to sustain and uplift us.

The faulty logic implied in such a view is that the "seeker" is already in a satisfactory spiritual condition. From such a subjective assumption, we would naturally presume that our own sense of comfort is the standard by which we can assess a system of beliefs. We are encouraged to assume that if a set of beliefs indicts our behavior, if it makes us feel uncomfortable with ourselves, then it must be "wrong for us." From this point of view, religion is no longer a source from which we derive our sense of values nor a source of truth about anything, whether we are evaluating other people or theories about physical or metaphysical reality. Religion in this context is not at the center of our lives as an integrating or organization principle; it is simply one among a myriad other descriptors we use to define ourselves.

LOVE AS AN "EVER-FIXÉD MARK"

In the same way that energy cannot be created or lost, only redirected or translated into different forms, so this metaphysical force of love that is the source of all metaphysical or spiritual life cannot be lost, only redirected or deflected. Consequently, it is entirely possible for a love relationship, one that is truly metaphysically based rather than physically based, to endure and evolve endlessly without ever degrading, so long as it is sustained by the "ever-fixéd mark," the unifying force of the love of God from which derive all other forms of affection we experience. In a beautifully poetic exegesis about "love" as the animating force of all forms of reality, 'Abdu'l-Bahá has penned the following verse:

Know thou of a certainty that Love is the secret of God's holy Dispensation, the manifestation of the All-Merciful, the fountain of spiritual outpourings. Love is heaven's kindly light, the Holy Spirit's eternal breath that vivifieth the human soul. Love is the cause of God's revelation unto man, the vital bond inherent, in accordance with the divine creation, in the realities of things. Love is the one means that ensureth true felicity both in this world and the next. Love is the light that guideth in darkness, the living link that uniteth God with man, that assureth the progress of every illumined soul. Love is the most great law that ruleth this mighty and heavenly cycle, the unique power that bindeth together the divers elements of this material world, the supreme magnetic force that directeth the movements of the spheres in the celestial realms. Love revealeth with unfailing and limitless power the mysteries latent in the universe. Love is the spirit of life unto the adorned body of mankind, the establisher of true civilization in this mortal world, and the shedder of imperishable glory upon every high-aiming race and nation. (*Selections*, no. 12.1)

Therefore, while we express our love relationships through physical actions, the underlying and animating source of those physical expressions is our participation in a metaphysical relationship.

But as with every other experience or process of learning or organic relationship, our understanding of this underlying reality that sustains and animates love is necessarily experienced and apprehended by degrees. Were it not for this gradualness, what Bahá'u'lláh describes as *qadar*, we would be incapable of deriving any meaningful experience from this most important of all forces at work in our lives.

LOVE AND "QADAR"

Bahá'u'lláh describes the concept of *qadar* ("degree" or "portion") in demonstrating how God's love for us is portioned out gradually over time according to our capacity in a given stage of our development. He states this axiom throughout His writings, perhaps most memorably in His comparison of the Manifestation to a divine physician:

> The All-Knowing Physician hath His finger on the pulse of mankind. He perceiveth the disease, and prescribeth, in His unerring wisdom, the remedy. Every age hath its own problem, and every soul its particular aspiration. The remedy the world needeth in its present-day afflictions can never be the same as that which a subsequent age may require. Be anxiously concerned with the needs of the age ye live in, and centre your deliberations on its exigencies and requirements. (*Gleanings*, no. 106.1)

Compared to the process of wise parental guidance and love, this analogy would translate into the wisdom with which parents must constantly change or upgrade their response to the needs and capacities of the growing child. Those rules and exhortations that might have been propitious expressions of love and protection a year or two ago, or even a few months ago, may need to be updated and altered as the child gains knowledge, skills, and powers.

Another feature of this concept of portioning out love and guidance according to the constantly changing condition of humankind is explained with the analogy of intensity. In a sublimely simple but wonderfully effective analogy, Bahá'u'lláh explains this concept of *qadar* with the cycle of a day:

Consider the sun. How feeble its rays the moment it appeareth above the horizon. How gradually its warmth and potency increase as it approacheth its zenith, enabling meanwhile all created things to adapt themselves to the growing intensity of its light. How steadily it declineth until it reacheth its setting point. Were it, all of a sudden, to manifest the energies latent within it, it would, no doubt, cause injury to all created things. . . . In like manner, if the Sun of Truth [Manifestations] were suddenly to reveal, at the earliest stages of its manifestation, the full measure of the potencies which the providence of the Almighty hath bestowed upon it, the earth of human understanding would waste away and be consumed; for men's hearts would neither sustain the intensity of its revelation, nor be able to mirror forth the radiance of its light. Dismayed and overpowered, they would cease to exist. (*Gleanings,* no. 38.1)

A third and related expression of *qadar* as demonstrated in the method of gradualness by which human beings are best assisted in development, whether by parents or by the Prophets, relates to the concept of "timeliness." Here again, wisdom and discernment on the part of the educator is absolutely essential to produce enlightenment and advancement rather than injury and retardation in the education of humanity. Some important truth or insight about reality could prove detrimental to humanity if it is not revealed in accordance with the principle of *qadar.*

> Oh, would that the world could believe Me! Were all the things that lie enshrined within the heart of Bahá, and which the Lord, His God, the Lord of all names, hath taught Him, to be unveiled to mankind, every man on earth would be dumbfounded.
>
> How great the multitude of truths which the garment of words can never contain! How vast the number of such verities as no expression can adequately describe, whose significance can never be unfolded, and to which not even the remotest allusions can be made! How manifold are the truths which must remain unuttered until the appointed time is come! Even as it hath been said: "Not everything that a man knoweth can be disclosed, nor can everything that he can disclose be regarded as timely, nor can every timely utterance be considered as suited to the capacity of those who hear it." Know of a certainty that in every Dispensation the light of Divine Revelation hath been vouchsafed unto men in direct proportion to their spiritual capacity. (*Gleanings,* no. 89.2–3)

THE STAGES OF LOVE

Because love is organic in nature, there are predictable stages of a love relationship we need to understand if we are to appreciate this inherent and relentless passion in our lives. Bereft of this understanding, we are destined to wander through our lives in an endless quest to discover the object of our yearning. We will likewise fall prey to the post hoc fallacy of assuming that responding to every new source of titillating distraction—whether sexuality, food, possessions, wealth, power, or prestige—is the possible solution to our desire.

In time we may discover that at the heart of each of these attractions is the manifestation or mimicry of some aspect of divine love. But we have a strategic advantage in the process of coming to understand this principal force in our lives if we know from the beginning that the manifestation of love in every relationship we encounter involves successive predictable stages of advancement.

A simple and accessible paradigm of the progress of love is portrayed by Bahá'u'lláh in His allegorical work the Seven Valleys. As the title implies, Bahá'u'lláh outlines seven stages of one's love relationship with God, though the paradigm is equally illuminating and valid in explaining human love relationships.

Comprehending the first four stages is the most helpful for us, inasmuch as beyond the fourth stage, the lover traverses about in the realms beyond physical limitations that are portrayed by Bahá'u'lláh in such poetic and ineffable terms that we are hard put to do much more than grasp the emotional indices He portrays as alluding to these exalted categories of spiritual experience.

The first stage of love is the process of searching for the beloved, a stage which requires that the seeker become receptive, pure of heart, and, above all else, aware of the nature of that which is sought. For example, if we understand the attributes of the beloved in ordinary human terms—if our criteria for the beloved consist solely of traditional signs of outward beauty—we are not very likely to discover the true source of our longing.

Here the analogy of physical training becomes useful. If we are striving to achieve a state of health, we would do well to follow the advice of a nutritionist rather than ingest those foods that are most appealing because of taste or appearance. But as we gradually train and become more healthy, we quickly discover that foods that are detrimental to our health lose their appeal. We become attracted to foods that give us the nourishment our body needs. In time we begin to avoid those foods that are unhealthy and perceive them as unappealing or even as repulsive.

This same principle holds true for our love relationships, particularly our search for the Manifestation. Whether we are searching for a life partner or for a Prophet of God, our faculty of discernment will be explicitly conditioned by our daily spiritual regimen, even as our quest for physical conditioning is predicated on a healthy spiritual regimen. If we are in a condition of depravity and mindlessly follow our appetitive nature, we are most likely going to be attracted to that which is detrimental to our spiritual development—that which appeals to our crass desire or base instincts.

It is doubtless in this vein that Christ exhorted His disciples to be ready to discover the return of the succeeding Manifestation of God by employing a simple analogy. If one is looking for a fig tree, one should attempt to discover a tree that has figs. In short, one can discern the quality or type of tree by the fruit it bears. Of course, also implicit in this analogy is that the seeker needs to know what figs look like.

Similarly, in our search for a Manifestation we need to know what the attributes of a Prophet of God are, as opposed to the attributes of someone falsely claiming to be one. Bahá'u'lláh observes that in this beginning stage of searching, the true seeker, in addition to knowing what signs characterize the beloved, must himself exhibit patience and persistence. Stated in the most ordinary terms, if the proper standards for search are applied, then in time the healthy seeker will discover one to whom he or she is strongly attracted.

The second stage of love or attraction consists of an overwhelming desire and longing to attain the presence of the beloved, the very same condition to which we have alluded as the commonplace definition of love itself. But as Bahá'u'lláh makes clear, this stage of enthrallment, while valuable and strategically important, is temporary and should lead one to another stage in the relationship, or else it will most surely become a source of destruction rather than the beginning of an ever-evolving relationship: "And if, confirmed by the Creator, the lover escapes from the claws of the eagle of love, he will enter the Valley of Knowledge and come out of doubt into certitude, and turn from the darkness of illusion to the guiding light of the fear of God" (The Seven Valleys, p. 11).

It is for this reason that 'Abdu'l-Bahá, in discussing the requisites of a process for discovering a marriage partner, advises us that attraction is important, but once that initial attraction has taken place, the couple must then become informed of each other's character to see if the attraction has a foundation based on something more healthy and enduring than sensual allure: "Bahá'í marriage is the commitment of the two parties one to the other, and their mutual attachment of mind and heart. Each must, however, exercise the utmost care to become thoroughly acquainted with the character of the other, that the binding covenant between them may be a tie that will endure forever" (*Selections*, no. 86.1).

This investigation of character in a personal relationship is parallel to the acquisition of knowledge of the character and teachings of the Manifestation in examining a religious belief. This is accomplished by practices such as examining the extent to which the life and actions of the Manifestation comply with His teachings, studying the logic and wisdom inherent in the teachings themselves, exploring the history of the religion, and becoming familiar with the quality of those who claim to be its adherents. The gradual acquisition of knowledge about that to which we are so strongly attracted will inform us if the relationship has a solid foundation and should be pursued, or is based on circumstantial or emotional appeal and should thus be abandoned.

The ultimate objective of this knowledge is conveyed by Bahá'u'lláh in terms that reverberate throughout the entirety of the Bahá'í texts. It is the pervasive concept of learning to discern "the end in the beginning." By this enigmatic phrase, Bahá'u'lláh explains that all knowledge, whether of material or spiritual laws about reality, ultimately leads us to an awareness that the source of all reality is God and that all creation takes its meaning and purpose according to the degree to which it manifests some attributes or understanding of the Creator. In terms of love between human beings (romantic love), we come to appreciate that we are drawn to each other by virtue of our having been created in God's image. And since God has no physical dimension per se, we come to realize that all creation is effectively the "temple" of God, the outer expression of His divine beauty. In short, our love of or attraction to any physical form or to any metaphysical concept is, when correctly comprehended, but a pathway leading us to the love of the Creator.

So it is that the "end" or objective of all knowledge is the understanding and subsequent love of God. In this sense, every aspect of physical creation and every experience we have in it are but a means to this end. We are, in effect, being led incrementally to that source from which we emanated as a breath of spirit, as essentially spiritual beings or human souls operating temporarily through a physical vehicle, the human temple.

And yet our body, our physical edifice that "houses" that essential self, no less exemplifies the Creator's handiwork. In the Qur'án we find the statement that "We have indeed created man in the best of molds," (95:4) a passage we might well infer to mean that we are physically appealing creations—we are created in beauteous forms. Our awareness of our own beauty, our own form, is manifested in obvious or overt terms by any cursory examination of art history. Our most fundamental awe is in contemplating our own physical makeup. We never grow tired of seeing images of the effulgence of that beauty.

Yet how much more amazed we become by this attraction once we begin to enter this third stage of love, the Valley of Knowledge. In this stage in the progress of love, we realize that both the primal source of this fascination and its end result is knowledge of the Creator in whose image we are made. Our attraction to that subtle form of ourselves derives not merely from sexual or biochemical reaction. We actually sense in that complex expression of beauty the form or idea of beauty as a divine attribute. Underlying our love of a concrete expression of a divine attribute is our attraction to a more lofty expression of that same affection, our love of the concept of beauty itself. And the ultimate source of our affection for all abstract realities (beauty, truth, justice, and the like) is the Creator (what Socrates calls "the Good").

Indeed, the fourth stage of love is the Valley of Unity, a subjective rather than a purely intellectual experience of the underlying integrity of creation and the coherence of God's plan. In this stage of love, all physical reality is understood as one organic expression of divine reality, and both physical and metaphysical aspects of reality are experienced as an emanation of the one Creator. This experience of unity from a personal perspective is hinted at by a passage Bahá'u'lláh cites from the Imám 'Alí: "Nothing have I perceived except that I perceived God before it, God after it, or God with it" (quoted in *Epistle to the Son of the Wolf*, p. 113).

In the Seven Valleys itself, Bahá'u'lláh presents several vivid analogies to illustrate this same experience. In this stage of enlightenment, the Valley of Unity, one realizes that all distinction or variation in creation derives solely from the perspective of the observer. By analogy, various terrains will appear with various hues, textures, and luminescence, even though all are illuminated by the light of the same sun. In other words, all variations appear because of distinctions among that which is illumined, even though the light of the sun remains constant and without variation.

Once we enter this stage, we sense or experience the essential unity of reality underlying all notions of distinction. In such a condition, concepts of first and last, of seen and unseen, cease to have importance because all creation is understood to be one organic expression of a single reality, the reality of the Creator: "Then what life have words, on such a plane, that 'first' and 'last' or other than these be seen or mentioned! In this realm, the first is the last itself, and the last is but the first" (The Seven Valleys, p. 28).

Having experienced the essential unity of creation, the seeker may then attain the fifth stage, the Valley of Contentment. This and the succeeding stages of "wonderment" and "true poverty and absolute nothingness" are so ineffable as to transcend the capacity of language to portray them adequately:

> The tongue faileth in describing these three Valleys, and speech falleth short. The pen steppeth not into this region, the ink leaveth only a blot. In these planes, the nightingale of the heart hath other songs and secrets, which make the heart to stir and the soul to clamor, but this mystery of inner meaning may be whispered only from heart to heart, confided only from breast to breast. (The Seven Valleys, p. 29)

Bahá'u'lláh alludes to the contentment the seeker or lover experiences at this stage in the evolution of the love relationship with several effective poetic passages. He observes that in this valley, the lover "burneth away the veils of want" and "from sorrow he turneth to bliss, from anguish to joy. His grief and mourning yield to delight and rapture," for on this plane, "the traveler witnesseth the beauty of the Friend in everything" (The Seven Valleys, p. 29).

THE NEED FOR GUIDANCE

If the evidence of the Creator is effectively inescapable, why is it necessary that we have a teacher or guide in this process of fulfilling our inherent purpose of coming to know the Creator? If we have further been created with an innate sense of curiosity, with an inherent love of discovery and learning, why are we not simply born into this rich storehouse of teaching devices and left to our own free will and creativity to figure things out for ourselves? In the next chapter we will discover the logical necessity for us human beings to have mentors from the outset.

3

HOW TO LOVE
AN UNKNOWABLE BELOVED

*How then can I sing and tell of Thine Essence, which the wisdom
of the wise and the learning of the learned have failed to
comprehend, inasmuch as no man can sing that which he
understandeth not, nor recount that unto which he cannot attain,
whilst Thou hast been from everlasting the Inaccessible, the
Unsearchable. Powerless though I be to rise to the heavens of
Thy glory and soar in the realms of Thy knowledge, I can
but recount Thy tokens that tell of Thy glorious handiwork.*
—'Abdu'l-Bahá

In a prayer revealed by 'Abdu'l-Bahá, the suppliant addresses the Creator in the following manner: "By Thy Glory! O Beloved of all hearts, Thou that alone canst still the pangs of yearning for Thee!" As we have noted, this love relationship we inherently yearn to attain is assisted by the fact that everything in creation manifests the attributes of the Creator. As we have also noted, because of this essential nature of creation to manifest some aspect of the divine, we might correctly consider physical reality as a classroom fashioned by the Creator precisely to teach us about our essential nature as spiritual beings. If we study this affection intelligently, we will become aware that the foundation

59

of all desire is our yearning to attain the knowledge of God, if we will but open the doors of perception. When we strive to attain this understanding, the knowledge we acquire is then capable of leading us to an eternally progressive love relationship with the Creator.

Therefore, while the Bahá'í writings give ample testimony to the fact that the Creator is *essentially* unknowable, we now realize that the word *essentially* is intended to be taken quite literally—we cannot know God's essence. However, what is also apparent is that we can know all manner of things *about* the Creator. As we have concluded, if everything in creation, including our own being, testifies to the nature of God, whether to a greater or lesser degree, then we can hardly escape knowing *about* God, even if His *essence* will ever remain veiled from complete or exact knowledge on our part.

THE LOGICAL NECESSITY FOR AN EDUCATOR

Even with all creation exhorting us to know and love the Creator so that we might benefit and progress from that knowledge, we still need important assistance. The fact is that we are not going to make any headway in our life's purpose without external assistance, without guidance, without a teacher. For unlike animal life, we as human beings are fashioned without a great deal of instinctive behavior. We need to be taught almost everything we learn.

In short, we can not spontaneously intuit the purpose of all these wonderful things around us, let alone the deeper metaphysical meaning of our relationships, without unremitting assistance from some teacher who possesses the knowledge and experience to nudge us in the right direction. By analogy, if we were to take an extremely bright child who had never been taught anything, and if we then placed this child in the best classroom our minds could devise—full of educational toys, computers, and teaching tools of every sort—we could hardly expect the child to learn anything at all if it were simply abandoned there.

Even after we have learned initial survival skills from our parents—walking, talking, nutrition, hygiene, and so on—we will not be able to progress further without continued assistance to provide us with constant and progressive increments of foundational skills and basic tools for living.

HUMANITY'S NEED FOR INTERCESSION

The observation about our need for assistance is logical and clear at the level of the individual, but if we consider humankind collectively on planet Earth the logic and wisdom of the need for help is no less pressing. Let us think of humanity as students in classroom Earth, and let us presume that most of us are at the same level of enlightenment, or lack of it. By analogy, we quickly realize that we will become no more educated than the brightest among us. And unless this person is a good teacher, we will never become even that bright. Furthermore, by the law of entropy, all the students of this teacher will become less astute by degrees so that over the course of time, the collective body politic will sink to the level of brutes.

This observation and conclusion can be upheld with a vast, intricate, and well-articulated analysis, but for our purposes, we need only acknowledge that the logical conclusion is inescapable. Without infusions of guidance from outside the physically closed system that is planet Earth, humankind would never have emerged from its rudimentary existence in caves. In fact, according to the law of entropy, without the infusion of outside information and guidance, the classroom of the children of men would degenerate into ineptitude.

Since the reverse of this has taken place and we have as a global community witnessed the ascent of humankind in terms of technological capacity and concepts of justice and global polity, it is only logical to conclude that there must have been in our history some external assistance in the form of Teachers who possessed "other worldly" knowledge—knowledge acquired from outside the confines of classroom Earth. Of course, we could theorize that each increment of human development or vast advance in human knowledge came about by chance or by trial and error. We saw fire happen with a lightning strike, so we fooled around with stuff until we could create fire ourselves by striking flint, rubbing sticks, or stealing fire from a burning brush after a lightning strike—a somewhat more chancy system. The discoveries by individuals that mark the major advances in physics and other sciences through the ages might seem to confirm this theory—ingenious minds started asking questions about how things work or how to make things work, and incrementally we advanced our understanding of reality.

The problem with this theory is that somebody had to raise these people and prime these minds. Someone taught them the foundational studies that enabled them to transform their potential for innovation and creativity into systematic thinking. Or to state the overall problem in terms of physical laws, a system cannot progress beyond the bounds of the energy that is infused into it. What is more, the source of that energy must be greater than the recipient of that energy. And if we could view human progress from its beginnings, we would realize that no progress could have been made without some initial infusion of instruction and guidance. Learning as an active creative and organic force cannot be set in motion without some external source of energy or stimulation.

Another aspect of this need for external prompting and guidance is that a single infusion of instruction is not sufficient. Again, physical law dictates that over time this single input of inspiration and energy will become diffused and dissipate. This observation holds true most especially for knowledge of metaphysical laws. For while we observe in primitive cultures the attempt to explain metaphysics in terms of nature-based beliefs that strive to explain the unexplainable, we soon observe a pantheon of divine forces with some systematic order. We further observe similar polytheistic concepts among diverse cultures that defy chance. In most cases, these similar concepts emerged at a time when communication was not possible between people on opposite sides of the globe.

For example, we need only compare the complex mythology of ancient Greece to the similarly complex Teutonic mythologies of the Germanic peoples to realize that the parallels in overall perspective and the systematic particularization of the function of deities, while based in nature, did not merely emerge spontaneously from observing nature. Some individual at some point must have introduced this abiding concept of nature as emulating metaphysical powers and forces.

Obviously, much of the religious beliefs among tribal cultures derive from a need to explain natural or physical phenomena that are for these peoples at their level of education otherwise incomprehensible, and yet extremely significant occurrences in their lives. Another bulwark for these tribal beliefs is the even deeper desire to discern some strategic and systematic purpose underlying the individual and collective lives of the ordinary members of the tribal community, especially as their lives interact with natural forces.

And yet it is not an adequate explanation for the emergence of these religions or the parallels among them to suggest that these needs were sufficient cause for the creation of beliefs, however much these desires may have buoyed or reinforced them. We may have heard, for example, how in some African tribal communities, the shaman could determine who was lying by touching the tongue of those under suspicion with an extremely hot stone. Because the tribe believed firmly in this power, those who had lied were in stark terror of being discovered and would experience a dryness in their mouths. The rock would burn them, but not those who, assured of their own innocence, would have moist tongues to deflect the initial pain the hot stone would inflict.

Here we see the power of superstition interacting with natural laws to empower a tribal belief that the shaman had supernatural powers. Furthermore we observe over time how some of the more widespread tribal beliefs seem to degenerate into cruel and, to our thinking, "unreligious" or "sacrilegious" acts of cannibalism or other forms of human sacrifice. In effect, what may have been initially noble attempts at understanding metaphysical concepts—especially as they apply to human attributes such as nobility, loyalty, truthfulness, and kindness—have become distorted, confused, or appropriated for use by those who desired to acquire power for perverse reasons of personal status and self-aggrandizement.

We can with a degree of certainty suppose that this is the pattern that these ancient religions followed, just as this same pattern is evident in the development of the more recent religions of Judaism, Christianity, and Islam. For though Paul in his second letter to Timothy states that "the love of money is the root of all evil" (6:10), money in and of itself has value only inasmuch as it provides power. Therefore we could reframe the axiom as it relates generally to human interaction, to state that the love of *power* is the source of all evil.

This revised axiom is certainly evident when religions and religious institutions founded for the explicit purpose of beatifying human behavior, especially as that behavior relates to social interaction, become politicized to uphold the desire for power and control on the part of an individual or some power-seeking segment of leaders within a religion.

We could obviously spend a great deal of time tracking this paradigm of infighting that crops up over time in the course of most religious history. Many volumes have been devoted to examining this process. This ostensibly "natural" course of religion is the central theme in Richard Dawkins' best selling book *The God Delusion*. Dawkins argues that society would have been better off without religion or belief in

God, since the passionate emotions and chauvinism associated with religious belief have been, and yet remain, the cause of so much strife, bloodshed, and inhumanity. A television documentary based on Dawkins' book takes its title "The Root of all Evil?" from Paul's axiom regarding the love of money, or power, as the source of discord and enmity among the peoples of the world.

THE DOUBLE-EDGED SWORD

Clearly power, like all forms of energy, is amoral. It can be used for good or ill. What is most interesting for our purposes is that religious beliefs, together with the passions and emotions associated with them, constitute one of the most powerful forces that drive social movements, particularly movements aimed at reformation. And yet this same power, if perverted or appropriated for purposes of personal power-seeking, can become an equally powerful force for social discord and destruction.

But again, this evidence does not logically demonstrate that religion or belief in a supreme being is in itself the cause of this history of grief. This is especially true when we consider that what often passes for religion—entrenched dogma and fanatical religious institutions—bears little similarity to what the Founders of the religions taught or intended. What this view of history demonstrates well is that beliefs and systems of belief are sources of incredible power and that power can be employed to build a great society or to oppress, enslave, and cause antipathy among the peoples of the world.

As we will discuss in more detail later, what can ensure that religion or religious doctrines do not become distorted or deranged is a logically and justly devised religious institution, a "new wineskin," as Christ called it, an institution capable of flexibility, growth, and change. But even if the creation of the institution devised by the Manifestation or

His followers is devised appropriately and benignly, there will over the course of time be the need for a new revelation and new institutional structures to befit the needs and capacities of an evolved human society. Indeed, 'Abdu'l-Bahá states that growth is a fundamental attribute of a religion and its institutions:

> Religion is the outer expression of the divine reality. Therefore it must be living, vitalized, moving and progressive. If it be without motion and non-progressive it is without the divine life; it is dead. The divine institutes are continuously active and evolutionary; therefore the revelation of them must be progressive and continuous. All things are subject to re-formation. . . . The divine prophets have revealed and founded religion. They have laid down certain laws and heavenly principles for the guidance of mankind. They have taught and promulgated the knowledge of God, established praiseworthy ethical ideals and inculcated the highest standards of virtues in the human world. Gradually these heavenly teachings and foundations of reality have been beclouded by human interpretations and dogmatic imitations of ancestral beliefs. The essential realities which the prophets labored so hard to establish in human hearts and minds while undergoing ordeals and suffering tortures of persecution, have now well nigh vanished. Some of these heavenly messengers have been killed, some imprisoned; all of them despised and rejected while proclaiming the reality of divinity. Soon after their departure from this world, the essential truth of their teachings was lost sight of and dogmatic imitations adhered to. Inasmuch as human interpretations and blind imitations differ widely, religious strife and disagreement have arisen among mankind, the light of true religion has been extinguished and the unity of the world of humanity destroyed. (*Foundations of World Unity*, p. 83)

HOW TRUE RELIGION EMANATES FROM THE WISH OR WILL OF THE CREATOR

If there is perfect love emanating from an omnipotent and benign Creator, and if that love becomes systematically expressed in this plane of existence through divinely revealed religions, we should naturally want to know how it is possible that these expressions of the divine will seem so imperfect. Or as we noted at the outset, if it is the plan of God that religion be the source of human enlightenment and progress, how could these same forces become a principal source of conflict, turmoil, and hatred—the very antithesis of what a loving Creator would *wish* or *will* to take place?

AUTHENTIC KNOWLEDGE REQUIRES FREE WILL

We noted before that as an omnipotent Creator, God could have created whatever He desired, but His wish to be known by beings capable of freely coming to appreciate and benefit from His unconditional love required that He fashion beings capable of acquiring knowledge and, subsequently, of choosing to apply that knowledge. Therefore, as a perfect educator, the Creator devised an indirect methodology in order to make knowledge available to humankind by degrees.

As we have also observed, this process is a requirement for all education. If our learning consists solely of memorizing axioms, then we have not acquired anything of enduring value. We are parroting what somebody else has learned. But when we are given gentle and subtle guidance, together with the essential tools for obtaining information for ourselves, we are no longer being indoctrinated. We are acquiring knowledge and, more importantly, we are learning how to learn!

True education or enlightenment is, therefore, not the acquisition of a body of fact, but the honing of the tools for acquiring understanding as we become gradually exposed to successively greater challenges and ever more complex questions. And to achieve this education, we must have a teacher to prime us. At every stage of this process, however, we must maintain an abiding desire to pursue this sometimes arduous and demanding task. We also need the freedom to exercise this desire.

The fact that free will is an essential part of enlightenment is at the heart of the logical requirement that the Creator fashion us as beings rich with potential for success, but capable of error and failure. This requirement is also the rationale behind all the indirection involved in our education. It is for this reason that we begin our lives in a physical classroom that emulates in symbolic or sensually perceptible terms the fundamental realities and relationships operant in the spiritual realm which we are being prepared to enter.

There is another equally important conclusion we draw from this understanding of the Creator's methodology in fashioning us to become participants in our own progress. If it is essential that in this life we acquire not merely information but the means of acquiring information and the means to express knowledge in action, then we necessarily must conclude that we will continue to need these same tools and processes after our transition to the spiritual realm.

Put another way, the ultimate goal of the education religion is revealed to teach us is that we become ever more aware of how our daily experience with reality, particularly with other human beings, can inform us about divine reality. And the ultimate purpose of that information and foundational training is to prepare ourselves, through God's systematic educational plan, for entrance into that reality. If we become aware of this objective and the educational system provided to attain it, then we will be less troubled by the seeming injustices of this realm. We will also be more likely to welcome that transition and perhaps be more prepared to navigate a metaphysical environment.

The fact that all our freely chosen efforts at acquiring knowledge are focused on our future existence should in no way be construed as devaluing or deemphasizing our existential or "earthly" experience.

Unlike the somber teachings of ascetically oriented religions and sects, the Bahá'í teachings exhort us to enjoy this life and take full advantage of all it has to offer. We should be ever mindful of our abiding purpose of extracting spiritual lessons from this educational experience, but this process necessarily requires that we indulge ourselves in the active pursuit of our own enlightenment, a quest that should exhilarate us, not render us grave, dour, and withdrawn from this world.

ACTION AS THE COMPLEMENT TO KNOWLEDGE

Action is a necessary complement to faith and knowledge. Stated in more practical terms, all personal knowledge is theoretical until it is expressed in some form of action. Even in science, we use the laboratory as a place to exercise our theories about reality, to test them in action. It is in this context that Shoghi Effendi describes our daily life in our community as a classroom or laboratory wherein we can exercise and develop our knowledge and capacities as spiritual and social beings:

> The Bahá'í community life provides you with an indispensable laboratory, where you can translate into living and constructive action the principles which you imbibe from the Teachings. By becoming a real part of that living organism you can catch the real spirit which runs throughout the Bahá'í Teachings. To study the principles, and to try to live according to them, are, therefore, the two essential mediums through which you can ensure the development and progress of your inner spiritual life and of your outer existence as well. (*The Compilation of Compilations,* 2:424)

This inextricable relationship between study and action, between theory and practice, constitute the twin pillars of true education. Once we have the subjective experience of a verity working in our lives, particularly in our relationships with other human beings attempting the same objectives, we not only confirm the validity of our theoretical learning, but we also appreciate the joy of acquiring this knowledge and are eager to learn more.

Stated in other terms, the act of learning is completed once the freely chosen task of acquiring knowledge is practiced in a series of freely chosen actions. We could learn an immense amount about riding a bicycle. We could study theories of balance, rules of the road, how the various parts of the bicycle work, and strategies for care and maintenance. However, the fact is that one afternoon of actually riding a bicycle instantly replaces what weeks and months of study might have attempted to teach. The subjective experience of balance, of how to turn toward the lean, about what it feels like to hold the handlebars stable as we pump our legs—all these actions instantly complete the process of transforming theoretical understanding into actual knowledge. What is more, the experience establishes a basis for further expansion of theoretical knowledge. Suddenly all the words describing the experience relate to and derive from our personal action of riding the bike, even if we have that experience only briefly.

The same process and principle holds true for metaphysical virtues. We could attend countless seminars instructing us about the nature and the value of kindness, particularly as this virtue applies to our relationships with other people. But if we simply engage in several possibly unrelated acts of kindness to other people and subsequently experience the emotional effect these simple acts have on others and on us, we will instantly become aware of the essential nature and existential benefit of this virtue.

From this point onward, the virtue of kindness will no longer consist of mere words and concepts. We will be capable of relating the concept to these particular instances in which we have felt the joy of bestowing and receiving kindness. And the more adept we become in the practice of the virtue, the more encompassing and complex our understanding and appreciation of this essential spiritual reality becomes.

Over time we discover that we can become experts in the art of kindness, of justice, of love, and of every other attribute. We can become refined practitioners in the art of Godliness. But to become successful at our profession, we must be willing to make this personal transformation an inalienable part of our daily lives. We must come to think of ourselves as becoming perpetual students in the divine art of becoming virtuous. No matter how proficient we may become, we can always be more adept at this art so long as we never come to believe we have achieved some final stage of advancement.

BRIDGING THE GAP

To a certain extent, we can now appreciate how physical exercises and processes are capable of completing our understanding of both our essential nature as spiritual beings and our spiritual purposes in coming to know (and subsequently to worship) the Creator. We begin with very rudimentary learning and progress as far as we are capable over the span of this earthly life. We then continue in the next life where we have left off here. We might assume, in other words, that this is how the gap between the Creator and ourselves is bridged.

But there is much more going on in that gap than we might first realize. In fact, understanding the nature of this gap and all that goes on within it constitutes the most important objective of the remainder of our study.

THAT SPACE BETWEEN THE FINGERS

The gap in Michelangelo's depiction of God empowering Adam demonstrates the artist's awareness that somehow the divine guidance of the Creator must traverse that divide between the metaphysical and physical aspects of reality. To accomplish this task, the Creator has devised specialized Beings, the Prophets or Manifestations of God, Who, according to Bahá'í scripture, preexist in and are fully aware of the spiritual realm but Who willingly take on the task of assuming human form in order to dwell among us that we might be educated by degrees.

THE MANIFESTATION AS GUIDE

While physical reality is replete with symbolic expressions of the attributes of the Creator, without the Manifestations as our guides none of these ingenious symbols would have much value for us. It is the Manifestations who exemplify and then explain to us the "names" of God that are also revealed in nature and in ourselves so that we may understand the means whereby we can become appreciative children, loving and adept parents, dutiful and caring husbands and wives, and faithful and friendly neighbors.

But clearly we, as children of God, are not able simply to intuit what we need to know. True, once we have been capably tutored and set in motion, we can build on what we have been taught. Yet because there is an infinite amount for us to learn, we will never outgrow our need for additional assistance, whether as individuals or as a society, whether in this life or in the life to come. Therefore, let us examine exactly how the Manifestations carry out Their mission as guides in an otherwise guideless realm.

4

THE MANIFESTATION
AS INTERMEDIARY

*The essence of belief in Divine unity consisteth in regarding Him
Who is the Manifestation of God and Him Who is the invisible, the
inaccessible, the unknowable Essence as one and the same. By this is
meant that whatever pertaineth to the former, all His acts and doings,
whatever He ordaineth or forbiddeth, should be considered, in all
their aspects, and under all circumstances, and without any
reservation, as identical with the Will of God Himself. This is
the loftiest station to which a true believer in the unity of God
can ever hope to attain. Blessed is the man that reacheth this
station, and is of them that are steadfast in their belief.*

—Bahá'u'lláh

Like most religions, the Bahá'í Faith asserts that the Creator has sent
Prophets or Messengers to teach and guide humankind. The distinctive nature of the Bahá'í belief about these Intermediaries is that where
some religions ascribe a variety of spiritual stations and capacities to
these Messengers, the Bahá'í scriptures are unambiguous about Their
nature and purpose. This understanding of terminology goes a long
way toward clarifying both the concept of what precise purpose these

Beings serve and how They are distinct from other important figures in religious history who, while influential and meritorious, do not possess the status or overall function as do the these divine Educators in carrying out the Creator's desire to be known and loved.

THE HINDU CONCEPT OF
DIVINE INTERMEDIARIES

The Hindu Faith, perhaps the oldest continuing religious tradition, portrays God (or Vishnu) as sending a sequence of Avatars, the ten most important of which are thought to incarnate the virtues of Vishnu, or else to be literal incarnations of Vishnu Himself. The best known of these Intermediaries are Krishna and Buddha, though the mythic traditions and variations of belief within both Hinduism and Buddhism hardly support a unified or consistent portrayal of some standardized theology or a consistent view of religious history.

THE JUDAIC CONCEPT
OF THE PROPHETS

The portrayal of Intermediaries or Prophets in the Torah (or Pentateuch), is distinct from the way in which these same figures are described later in the Qur'án. According to the Old Testament, the Prophets of Judaic religious history, particularly the antediluvian patriarchs Adam and Noah, are perceived not so much as divine Emissaries as they are ordinary human spiritual leaders to whom God gives explicit instructions. The later central Prophets of Judaism—Abraham and Moses—are also portrayed as extraordinary religious leaders directed by God, but not as divine beings sent from the spiritual realm. They are portrayed as fallible individuals whom God anoints to carry out specific missions. After this transformative anointing, these figures assume leadership based on incremental guidance given to them directly by God.

In the Old Testament this process is portrayed in literal terms. God speaks directly to these individuals and explains exactly what they should do and how they should go about accomplishing their tasks. And though they may have been chosen because of some inherent capacity or nobility of character, they are sometimes portrayed as being relatively clueless about their station or purpose until God reveals Himself bit by bit. Furthermore, they are inclined now and again to become impatient and evoke God's wrath and punishment, or so the chronicles of these events would have us infer.

THE CHRISTIAN MESSIANIC BELIEF

In the majority of interpretations of Christian theology, the principal intermediary between God and humankind is God Himself. According to the Trinitarian doctrine, God temporarily assumes the guise of an ordinary human being, Christ (the Messiah or "Anointed One"). God in the form of an ordinary human persona is thereby able to fulfill the prophecies regarding the advent of the Messiah, bring the new law, and sacrifice Himself on the cross as recompense or atonement for the sins of humankind that began with the fall of Adam and Eve (humankind) from grace.

According to most Christian belief, particularly as discussed in Paul's letters, the prophets of the "Old Testament" are still important spiritual leaders, but their function historically was to prepare people for the advent of the "Savior," the Messiah who would effectively set things right for all time. From this Christian perspective, Judaism was a part of God's plan, but the ultimate expression of God's intervention in human history is the advent of Christ. Likewise, the conclusion of human history, according to many interpretations of Christ's words about His return, together with the symbolic expressions of eschatology in the Revelations of St. John the Divine, will be the Last Judgment that will occur with the Second Coming of Christ at the time of "the end."

75

THE ISLAMIC CONCEPT OF THE MESSENGERS

Islamic belief as set forth in the Qur'án establishes a very clear distinction between the Prophets or Apostles of God, and God Himself. This is possibly the foremost theme of the Qur'án—the absolute supremacy of God the Creator. All besides God is created by Him and functions according to His will.

Muḥammad repeatedly alludes to the plan whereby God sends a sequence of divinely empowered Apostles or Messengers of God, all of whom are of equal status and rank, but each of whom has a specific part to play in the ongoing spiritual enlightenment and education of humankind. Therefore, frequently throughout the Qur'án Muḥammad lists these Intermediaries and sometimes describes the trials and tribulations they endure when, ironically, they are rejected by the very people to whom they are sent in fulfillment of prophecy.

Muḥammad observes that in spite of the proofs of Their station and Their capacity to reveal guidance, these Messengers suffer, are rejected, and only later are appropriately recognized, most often because of the salutary influence Their advent has manifested among the peoples who become influenced by Their teachings. Furthermore, according to the Qur'án, Adam is not an ordinary human being who sins against God, but is one of these divinely empowered Messengers sent by God to teach humankind the "names" (spiritual attributes) manifested in all created things.

THE BAHÁ'Í CONCEPT OF THE MANIFESTATION

The Bahá'í Faith amplifies and further clarifies the description in the Qur'án of the divinely created process by which humankind is uplifted and educated. First, the term "Manifestation" is employed to replace the Islamic term "Messenger" to emphasize the fact that these specialized Emissaries are not ordinary human beings, but an order of representatives from the divine realm Who perfectly incarnate or "manifest" all the attributes of God but are not of the same "essence" as God—that is, They are not incarnations of God Himself, but of His qualities.

Second, Bahá'u'lláh explains that this process has existed ever since the emergence of humankind on Earth and will continue so long as Earth endures. In this sense, no Manifestation is individually superior to another in rank or capacity. But because this is an ongoing educational program, each successive Manifestation necessarily sums up all that has preceded Him and then takes the process a stage further. It is in this sense that each Manifestation "seals up" or is the "end" or culmination of all that has gone before, and yet is the "beginning" of a new revelation, another stage in human development.

It is in this context that Christ says He is the "alpha and the omega" (Rev 1:10), and Muḥammad observes similarly that He is the first Adam:

> These Manifestations of God have each a twofold station. One is the station of pure abstraction and essential unity. In this respect, if thou callest them all by one name, and dost ascribe to them the same attributes, thou hast not erred from the truth. Even as He hath revealed: "No distinction do We make between any of His Messengers"[2:285]. For they, one and all, summon the people of the earth to acknowledge the unity of God, and herald unto them the Kawthar of an infinite grace and bounty. They are all invested with the robe of prophethood, and are honored with the mantle of glory. Thus hath Muhammad, the Point of the Qur'án, revealed: "I am all the Prophets." Likewise, He saith: "I am the first Adam, Noah, Moses, and Jesus." (Bahá'u'lláh, Kitáb-i-Íqán, ¶161)

THE BAHÁ'Í CONCEPT OF THE COVENANT

Bahá'u'lláh explains the distinction between two categories of covenants relevant to the education of humanity. There is the Eternal Covenant between God and humankind represented most notably in recorded religious history by God's covenant with Abraham. According to this pact, God will never leave humanity without appropriate guidance and assistance in the form of these Emissaries and the guidance They bring. This eternal Covenant is sometimes alluded to in the authoritative Bahá'í texts as the "Major Plan of God" or as the "Most Great Covenant," and it designates the entire systematic process whereby God sends successive Manifestations to educate humankind by degrees with the abiding objective of fashioning a global society run according to spiritual principles. Or stated in the terms Christ employs, the purpose of the Major Plan is the gradual construction of the Kingdom of God on Earth.

The role of humankind in this agreement or covenant is to seek out the Manifestations whenever They appear. Once we have discovered Them, we are then obliged to abide by whatever guidance They reveal until such time as another Manifestation appears to continue this program of human advancement.

The second sort of covenant is that agreement between each Manifestation and His followers. The Manifestation assures us that His teachings will enlighten and guide us until the appearance of the succeeding Emissary. The role of humankind in this pact is that we must uphold His teachings for our personal comportment and refinement and also be faithful to whatever instructions He provides for the promulgation and security of the Faith. In particular, this pact requires we follow whatever successors or institutions the Manifestation has designed or designated to endure after His passing.

These covenants thus establish the systematic basis of the link or communication between the metaphysical realm and the physical realm. They also describe the means by which humanity can establish the beginning stage of our intimate and enduring love relationship with a Being we personally have neither seen nor heard in any direct physical sense. We thus come to communicate with God and effectively "enter His presence" by virtue of our covenant with God through His Manifestations.

By appearing periodically in human history, the Manifestations advance by degrees our understanding of the Creator and facilitate the progress of our love relationship with Him. In fact, the Bahá'í writings assert that without these Intermediaries, the gap between the Creator and ourselves would not be bridged, and our own individual and collective advancement would be impossible.

SYMBOLIC EXPRESSIONS OF THE INTERMEDIARY PROCESS

There are a number of very useful symbolic and metaphorical expressions of this intermediary relationship between God and humankind that provide significant insight and logical elucidation about the divinely ordained process portrayed in Bahá'í scripture.

THE PRISM

Examining the nature of a prism can be an extremely useful analogy for explaining how the Manifestations function as intermediaries between the Holy Spirit—the attributes and powers emanating from God—and humanity as the recipients of this bounty. Of particular value is the capacity of the prism to demonstrate how the Manifestation is capable of making that which is unseen or invisible to the naked eye (the metaphysical nature and powers of the Holy Spirit) become visible and apparent.

By refracting the array of light lengths into a rainbow of colors latent in the pure white light of the Sun, the prism becomes an intermediary whereby we glimpse the complexity of what is otherwise beyond our immediate comprehension. Likewise, the Manifestation has the capacity to demonstrate to us in sensually and intellectually comprehensible terms the attributes of the Holy Spirit emanating from God. All of the Manifestation's words and actions translate for us this otherwise imperceptible spiritual force into advice, laws, exhortations, and visual examples of all we are able to comprehend and apply to our daily lives for a specific dispensation or "Day" of God.

Naturally, we will never understand God directly, not even in the continuation of our lives beyond our physical experience. But it would be totally erroneous to conclude that we cannot know God. We are given the opportunity through the appearance and guidance of the Prophets to comprehend all the attributes of God. What we can never comprehend, however, is the *essence* of God—His essential reality. The essential reality of God is beyond the comprehension of any being but Himself. It is in this literal sense that we say God is "essentially unknowable." This verity is also at the heart of what is meant in the ḥadíth of the Hidden Treasure when God states that "I was alone."

THE MIRROR

Another useful analogy for understanding the function and the unity of the Manifestations is the relationship between sunlight and a mirror. If we think of each of the Manifestations as a distinctly perfect reflection of sunlight, we can appreciate that each is capable of conveying to us flawlessly all the attributes of the Sun. Consequently, the Sun need not come down to Earth nor even shine upon the Earth directly for us to receive its bounties. Were there perfect mirrors in space capable of reflecting that light to us, we would not be able to distinguish between the two sources (the Sun or the Mirror), nor would we need to.

Each Manifestation thus reflects the same light from the same Sun. And yet because each Manifestation appears at a distinct time in a distinct persona, we understandably view them as distinct sources of guidance. It is in a similar vein that we give different names to the different days of the week even though on each new day the same sun dawns with the same rays and attributes:

> These Tabernacles of holiness, these primal Mirrors which reflect the light of unfading glory, are but expressions of Him Who is the Invisible of the Invisibles. By the revelation of these gems of divine virtue all the names and attributes of God, such as knowledge and power, sovereignty and dominion, mercy and wisdom, glory, bounty and grace, are made manifest. (Bahá'u'lláh, the Kitáb-i-Íqán, ¶109)

From this analogy we can also appreciate the Bahá'í axiom that each of these sequential "Mirrors" are equally capable of reflecting all of the Creator's divine attributes with whatever intensity They wish. That each "illumines" humanity only to the extent that we are capable of receiving that light at a given historical context, can be attributed to Their infinite wisdom as divine Educators. They reveal only so much light as we are able to comprehend and find useful at a given stage in our continuous social and spiritual advancement.

In this sense, whatever portion we receive is pure and flawlessly conveyed, though we will never receive all of the "enlightenment" available. Were this to occur or were we to receive more light than would be tolerable, we would become blinded. Instead of being assisted and educated, we would become totally confused and dumbfounded:

> Know of a certainty that in every Dispensation the light of Divine Revelation hath been vouchsafed unto men in direct proportion to their spiritual capacity. Consider the sun. How feeble its rays the moment it appeareth above the horizon. How gradu-

ally its warmth and potency increase as it approacheth its zenith, enabling meanwhile all created things to adapt themselves to the growing intensity of its light. How steadily it declineth until it reacheth its setting point. Were it, all of a sudden, to manifest the energies latent within it, it would, no doubt, cause injury to all created things. . . . In like manner, if the Sun of Truth were suddenly to reveal, at the earliest stages of its manifestation, the full measure of the potencies which the providence of the Almighty hath bestowed upon it, the earth of human understanding would waste away and be consumed; for men's hearts would neither sustain the intensity of its revelation, nor be able to mirror forth the radiance of its light. Dismayed and overpowered, they would cease to exist. (Bahá'u'lláh, *Gleanings*, no. 38.1)

THE SUN, THE LIGHT, AND THE MIRROR

Because these Mirrors are perfect, the attributes of God are manifest in them as completely and flawlessly as if They were God incarnate. And yet each is careful to inform us that He is *not* God. By analogy, we can imagine how easy it would be for the untrained eye to conclude that the prism itself is the source of the wondrous array of colors and powers, not the invisible sunlight shining through it. The same problem holds true for the mirror analogy. If the light shining from the sun is completely and immaculately reflected in the Mirror, we can appreciate why the followers might be tempted to deify the Manifestation or conclude that He is God incarnate.

It is precisely for this reason that the Manifestations emphasize time and again to Their followers that while They are the only way by which the believer can gain access to God, They are distinct from the essence of the Creator. They are His dutiful Servants and by no means His peer or copartner.

For example, Christ compares Himself to a vine and God to the vinedresser: "But that the world may know that I love the Father; and as the Father gave me commandment, even so I do. Arise, let us go hence. I am the true vine, and my Father is the husbandman" (John 14:31–15:1). Likewise, in the Qur'án we find Muḥammad asserting that He cannot alter anything in the Qur'án because it emanates not from Him but from God: "But when Our Clear Signs are rehearsed unto them, those who rest not their hope on their meeting with Us, say: 'Bring us a Reading other than this, or change this.' Say: 'It is not for me, of my own accord, to change it: I follow naught but what is revealed unto me: if I were to disobey my Lord, I should myself fear the Penalty of a Great Day (to come)'" (10:15). Bahá'u'lláh likewise says, "This thing is not from Me, but from One Who is Almighty and All-Knowing. . . . This is but a leaf which the winds of the will of thy Lord, the Almighty, the All-Praised, have stirred" (*Epistle to the Son of the Wolf*, p. 11). Even so, Bahá'u'lláh makes two statements that reaffirm that for human beings, spiritual proximity to the Manifestation is tantamount to entering the presence of God.

First, Bahá'u'lláh observes that the object of human creation is, as we have noted, to know and worship God: "The purpose of God in creating man hath been, and will ever be, to enable him to know his Creator and to attain His Presence" (Bahá'u'lláh, *Gleanings*, no. 29.1).

But in another passage, Bahá'u'lláh notes that attaining the spiritual presence of the Manifestations by recognizing them and obeying Their guidance is equivalent to attaining the presence of God: "Therefore, whosoever, and in whatever Dispensation, hath recognized and attained unto the presence of these glorious, these resplendent and most excellent Luminaries, hath verily attained unto the 'Presence of God' Himself, and entered the city of eternal and immortal life" (Bahá'u'lláh, the Kitáb-i-Íqán, ¶151).

CYCLES OF DAYS AND YEARS

An enduring analogy that is useful in understanding almost all aspects of the program by which the Creator educates humanity is the process by which we nourish and strengthen our bodies. For example, no matter how well or healthily we may eat one day, we will still need to take nourishment the next. Likewise, if we wish to become physically strong, no matter how completely and intelligently we exercise one day, we cannot progress without a program of exercise carried out over an extended period of time.

Similarly, these plans or programs of pursuing physical health and development never cease. If we stop eating decent foods on a regular basis or become lax in our exercise, the progress we have made will cease and all the development attained will begin to dissipate.

The principle of gradualness in both processes is likewise comparable. We may wish we could advance quickly and attempt to exercise more strenuously than we are prepared to, in which case we may damage our body. Patience and incremental advancement constitute the most crucial components in any program of human development, whether physical, mental, or spiritual.

It is for this reason that someone other than ourselves—one who is an expert in training the body or the mind or the spirit is essential for our individual and collective development. This is the reason that a single divine revelation is insufficient to guide humankind for all time. The social, intellectual, and spiritual advancement of humanity is a process that is never finalized or completed.

Additionally, we as a human family on planet Earth will never reach a point where we no longer need this external assistance, precisely because we have never seen this program carried out before. We cannot possibly intuit what should be the next stage in our refinement or when it should be undertaken or administered any more than a patient can diagnose a disease, prescribe the best course of treatment, and then apply the treatment intelligently.

OUR DEPENDENCY ON
THE MANIFESTATIONS OF GOD

It is in light of the incremental nature of this program of human development that 'Abdu'l-Bahá explains that without the periodic infusion of grace and guidance released with the advent of these Intermediaries from the celestial realm, human civilization would be incapable of evolving, and that we would never have emerged from our primitive stage of existence:

> The enlightenment of the world of thought comes from these centers of light and sources of mysteries. Without the bounty of the splendor and the instructions of these Holy Beings [the Manifestations] the world of souls and thoughts would be opaque darkness. Without the irrefutable teachings of those sources of mysteries the human world would become the pasture of animal appetites and qualities, the existence of everything would be unreal, and there would be no true life. That is why it is said in the Gospel: "In the beginning was the Word" (John 1:1), meaning that it became the cause of all life. (*Some Answered Questions*, p. 162)

Two other passages further help us to appreciate the logical necessity for the appearance of the Manifestations to instigate and sustain human progress. The first of these passages is an all-encompassing statement by Bahá'u'lláh that everything we know or wish to know ultimately is accomplished through our knowledge of God. A corollary of this principle is that all knowledge of God is derived solely from the advent of the Manifestations: "The source of all learning is the knowledge of God, exalted be His Glory, and this cannot be attained save through the knowledge of His Divine Manifestation" (Words of Wisdom, in *Tablets of Bahá'u'lláh*, p. 156).

A second passage attesting to this same principle is articulated by Shoghi Effendi. This passage asserts the absolute necessity of the appearance of divine Intermediaries for the advancement of human progress. He also explains why it is therefore entirely permissible and efficacious for us to pray to the Manifestations in Their capacity as God's representatives: "We cannot know God directly, but only through His Prophets. We can pray to Him realizing that through His Prophets we know Him, or we can address our prayer in thought to Bahá'u'lláh, not as God, but as the Door to our knowing God" (*Lights of Guidance*, no. 457).

PART 2

THE NATURE OF
THE PROPHETS OF GOD

Briefly, the Holy Manifestations have ever been, and ever will be,
Luminous Realities; no change or variation takes place in Their
essence. Before declaring Their manifestation, They are silent and
quiet like a sleeper, and after Their manifestation, They speak
and are illuminated, like one who is awake.

—'Abdu'l-Bahá

5

WHO DO YOU SAY I AM?

When Jesus came into the coasts of Caesarea Philippi, he asked
his disciples, saying, "Who do men say that I the Son of man am?"
And they said, "Some say that thou art John the Baptist: some,
Elias; and others, Jeremias, or one of the prophets."He saith
unto them, "But who say ye that I am?"
—Matt: 16:13–15

The diverse and differing opinions about the essential nature—the ontology or "being"—of the Prophets or Messengers is possibly the greatest source of chauvinism and conflict among the world religions. For even though few can deny the fundamental efficacy of the teachings They bring, it is also apparent that much of the turmoil and slaughter which characterizes the narrative of human history results from contention among religions about the issue of Who exactly these Beings are and which among Them has primacy in Their successive appearances among us.

HISTORICAL INFLUENCE OF THE PROPHETS

The charismatic effect of the appearances of the Intermediaries or Manifestations of God is undeniable. The powers of the social and religious movements and reforms that emanate from Their appearances testify to Their influence on society as a whole and, in the long run, on the advancement of the world of ideas. Yet, while They live among us on earth in a human form, They appear as relatively unobtrusive, meek, humble, and thoroughly kind individuals who attract a following only when They begin to articulate ideas that seem at odds with the beliefs of those in power, particularly with the staunchly held views of priests, clerics, divines, and religious authorities associated with the prior revelation. This conflict quickly evokes controversy, especially in those societies that are governed by a theocracy or a political authority aligned with the religious institutions in place from the dispensation of the previous Manifestation.

The end result of the appearance of virtually every Manifestation of God is that these Figures are almost inevitably rejected, ridiculed, and persecuted by those who feel threatened by Their teachings. This clash occurs in an especially vehement manner when the teachings of the new Manifestations seem to contradict or alter portions of the worldview held by followers of the previous revelation. Consequently, the religion that in time emerges from the appearance of a new Manifestation usually does not take shape until some time after the Manifestation's death.

During Their earthly lives, the teachings of the Manifestation are known mostly by a small cadre of dedicated and courageous individuals who themselves face persecution and, in many cases, imprisonment or martyrdom. Likewise, the intended objective of the new Manifestation in bringing about social and spiritual change would seem to have failed from the point of view of those living during Their lifetime because the Manifestations most often depart this life in relative obscurity.

In terms of contemporary society, Their executions or imprisonments would probably not make the front page of our local papers. In fact, those of us who live in relatively comfortable material circumstances would probably pay little attention to news of the imprisonment or execution of the leader of some obscure, radical religious/political sect of "trouble makers." The crucifixion of Christ, for example, was probably little noticed by the upper middle-class Jews—He would have been merely one among a number of convicted criminals crucified that day in Jerusalem.

By the early part of the seventh century when Muḥammad declared Himself a Messenger of God with an authority and spiritual station identical to that of Christ, Christianity had three hundred years earlier in 324 at the Council of Nicaea already decided that Christ was not a Messenger or Prophet of God, but God in the flesh. Therefore, Muḥammad's repeated assertion in the Qur'án about His own station being equal to that of Christ, as well as His explicit denunciation of the literalist concept of the Trinitarian doctrine, would have made it impossible for most Christians to recognize Muḥammad as fulfilling Christ's prophecies about sending a "Comforter" to pick up where He had left off. Indeed, this same attitude about Islam still abides among most Christian communities who believe that Christ's appearance was the climax of religious history on planet Earth.

Likewise, the Muslim occupation of the Holy Land gave Christendom sufficient reason to war against what they considered to be a pagan occupation of their most sacred shrines, while the Muslim soldiers, believing Muḥammad to be the divine successor to Christ, felt equally justified in securing this sacred land for the new Manifestation for Whom this was likewise sacred ground. And yet, while Islam spread rapidly after Muḥammad's death, it did not achieve what religious historians refer to as its "Golden Age" until the middle of the thirteenth century, more than seven hundred years after His passing.

Thus it is that historically the efflorescence of a religion, together with its subsequent influence on human learning and social structures, has not become readily apparent until a significant period of time after the Manifestation has appeared. To a certain extent, the gradualness of this ascent might be the result of the Manifestation's choice not to contend with temporal authority nor to seek any sort of secular or popular status. Furthermore, even though They bring progressive enlightenment for humankind, Their teachings often challenge directly the orthodoxy of the presiding system of belief that has become entrenched among the so-called learned of the day. Thus it is only among the early followers of a new Manifestation that the renovated worldview and spiritual insights become received as liberation from past beliefs, and that the traditions and authority of the previous revelation are understood to be inadequate to describe reality or to provide needed social and spiritual guidance.

The dramatic alteration in the worldview that occurred with the advent of Islam offers us a prime example of how this transition from one revelation to another challenges and tests humankind. By the time of the appearance of Muḥammad, the Christian view of cosmology was importantly aligned with and dependent on the Ptolemaic geocentric theory that the earth is the center of the universe. While the eventual acceptance of an altered view of cosmology in Christendom—the heliocentric solar system—is often attributed to the sixteenth century European Christian Renaissance scholar Nicolaus Copernicus, the heliocentric theories were initially set forth by Islamic scholars some three centuries earlier. Furthermore the European Renaissance that lifted western Christendom out of the so-called dark ages was instigated, as many scholars now readily acknowledge, by the influence and effulgence of Islamic scholarship.

CATALOGUING THE PROPHETS

Needless to say, we could explore volumes upon volumes analyzing the succession of religions and the historical conflicts among them, but ultimately we would be forced to choose from among several possible conclusions regarding the divine plan of the Creator to bring about the spiritualization of planet Earth.

The first possibility is that the theory of progressive revelation (God in history) is wrong. In effect, there is no systematic plan of a Creator to assist us. All those who have claimed the position of teaching us on behalf of God are liars, and all their followers are deceived. A second possibility is that the system devised by the Creator to educate us is not working terribly well because humankind simply cannot or will not change—that's human nature! We are just obstinate, incorrigible, and unteachable. A third alternative is that the system is working exactly as it should, given our free will and the time it takes for us to achieve sufficient collective understanding to become united in our appreciation of our nature, our purpose, and the necessity of our obedience to the guidance of the Manifestations to bring about global change.

Of course, there is at least one other possibility, a theory that has currency among a great number of contemporary scholars—that metaphysical reality, together with the Deity that governs it, are fictional anthropomorphic creations we have devised to comfort ourselves in our pitiful attempt to make sense out of a reality that has no inherent purpose or justice of its own. In other words, we have created God from the vain images of our own imagination.

If the concept of a God who sends successive Emissaries or Messengers or Prophets to assist us is a myth, it is a strangely persistent and consistent one. We have already noted the similar stages of religious belief among tribal cultures, however remote in time and geography they may be from one another. Similarly, we have noted that in some of the ancient Dharmic[1] religions we find a list of successive Avatars that parallels the list of Prophets we find in the Pentateuch (or Torah), as well as lists of Apostles in various súrih of the Qur'án, and of Manifestations cited in the Bahá'í texts.

---

1. The term *Dharma* has various meanings, the most general of which is the concept of a primal or principal animating force of the universe. Among those religions most closely associated with this line are Hinduism, Buddhism, Zoroastrianism, together with several philosophical offshoots of these, such as Sikhism, and Jainism.

BIBLICAL ALLUSIONS

Those Prophets most familiar to us from the Old Testament are Noah, Abraham, and Moses, though there are a number of other figures considered by Judaism and Christianity to be minor prophets. Among these in the Jewish tradition are Isaiah, Jeremiah, Ezekiel, and Daniel, and, to a lesser extent Hosea, Joel, Amos, Obadiah, Jonah, Micah, Nahum, Habakkuk, Zephaniah, Haggai, Zechariah, and Malachi.

Christ often alludes to the prophets of the past, but more importantly, almost every statement of Christ contains allusions to passages from these figures, something any decent edition of the Bible will explain in footnotes. What is also clear is that Christ's audience usually does not recognize these allusions to their own scripture. The most salient example of this tactic is Christ's allusion to Psalm 22 as He is dying on the cross: "And about the ninth hour Jesus cried with a loud voice, saying, '*Eli, Eli, lama sabachthani?*' that is to say, 'My God, my God, why hast thou forsaken me?'" (Matt 27:46). While those who hear Him are bewildered, their own Psalms of David both prophecy this event and explain how this event fits into the divine plan of God:

> My God, my God, why hast thou forsaken me? why art thou so far from helping me, and from the words of my roaring? O my God, I cry in the day time, but thou hearest not; and in the night season, and am not silent. But thou art holy, O thou that inhabitest the praises of Israel. Our fathers trusted in thee: they trusted, and thou didst deliver them. They cried unto thee, and were delivered: they trusted in thee, and were not confounded. But I am a worm, and no man; a reproach of men, and despised of the people. All they that see me laugh me to scorn: they shoot out the lip, they shake the head, saying, "He trusted on the LORD that he would deliver him: let him deliver him, seeing he delighted in him." (Matt: 22:1–8)

Likewise Christ sometimes explicitly compares Himself and His advent to that of Abraham or Moses. We have no record of Him cataloging the sequence of Prophets preceding Him, but He does make several significant comments about the fate of the Prophets sent by God to guide humanity. Perhaps the most memorable of these is His lengthy diatribe against the learned scribes and Pharisees:

> Ye serpents, ye generation of vipers, how can ye escape the damnation of hell? Wherefore, behold, I send unto you prophets, and wise men, and scribes: and some of them ye shall kill and crucify; and some of them shall ye scourge in your synagogues, and persecute them from city to city: That upon you may come all the righteous blood shed upon the earth, from the blood of righteous Abel unto the blood of Zacharias son of Barachias, whom ye slew between the temple and the altar.
>
> Verily I say unto you, All these things shall come upon this generation. O Jerusalem, Jerusalem, thou that killest the prophets, and stonest them which are sent unto thee, how often would I have gathered thy children together, even as a hen gathereth her chickens under her wings, and ye would not! Behold, your house is left unto you desolate. For I say unto you, Ye shall not see me henceforth, till ye shall say, Blessed is he that cometh in the name of the Lord (Matthew 23:33–39).

QUR'ÁNIC ALLUSIONS

What, then is the distinction between the Prophets who are Manifestations and the minor prophets who, while divinely assisted and inspired, are not the same category of Being?

Throughout the Qur'án, Muḥammad alludes to the sequence of Messengers God has sent to guide humankind. However, He employs two distinctly different Arabic terms to differentiate between two categories of prophets. Some are alluded to as Messengers (*rasul*), while others are said to be prophets (*nabi*). The "Messengers" unfold a new revelation—what Muḥammad refers to as another part of "the Book," the continuous revelation from God. The Messengers (that is, Manifestations) also bring a new religion that supersedes and abrogates the religion of the previous Messenger.

On the other hand, the minor prophets (*rasul*) may receive inspiration from God to assist in providing spiritual guidance, but they do not produce a new "Book" that constitutes the basis for a new "dispensation" in the spiritual education of humankind. They never claim to bring forth a new revelation, nor do they attempt to instigate a new religion.

In the Qur'án Muḥammad mentions twelve Messengers (though these are sometimes alluded to as Prophets as well), and ten prophets for whom He does not employ the term *rasul* ("Messenger"). The twelve Messengers, each of whom brings a new revelation and new dispensation, are Noah, Houd, Saleh, Abraham, Lot, Ishmael, Jethro, Moses, Elijah, Jonah, Jesus, and Muḥammad. The term *rasul* is not employed in alluding to Adam, though He is regarded by Muslims as the first Messenger, even as Muḥammad is deemed to be the last or final Messenger.

The *nabi* ("prophets") listed in the Qur'án usually appear to reaffirm and reinvigorate the dispensation of the previous Messenger in whose shadow they appear. Those mentioned as being *nabi* but not as *rasul* are Enoch, Isaac, Jacob, Joseph, Job, Aaron, David, Solomon, Elisha, Zechariah, and John the Baptist.

MANIFESTATIONS AND PROPHETS
IN THE BAHÁ'Í TEXTS

In the Bábí and Bahá'í texts, there is a similar distinction made between those who are "Manifestations" of God and those minor prophets who appear in the historical context of a dispensation to assist or reinforce the teachings of the Manifestation. For example, the Old Testament prophets Ezekiel and Daniel appear in the context of the continuity of the dispensation of Moses. They did not set out to instigate a new religion nor did they assert that they were revealing a new "Book," even though their inspired prophecies are considered to be from God and thus valid.

The Messengers who are alluded to in the Bahá'í authoritative texts as being "Manifestations" are Adam, Noah, Húd, Sálih, Krishna, Moses, Abraham, Zoroaster, Buddha, Jesus, Muḥammad, the Báb, and Bahá'u'lláh. This list is not intended to be a definitive or complete list of the Manifestations. The Bahá'í writings observe that entire cycles of Manifestations are lost to the collective memory of man, and all evidence of Their dispensations has been entirely eradicated. However, in the Bahá'í texts are cogent discussions about the nature of the Manifestations, as well as elucidations about the distinctions between Manifestations and the "minor prophets."

'Abdu'l-Bahá notes that the independent Manifestations of universal prophethood are like the sun, while lesser prophets are like moons reflecting the power of the Manifestation. Thus Moses was a Manifestation of God while his brother Aaron was a minor prophet. Stated another way, where Moses spoke on behalf of God (a revelation direct from God), Aaron spoke on behalf of Moses:

> Universally, the Prophets are of two kinds. One are the independent Prophets Who are followed; the other kind are not independent and are themselves followers.
>
> The independent Prophets are the lawgivers and the founders of a new cycle. Through Their appearance the world puts on a new garment, the foundations of religion are established, and a new book is revealed. Without an intermediary They receive bounty from the Reality of the Divinity, and Their illumina-

tion is an essential illumination. They are like the sun which is luminous in itself: the light is its essential necessity; it does not receive light from any other star. These Dawning-places of the morn of Unity are the sources of bounty and the mirrors of the Essence of Reality.

The other Prophets are followers and promoters, for they are branches and not independent; they receive the bounty of the independent Prophets, and they profit by the light of the Guidance of the universal Prophets. They are like the moon, which is not luminous and radiant in itself, but receives its light from the sun.

The Manifestations of universal Prophethood Who appeared independently are, for example, Abraham, Moses, Christ, Muhammad, the Báb and Bahá'u'lláh. But the others who are followers and promoters are like Solomon, David, Isaiah, Jeremiah and Ezekiel. For the independent Prophets are founders; They establish a new religion and make new creatures of men; They change the general morals, promote new customs and rules, renew the cycle and the Law. Their appearance is like the season of spring, which arrays all earthly beings in a new garment, and gives them a new life.

With regard to the second sort of Prophets who are followers, these also promote the Law of God, make known the Religion of God, and proclaim His word. Of themselves they have no power and might, except what they receive from the independent Prophets. (*Some Answered Questions*, p. 164)

WHY THE MIDDLE EAST IS THE "HOLY LAND"

We might well then pose the question that if this divine plan of global enlightenment is so logical and carefully devised, why does it not seem to play out very clearly, openly, or obviously? Why, for example, do the major religions seem to originate in the Middle East? Why do they not originate in the Americas or in Africa, in Australia, or elsewhere?

One poetic answer might be that since the river basin of the Tigris and Euphrates is the cradle of the beginnings of civilization as we understand it, it is a logical and symbolic culmination of this Plan that the turning point in human history—which this age we live in is designated by Bahá'í scripture to be—coalesce there.

Another less poetic but possibly more viable answer is that these processes did indeed play out in all these other places and that the evidence of ancient religions and religious traditions can be discovered in every culture. In places in Central and South America, for example, there is evidence of once great civilizations, each with a complex set of beliefs about the interplay between metaphysical reality and everyday life and each with an exacting set of religious practices.

We find the same sort of evidence with the mysterious monoliths of Stonehenge or with the amazing remnants of Minoan, Greek, and Trojan civilizations. There are likewise remnants and artifacts that demonstrate the remains of incredible cultures and kingdoms in the African continent, even as 'Abdu'l-Bahá asserts when He alludes to bygone cycles now lost to the memory of humankind:

> When a cycle is ended, a new cycle begins; and the old one, on account of the great events which take place, is completely forgotten, and not a trace or record of it will remain. As you see, we have no records of twenty thousand years ago, although we have before proved by argument that life on this earth is very ancient. It is not one hundred thousand, or two hundred thousand, or one million or two million years old; it is very ancient, and the ancient records and traces are entirely obliterated.

Each of the Divine Manifestations has likewise a cycle, and during the cycle His laws and commandments prevail and are performed. When His cycle is completed by the appearance of a new Manifestation, a new cycle begins. In this way cycles begin, end and are renewed, until a universal cycle is completed in the world, when important events and great occurrences will take place which entirely efface every trace and every record of the past; then a new universal cycle begins in the world, for this universe has no beginning. (*Some Answered Questions*, p. 159)

ABUNDANT ACCESS TO GOD

This concept likewise seems to corroborate the observation of Muḥammad that God has sent Messengers to every people at some point in their history and that no one on the planet is without some form of moral perspective about what it means to be a "good" or "moral" person. Indeed, in the Qur'án Muḥammad observes that some peoples may complain that they have worshipped false gods because Alláh did not will to send them a Manifestation. He then states that this is no excuse for immorality or idol worship because at some point in history, all peoples have received guidance from God through a Messenger or Manifestation:

> The worshippers of false gods say: "If Alláh had so willed, we should not have worshipped aught but Him—neither we nor our fathers—nor should we have prescribed prohibitions other than His." So did those who went before them. But what is the mission of Messengers but to preach the Clear Message? For We assuredly sent amongst every People a Messenger, (with the Command), "Serve Allah and eschew Evil": of the people were some whom Allah guided, and some on whom Error became

inevitably (established). So travel through the earth, and see what was the end of those who denied (the Truth). (16:35–36)

Bahá'u'lláh confirms the same verity when He reveals the following often cited passages concerning the personal responsibility of each person to recognize and abide by the moral principles espoused by these Emissaries or their followers:

> It follows, therefore, that every man hath been, and will continue to be, able of himself to appreciate the Beauty of God, the Glorified. Had he not been endowed with such a capacity, how could he be called to account for his failure? If, in the Day when all the peoples of the earth will be gathered together, any man should, whilst standing in the presence of God, be asked: "Wherefore hast thou disbelieved in My Beauty and turned away from My Self," and if such a man should reply and say: "Inasmuch as all men have erred, and none hath been found willing to turn his face to the Truth, I, too, following their example, have grievously failed to recognize the Beauty of the Eternal," such a plea will, assuredly, be rejected. For the faith of no man can be conditioned by any one except himself. (*Gleanings,* no. 75.1)

A "WORLD" RELIGION

Most likely the reason that the Middle East is now considered the "Nest of the Prophets" ('Abdu'l-Bahá, quoted in Shoghi Effendi, *Citadel of Faith,* p. 95) is that for the most recent universal revelations of Christianity, Islam, and the Bahá'í Faith, the Holy Land plays such a critical role in their history and administration. But at what point can we consider that one of the religions revealed by God has been intended to be applicable to the entire planet rather than the limited region of the world it could reach during the period of its dispensation? Is there a point in our history that a religion was established that was designed to be "universal" both in its global acceptance and in its spiritual and social guidance?

For example, Judaism became widespread only because Christianity included the Pentateuch together with the rest of the Old Testament as part of its own scriptural texts. Therefore, as Christianity became the state religion of the Roman Empire, the knowledge of Judaism also spread, even as did the knowledge of Judaism with the Diaspora of the Jews as they were persecuted from place to place.

But if we accept the Bahá'í and Islamic view of religious history, then Christianity as the religion it was intended to be effectively ended with the advent of Muḥammad in 622. That is, according to the Bahá'í concept of religious history, a new revelation appears whenever humankind is ready for further advancement and when the previous religion has become stagnant, distorted, and incapable of meeting the needs of humankind. The previous religion may still provide spiritual sustenance for some, but the religion as an institution and as a force for human progress has become irreparably damaged and dysfunctional.

It is well worth noting that in 622, the beginning of the Islamic dispensation, Christianity was confined to a rather small portion of the planet. Furthermore, the Roman Empire had been overrun by tribal invasions, by peoples who possessed totally different religious beliefs. As a result, Europe entered the so-called "dark ages" in which the efficiency and material magnificence of the Roman Empire dissipated and all but vanished.

Consequently, it is theoretically feasible to assert that the subsequent spread of the Christian religion throughout the world as these tribes became Christianized, while doubtless propitious in some instances, probably caused more consternation, conflict, and destruction than any force previously known in world history. At the very least, such an argument is worthy of reflection and consideration. Certainly, it can be argued that without the resurrection of Christian civilization instigated by the advent of Islam, the Renaissance and the subsequent spread of "Western" culture would never have occurred.

ISLAM

It is only with the advent of the revelation of Muḥammad, therefore, that we see a religion appearing during an historical period in which the term *universal* might conceivably be used to imply the entire planet. It was during this dispensation that most of the peoples of the world became discovered and the various territories and climes of the globe had been explored.

The following ḥadíth, attributed to Muḥammad, would seem to support this argument: "Every Prophet used to be sent to his [own] nation exclusively, but I have been sent to all mankind" (Sahih Bukhari, volume 1, ḥadíth no. 4). But as with so many revelations before Islam, what is intended by the Manifestation can become diverted and perverted in the hands of the clerics and believers, even as Christ's description of His station became totally misunderstood and ultimately distorted by the assembled Christian scholars at the Council of Nicaea.

In the same manner, the basis for the major schism in Islam—the division between the Shi'íh and Sunni factions—occurred at the moment of Muḥammad's death. Likewise, many of the teachings of Muḥammad became misinterpreted and misapplied, while other perverse and baseless teachings were gradually appended to the evolving *Sharia,* an Arabic term meaning the "path," an allusion to the total collection of Islamic religious law. The Sharia contains teachings and constraints that sometimes bear little resemblance to the teachings of Muḥammad or to what might be considered authoritative ḥadíth.

What is more, once the spread of Islam was deterred from advancing into the totality of Europe, going as far as France in the West and as far as Bulgaria in the East, the so-called Holy Roman Empire remained secure, such as it was, and the resurgence of the various Christian European cultures reemerged after the Renaissance as dominant powers in the West.

This is not to say that this concept of Islam as a world religion has declined in the hearts and minds of Muslims, especially those Islamic fundamentalists who still strive to create a global Islamic state, even as Muḥammad seemed to imply it should. The problem with this concept from the standpoint of religious history, at least according to a Baháʼí perspective, is that Islam, like Christianity, long ago strayed from the central doctrines Muḥammad purveyed. Texts were added and manmade institutions were devised that bore little resemblance to anything described or envisioned by Muḥammad. Thus the Sharia, the Islamic compilation of law, once reviewed in the context of its historical evolution, cannot be said to represent law derived from authoritative sources. Furthermore, from the point of view of the Major Plan of God, once another Manifestation appeared in the person of the Báb, the Islamic dispensation officially ended and its laws and institutions were abrogated.

THE BÁBÍ AND BAHÁʼÍ RELIGIONS

Most critical of all from the Baháʼí perspective is the fact that in 1844 the Báb (Siyyid ʻAlí-Muḥammad Shírází) proclaimed Himself to be the promised Qáʼim, Whose advent was to usher in the long-awaited resurrection alluded to by Muḥammad throughout the Qurʼán as the climax to all previous human history. The Báb in His own revealed writings (which far surpass in volume the sum total of all previously revealed scripture) clarified the "resurrection" as heralding not the end of humankind or human history, but the end of the Prophetic

Age—an age of preparation and basic training of humankind—and the advent of the union and resurrection of the spiritual life of humankind worldwide.

Before His execution by firing squad in 1850 in Tabríz, the Báb set forth in explicit terms what He alluded to as the "Latter Resurrection" of "Him Whom God will make Manifest," a Manifestation who would appear in the year nine of His own revelation (1853). The appearance of this Manifestation, the Báb asserted, would effectively end the Bábí dispensation, which would have thus served to prepare humanity for this same Manifestation Who, as prophesied in every previous religion, would unite the peoples of the world under the banner of a global peace and a unified faith in God.

RELIGIOUS CONFLICT AND
THE NATURE OF THE PROPHETS

Again, one might well question why a plan devised by an omnipotent Creator could not work better. Why should the intervention intended to guide us to spirituality and accord so often have had the exact opposite result? As in our previous discussion, the answer is ever the same—the free will bequeathed us by the Creator. The same freedom we have to discover the source of our help and salvation also allows us to fall prey to distractions from our true purpose and from learning about how this system is intended to work. In short, the system or plan is working fine, though we have not used it as well as we could have. Even so, our past failures become useful sources of learning for our present and future responses to God's plan.

Of course, not all bloodshed arising out of disputes among religions has resulted solely from disagreements about the spiritual station of the Founders of the religions, but a great deal of it has. Debate and confusion about the essential nature of these Beings, especially regarding Their relationship to God, has been the central cause of much chauvinism and almost all of the failure on the part of humanity to understand the underlying unity and integrity of the divine system of progressive revelation.

Lord Krishna is perceived to be largely a figure of ancient mythic traditions by some Hindus, a deity by others, and an incarnation of God or Vishnu by others. Buddha is presently considered to have been a great philosopher and teacher who, according to contemporary interpretations, speaks little of monotheistic belief and, according to some, even denies the reality of such a Being:

> The beliefs and rites of the Buddhists and Confucianists have not continued in accordance with their fundamental teachings. The founder of Buddhism was a wonderful soul. He established the Oneness of God, but later the original principles of His doctrines gradually disappeared, and ignorant customs and ceremonials arose and increased until they finally ended in the worship of statues and images. ('Abdu'l-Bahá, *Some Answered Questions*, p. 164)

Likewise, Zoroastrianism was founded by a figure titled Zoroaster whose life is veiled in mystery. He is considered to have been a Prophet and poet who penned the part of the *Avesta* called the *Gathas*. The religion that bears His name was founded in western Persia and spread all the way to the Indian subcontinent, but no abiding understanding of Zoroaster's life or station remains, even though the religion itself is still extant.

The patriarchal Prophets of the Old Testament—such as Noah, Abraham, and Moses—are viewed by most sects of Judaism as Emissaries or Prophets of God, but also as thoroughly human individuals who had foibles and flaws, who, from time to time went astray, or, according to Biblical accounts, failed God in some way. In short, these figures are perceived as possessing a degree of divine authority and as conveying binding laws from God, but they are not perceived as being superhuman or as having powers beyond those God temporarily endowed them with from time to time.

HOW THE MANIFESTATIONS
DESCRIBE THEMSELVES

Clearly all of us are capable of becoming spiritual to a greater or lesser degree. Perhaps it could be said that each of us is capable of becoming a spiritual leader of sorts, even if only within the context of our own family or neighborhood. At the same time, few of us would dare claim we are emissaries from God, that we are endowed with power of prophecy, or that we have come to bring a world-changing message of spiritual renewal and rebirth given to us directly from God.

Therefore, one important object of our quest in this study is to discover the distinguishing characteristics of these individuals, Whom Muḥammad calls "Messengers," or *rasul*, and Whom the Bahá'í writings call Manifestations. According to Bahá'í theory, these figures are responsible for the ascent of civilization itself. In effect, we need to deal head-on with the very dilemma that faced those attending the tempestuous synod that was the Council of Nicaea where Christian scholars, under the mandate of Constantine the Great, determined to come to some conclusive and binding decision about the essential nature or "ontology" of Christ.

We, however, are trying to determine the same thing about *all* the Manifestations. Are these ordinary individuals suddenly anointed or appointed by God with extraordinary powers to accomplish superhuman tasks? Or are these Beings inherently distinct from us ordinary human beings? Do the Manifestations of God belong to a higher order of being than us, thereby relieving us of the secret guilt and envy we might harbor for being hopelessly incapable of emulating them?

The Bahá'í writings help resolve most of the questions we might have about this major húrí, but we need to lay the groundwork for approaching the answers these texts proffer. In addition, how we interpret these explanations depends in large part on the context in which they are enunciated. Therefore, before we attempt to "unveil" this húrí, let us review carefully what the Manifestations have to say about themselves.

6

WHAT'S IN A NAME?

Neither shall thy name any more be called Abram, but thy name shall be Abraham; for a father of many nations have I made thee. And I will make thee exceedingly fruitful, and I will make nations of thee, and kings shall come out of thee. And I will establish my covenant between me and thee and thy seed after thee in their generations for an everlasting covenant, to be a God unto thee, and to thy seed after thee.

(Genesis 17:5–7)

We frequently employ titles to designate profession, rank, or status. Naming is one of the initial powers that language itself bestowed upon humankind. Therefore if we wish to discover the essential nature of the Manifestations of God, we should obviously begin with what They say about Themselves. These statements, together with what accepted authoritative scripture says about Them, should establish for us a decent beginning in our attempt to approach what is possibly the single most critical question one can pose about the Manifestations of God: What is the exact nature of these mysterious Beings?

SYMBOLIC TITLES OF THE MANIFESTATIONS

What is especially worth noting is that the Manifestations often assume a symbolic title once They announce Their station as Emissaries of God. For example, it is fairly common knowledge that the "Buddha" (the "awakened one" or the "enlightened one") is a title adopted by Siddhartha at age thirty-five after He had meditated for forty-nine days and had arrived at an insight about how the single cause of human suffering is ignorance. According to Buddhist tradition, He also began to reveal a solution to this problem and to articulate guidance about spiritual development. He discussed what has become known as the path of moderation, a middle path between the extremes of self-indulgence and self-mortification.

In the Old Testament, some information is provided about the names of what are referred to as the "Antediluvian Patriarchs," Adam and Noah, Who are considered Manifestations by Islam and by the Bahá'í Faith. The information about their lives is so scant and mythically charged that we have no exact sense of the point of transformation in which their names attain their symbolic value. For example, one etymology of the word *Adam* is the masculine form of the word *adamah* meaning "ground" or "earth," an appropriate appellation for one who symbolizes a cognitive being (the human being) fashioned by the Creator from water and clay. The Manifestation Noah, according to the account in Genesis, was named by his father Lamech to symbolize the fact that Noah would introduce agriculture to the people. The name Noah, meaning "rest" in Hebrew, signified that teaching people this essential skill would turn them from nomadic hunter-gathers into settled communities.

ABRAHAM AS A POINT OF BEGINNING

It is with Abraham that we begin to discern a religious history in the Abrahamic line of Manifestations sufficiently complete in both biblical and Qur'ánic sources. In the case of Abraham, the name or title of the Manifestation is related explicitly to the revelation of a covenant with God and to an explicit mission associated with that covenant. It is important to note, however, that from a Bahá'í perspective, the only totally reliable scriptural texts from any Manifestations are the Qur'án (which was dictated by Muḥammad), the writings of the Báb, and the writings of Bahá'u'lláh. The New Testaments are accepted as containing valuable and probably reliable information about many of the things Christ said, but as scholarship acknowledges, the four gospels were written after Christ's crucifixion as recorded from notes taken by largely unknown or historically unauthenticated sources.

Contemporary scholarship dates Abraham as having lived somewhere between 2000–1500 BCE. Regardless of the accuracy of the dating of His dispensation, according to both biblical and Qur'ánic accounts, the appearance of Abraham is portrayed as a milestone in religious history. Part of His station is indicated in the biblical account of the changing of His name or title from "Abram" ("revered father") to "Abraham" ("father of many" or "progenitor of many peoples"). This change in title resulted from His covenant with God as signaled by the commandment that all male followers be circumcised. Biblically, Abraham represents the Prophet who establishes for all time the monotheistic doctrine associated with the Abrahamic line of prophets.

The Qur'ánic allusions to the life and importance of Abraham are markedly different from the Biblical accounts. While the Bible portrays Abraham as agreeing to sacrifice His firstborn son Isaac, the Qur'án asserts that it was Ibrahim's firstborn son Ishmael. Likewise, the Bible focuses on Isaac, who becomes the progenitor of the Hebraic peoples and of the Manifestations, Moses and Christ. The Qur'án, on the other hand, focuses on Ishmael as the progenitor of the Arabic nation and the Arabic line of Manifestations, Húd, Sálih, and Muḥammad.

MOSES (1228–1108 BCE)

The story of Moses ("Músá" in the Qur'án) depicted in the Old Testament does not seem to allude to a name or title change associated with any particular point in His storied and widely known life. The name has etymological roots in Egyptian culture (into which Moses was born) with the words *birth* and *protect* ("protected birth") implicit in its meaning. In other scholarship, the name is associated with roots alluding to his having been drawn out of the water by Pharaoh's daughter (in the Bible) and by Pharaoh's wife (in the Qur'án). The Arabic *Músá* is likewise associated with roots alluding to "water" and "reeds" or "wood," possibly referring to the basket-boat in which He floated as an infant among the reeds.

Hermeneutically, the water takes on a greater symbolic value in terms of two miraculous events associated with the life of Moses—His parting of the Red Sea to save His people from Pharaoh's army, and toward the end of life, His tapping a stone with His staff on Mt. Horeb to bring forth water for His people. However, the miraculous events most commonly associated with Moses are His rod as a symbol of His station, a staff which He transforms into a snake as a sign of His power before Pharaoh, His providing the manna for His people in the wilderness, and most pivotal of all, His receiving of revelation direct from God when He ascends Mt. Sinai alone and beholds the burning bush.

From the Qur'ánic account, Moses first ascends the mountain alone while He and His family are on a return trip to Egypt. He had escaped from Egypt for being accused of murder and had become a shepherd for the Prophet Shoaib, who immediately recognizes Moses' divine station. Moses then marries Safoorah, the daughter of the Shoaib, and, after about ten years, He decides to return to the land of His birth.

As they travel, Moses beholds a fire burning on Mt. Sinai, tells his family to wait, and proceeds toward the flame so that he might obtain material for their own needs. As He approaches the fire, the voice of God speaks out: "Verily I am thy Lord! Therefore (in My presence) put off thy shoes: thou art in the sacred valley Tuwa. 'I have chosen thee: listen, then, to the inspiration (sent to thee). Verily, I am Allah: there is no God but Me: so serve Thou Me (only), and establish regular prayer for celebrating My praise'" (Qur'án 20: 12–14).

Because of this "encounter" with God, and His subsequent second ascent of the same mountain when He received the Ten Commandments, Moses receives the title in the Qur'án of *Kalim Alláh* ("He who speaks with God, or He whose speaks on behalf of God"). Bahá'u'lláh refers to Moses with a similar title, "He Who held converse with the Almighty."

JESUS THE CHRIST (CA 2 BCE–CA 26 CE)

According to the Synoptic Gospels of Matthew and Luke, Jesus was born in the genealogical line descending from David, and thence from Abraham. While the Gospels of Matthew and Luke narrate the familiar story of Christ's birth, all four gospels give great importance to the appearance of John the Baptist as forerunner or herald of the advent of the Messiah (Hebrew for "the anointed one"), as prophesied explicitly in Isaiah. John immediately recognizes Jesus as the Christ and proceeds at Jesus' insistence to baptize or anoint Him. From this point on, Jesus is alluded to as Christ as a symbol of His having assumed His station in fulfillment of Judaic prophecies and traditions regarding one who would appear from the Davidic line to bring about a "Messianic Age."

To all appearances, Jesus was a simple carpenter, an artisan living an uneventful and unspectacular life until His encounter at the Jordan River with John the Baptist, an itinerant preacher who taught that one greater than himself would soon appear. This Messiah, he foretold, would redeem occupied Jerusalem by instigating a spiritual reformation. John the Baptist exhorted everyone—his followers and even political figures—to prepare for this advent by repenting for their sins. As a symbolic ritual of their preparation for and dedication to this apocalyptic prophecy, John immersed his followers in the waters of the Jordan River.

The three synoptic gospels (Matthew, Mark, and Luke) then describe the baptism of Christ by John (the gospel of John omits this event), though they differ as to the particulars. The most memorable description of the event in terms of a transformative epiphany for Jesus occurs in Mark: "And it came to pass in those days that Jesus came from Nazareth of Galilee and was baptized of John in Jordan. And straightway coming up out of the water, He saw the heavens opened, and the Spirit like a dove descending upon Him. And there came a voice from heaven, saying, 'Thou art my beloved Son, in whom I am well pleased'" (1:9–11).

In the gospels, this event marks the beginning of the narration of Christ's ministry. Likewise, it is from this point forward that Jesus of Nazareth assumes the title "Christ," a word derived from the Greek *Khristós,* meaning "the Anointed One," an obvious allusion to both His baptism and to His fulfillment of the Hebrew expectation of the Messiah, a term that also means "anointed."

Thus later in His ministry when Christ questions His own disciples about who people say He is and, in particular, about who the disciples say He is, Christ cautions them not to withhold divulging to anyone what Peter has just discerned—that Jesus is "the Christ," the Promised Messiah:

> When Jesus came into the coasts of Caesarea Philippi, he asked his disciples, saying, "Who do men say that I the Son of man am?"
>
> And they said, "Some say that thou art John the Baptist: some, Elias; and others, Jeremias, or one of the prophets."
>
> He saith unto them, "But who say ye that I am?"
>
> And Simon Peter answered and said, "Thou art the Christ, the Son of the living God."

And Jesus answered and said unto him, "Blessed art thou, Simon Barjona: for flesh and blood hath not revealed it unto thee, but my Father which is in heaven. And I say also unto thee that thou art Peter, and upon this rock I will build my church; and the gates of hell shall not prevail against it. And I will give unto thee the keys of the kingdom of heaven: and whatsoever thou shalt bind on earth shall be bound in heaven: and whatsoever thou shalt loose on earth shall be loosed in heaven."

Then charged He his disciples that they should tell no man that He was Jesus the Christ. (Matt: 16:13–20)

MUHAMMAD (570–632 CE)

The early life of Muḥammad is complex but ostensibly unrelated to His station of Prophethood. His father died before He was born, and his mother died when Muḥammad was six. He was then passed to the care of His paternal grandfather. When the grandfather died two years later, He was given to the care of His uncle Abu Talib, head of the Banu Hashim tribe and a merchant and trader by profession.

It was at age ten while accompanying His uncle on a journey to Syria that Muḥammad first encountered someone who seemed to discern in Him a sign of future greatness. In the Syrian town of Bosra, Muḥammad encountered Bahira, a Christian monk. From his study of Christian scripture, Bahira recognized in Muḥammad the one Who would fulfill Christ's prophecy about sending a "Comforter" or Paraclete: "But the Comforter, which is the Holy Ghost, whom the Father will send in my name, he shall teach you all things, and bring all things to your remembrance, whatsoever I have said unto you" (John 14:26).

This allusion to the childhood of Muḥammad immediately calls to mind the single episode (cited in Luke 2:39–52) regarding Jesus' own childhood. At age twelve Jesus was found in the temple by his frantic parents who had thought the twelve-year-old to be lost:

> And it came to pass, that after three days they found him in the temple, sitting in the midst of the doctors, both hearing them, and asking them questions. And all that heard him were astonished at his understanding and answers. And when they saw him, they were amazed, and his mother said unto Him, "Son, why hast thou thus dealt with us? Behold, thy father and I have sought thee sorrowing."
>
> And he said unto them, "How is it that ye sought me? Wist ye not that I must be about my Father's business?" And they understood not the saying which He spake unto them." (Luke 2:46–50)

The transformative episode which marks the beginning of Muḥammad's presumed awareness of His station and mission did not occur until He was forty. In the meantime, He had acquired the nickname of *"Al Amín"* ("The Trusted One") because of His honesty and upright character. He also had a felicitous marriage to a wealthy widow named Khadíjah, whom He married when He was twenty-five and she was forty.

Sometime during the next decade, Muḥammad began to make it a practice to spend several weeks each year meditating in a cave on Mt. Hira. In the year 610, the Angel Gabriel appeared to Muḥammad and commanded Him to recite verses. Over the next three years, He developed a regimen of prayer and meditation, parallel thematically to Christ's forty days of meditation in the dessert following His own epiphany.

During this period, the revelations continued and in time He began to preach the messages revealed to Him. The first to believe in His station as both a Prophet (*nabí*) and a Messenger (*rasul*) was His wife Khadíjah, and the second was his young cousin ʻAlí, who was but ten years old at the time. 'Alí would later marry Muḥammad's daughter Fatimah and, according to Shí'ih belief, would become the designated successor to Muḥammad, or the first Imám.

While the spiritual, social, and political processes that followed these initial stirrings of the revelation of Muḥammad are well worth recounting, the date usually given for the beginning of Islam is 622, when, with the help of 'Alí, the fifty-two-year-old Prophet emigrated from Mecca to Medina where He began to establish laws, to secure pacts for peaceful relationships among the various tribal groups, and thereby to establish the first Muslim community. This first community would thenceforth become the model for the process whereby spiritual principles could become inculcated into an ingenuous and effective political system. By this time, the Roman Empire had collapsed, and tribal migrations conquered the former Roman colonies, including Gaul (France) and Britannia (England).

THE BÁB (1819–1850) AND THE BAHÁ'Í ERA

Though it is not well documented in the histories of the more ancient religions, a precursor or herald always appears prior to the advent of the Manifestation Himself. This individual will sometimes be the first to recognize the Manifestation prior to His first revelatory experience, or else someone who assembles a following to teach them that the time for the advent of the next Prophet is at hand. Though the Báb is presently best known as being the herald or forerunner of Bahá'u'lláh, He was a Manifestation in His own right. Consequently, there was a foreshadowing of the advent of the Báb in the form of two prominent teachers who proclaimed that the time for the appearance of another Manifestation had arrived.

The first of these figures was Shaykh Aḥmad-i-Ahsá'í (1753–1826), and the second was his successor, Siyyid Kázim-i-Rashtí (1793–1843).

Both of these individuals wrote and taught extensively that the time was at hand for the appearance of the promised *Qá'im* ("He who will arise"), sometimes alluded to as the *Mahdí* (the "Guided One"). According to <u>Shí</u>'ih belief, the Qá'im would be a lineal descendant of Muḥammad who would appear to usher in an age of righteousness.

Among the students of Kázim-i-Ra<u>sh</u>tí in Karbilá during the year 1840 was a young man of twenty years of age, Siyyid 'Alí-Muḥammad <u>Sh</u>írází. On a pilgrimage to Karbilá from his native city of Shiraz, Siyyid 'Alí-Muḥammad (Who would assume the title, "the Báb") was at the time a young merchant working for His uncle in Bushihr, a coastal town on the Persian Gulf. It is said that during these classes, Siyyid Kázim paid special attention to Siyyid 'Alí-Muḥammad, at one time alluding to him while discussing the imminent appearance of the Qá'im.

This was hardly the first time someone had noted the special status of the Báb. As with Christ and Muḥammad, the childhood of the Báb is marked by instances in which His transcendent knowledge was apparent to fellow students and teachers alike. When 'Alí-Muḥammad was nine years old, His father, Muḥammad-Riḍa, died. His mother, Fatimih-Bagum, was assisted by her three brothers in raising Him, with His uncle Haji Mirzá Siyyid 'Alí playing the most critical role. One of the first indications of the boy's superior intellect occurred when He was first sent by this same uncle to be instructed by <u>Shaykh</u> Abid: "When He was sent to school, He so surprised the schoolmaster, <u>Shaykh</u> 'Abid, with His wisdom and intelligence that the bewildered man took the child back to His uncle and said that he had nothing to teach this gifted pupil: 'He, verily, stands in no need of teachers such as I'" (H. M. Balyuzi, *The Báb,* p. 33).

Nevertheless, at the insistence of His uncle, the Báb continued to study under <u>Shaykh</u> Abid. During this period many other examples of His inherent knowledge became evident. For example, <u>Shaykh</u> Abid began to observe that 'Alí-Muḥammad cared little for ordinary childhood pastimes but instead desired to concentrate on prayers and mediations. Consequently, when the boy began to come late to school, the teacher became concerned about why his best student was becoming negligent.

Shaykh Abid sent some of the Báb's fellow students to the Báb's home to ask Him to come to school. When the boy arrived and was asked why He had come late to school, the Báb answered that He had been in His grandfather's house. Since the Báb had no living grandfather, the teacher knew that He was referring to the Prophet Muḥammad. The Báb was a Siyyid, a descendant of the Prophet Muḥammad, and sometimes Siyyids would refer to Muḥammad as their "grandfather." What was more, the teacher understood that being "in His Grandfather's house" meant that He had been praying, meditating, and communing with the soul of the Prophet Muḥammad.

The Bábí religion is considered to have begun on the evening of May 23, 1844, in Shiraz when 'Alí-Muḥammad declared to an avid follower of Siyyid Kázim, named Mullá Ḥusayn, that He, Siyyid 'Alí-Muḥammad, was the Qá'im and that His title was to be the Báb (meaning in Arabic, "the Gate") because the purpose of His revelation would be to prepare the way for "Him Whom God will Manifest," another Manifestation or Messenger Who would transform the entirety of the world community.

The entrancing narration of that evening in the account by Mullá Ḥusayn is a remarkable testimony to the power and influence of the Báb. Mullá Ḥusayn was extremely learned and well versed in the traditions and requirements that would qualify anyone laying claim to the station of Qá'im. One of the confirmations Mullá Ḥusayn sought was the fulfillment of a secret proof of his own devising—that the real Qá'im would, unasked, spontaneously reveal for him a commentary on the enigmatic Súrih of Joseph from the Qur'án. After Mullá Ḥusayn had satisfied himself that all other qualifications were evident in the personage of 'Alí-Muḥammad, the Báb, unasked, began to reveal the first chapter of "that 'first, greatest and mightiest' of all books in the Bábí Dispensation, the celebrated commentary on the *Súrih of Joseph*" (Shoghi Effendi, *God Passes By*, p. 6).

THE EPIPHANY OF THE BÁB

While this evening marked a milestone in beginning the overt declaration of the Báb's station and mission, this celebrated event did not mark the point at which the Báb Himself had His own "epiphany" or awakening to the fact that the time for His own revelation had come. The event comparable to Moses' vision of the Burning Bush, Christ's baptism in the Jordan, and Muḥammad's vision of the Angel Gabriel occurred to the young Prophet in a dream as described in the authoritative account by Shoghi Effendi: "[I]n a dream He approached the bleeding head of the Imam Ḥusayn, and, quaffing the blood that dripped from his lacerated throat, awoke to find Himself the chosen recipient of the outpouring grace of the Almighty" (*God Passes By*, p. 92).

The Báb's own account of this awakening to the beginning of His ministry is most moving. He experienced this dream-vision in 1843, a year before His declaration of His station to Mullá Ḥusayn, and He penned a fairly detailed recollection of that experience:

> The spirit of prayer which animates My soul is the direct consequence of a dream which I had in the year before the declaration of My Mission. In My vision I saw the head of the Imám Ḥusayn,[1] the Siyyidu'-sh-Shuhadá', which was hanging upon a tree. Drops of blood dripped profusely from His lacerated throat. With feelings of unsurpassed delight, I approached that tree and, stretching

---

1. In the year 680 the Imám Ḥusayn, the grandson of Muḥammad, was killed and beheaded at the battle of Karbilá.

forth My hands, gathered a few drops of that sacred blood, and drank them devoutly. When I awoke, I felt that the Spirit of God had permeated and taken possession of My soul. My heart was thrilled with the joy of His Divine presence, and the mysteries of His Revelation were unfolded before My eyes in all their glory. (Quoted in, Nabíl-i-Aẓam, *The Dawn-Breakers*, p. 253)

Similar in its symbolism to Christ's request that His disciples partake of the wine as if it were His own blood, this dream obviously relates to the Báb's heritage as a direct descendant of the Imám Ḥusayn as well as His inheritance of the mantle of the authority that, according to S͟híʻih belief, befell each of the twelve Imáms.

BAHÁ'U'LLÁH (1817–1892)

According to Baháʼí belief, the most recent Manifestation of God is Baháʼuʼlláh, the Prophet and Founder of the Baháʼí Faith. Baháʼuʼlláh ("the Glory of God") is the title bestowed on Mírzá Ḥusayn-ʻAlí, an early follower of the Báb who was born in Tehran, imprisoned, then exiled successively to Baghdad, Constantinople, Adrianople, and finally to ʻAkká. He passed away in 1892, and His remains are entombed in a shrine outside ʻAkká in northern Israel, a site considered by the worldwide Baháʼí community as the qiblih ("the point of adoration") for this dispensation.

Born into a noble family, Mírzá Ḥusayn-ʻAlí had the opportunity to succeed His father, Mírzá Buzurg, who served as a vizier and as a governor under the king of Persia, Muḥammad S͟háh. In 1839 when Mírzá Husayn-ʻAlí was twenty-two, his esteemed father died, but the youth had no desire for public office and rejected the opportunity to take his place. He would continue the rest of His life to reject any sort of public position, focusing all His attention instead on spiritual concerns, whether in helping the poor in His midst or preparing for that time when He Himself would receive the first intimations of His own revelation.

As with Christ, Muḥammad, and the Báb, the upbringing of Mírzá Husayn-'Alí and the stories associated with his childhood are demonstrative of His inherent knowledge and uncanny wisdom:

> When Bahá'u'lláh was a child of five or six years, He dreamt that He was in a garden where huge birds were flying overhead and attacking Him, but they could not harm Him; then went to bathe in the sea, and there he was attacked by fishes, but they too could cause Him no injury. Bahá'u'lláh related this strange dream to His father, and Mírzá Buzurg sent for a man who claimed to interpret dreams. After making his calculations, he told Mírzá Buzurg that the expanse of the sea was this world in its entirety, and the birds and fishes were the peoples of the world assailing his Son, because He would promulgate something of vital importance related to the minds of men. But they would be powerless to harm Him, for He would triumph over them all to achieve a momentous matter. (Balyuzi, *Bahá'u'lláh: The King of Glory*, p. 19)

A LETTER FROM THE BÁB

Skipping over many details from the years when, after His father's death, Mírzá Ḥusayn-'Alí took over the family affairs, including the raising of His young brother Mírzá Yaḥyá, we come to a turning point in the life of the Manifestation with His recognition of the Báb as Qá'im and His subsequent role in the rapidly emerging Bábí religion.

Soon after declaring His station to Mullá Ḥusayn in May of 1844, the Báb sent this first of His followers on a strategic mission—to take a scroll wrapped in cloth containing a letter of the Báb to "Him Whom

God will Manifest." To accomplish this, Mullá Ḥusayn was told by the Báb to travel from Shiraz "towards the north, and visit on your way Iṣfahán, Kashan, Qum, and Ṭihrán." The Báb went on to explain that Mullá Ḥusayn should "Beseech almighty Providence that He may graciously enable you to attain, in that capital, the seat of true sovereignty, and to enter the mansion of the Beloved. A secret lies hidden in that city. When made manifest, it shall turn the earth into paradise. My hope is that you may partake of its grace and recognize its splendour" (Balyuzi, *Bahá'u'lláh,* p. 32).

Mullá Ḥusayn made his way to Tehran as instructed by the Báb. Ultimately he succeeded in delivering this same scroll to Mírzá Ḥusayn-'Alí by securing the aid of a young student who served as intermediary for this purpose. Upon reading the tablet conveyed to Him by the young student, Bahá'u'lláh reacted with instant recognition of the station of the Author of the message. The report of the student to Mullá Ḥusayn described the event as follows:

> Unfolding the scroll, He glanced at its contents and began to read aloud to us certain of its passages. I sat enraptured as I listened to the sound of His voice and the sweetness of its melody. He had read a page of the scroll when, turning to His brother, He said: "Musa,[2] what have you to say? Verily I say, whoso believes in the Qur'án and recognizes its Divine origin, and yet hesitates, though it be for a moment, to admit that these soul-stirring words are endowed with the same regenerating power, has most assuredly erred in his judgment and has strayed far from the path of justice." (Quoted in Nabíl-i-Aẓam, *The Dawn-Breakers,* p. 106)

---

2. Mírzá Músá (Áqáy-i-Kalím) was a younger brother of Bahá'u'lláh who remained a faithful follower of his brother for the remainder of His storied life.

From this point on, Bahá'u'lláh was a staunch follower of the Báb and immediately began promulgating the Bábí Cause throughout His native province of Mázindarán.

TURMOIL AND EPIPHANY

For the next six years, life for the Báb and for the Bábí community was a whirlwind of activity and, before long, a wildfire of persecution, torture, and executions. In 1847 the Báb, Who had been under various forms of house arrest since His return from pilgrimage in 1845, was imprisoned in the remote mountain fortress of Máh-Kú in the northwest of Adharbáyján.

The Báb remained imprisoned there for nine months, after which He was removed to further imprisonment in the fortress of Chihríq, also in Adharbáyján, where He remained for the next two years. On July 9, 1850, He was executed by a government firing squad in the barracks square of Tabríz under miraculous circumstances. But during the six years of the Báb's ministry, Bahá'u'lláh was, at the Báb's behest, steadily guiding the Bábí Faith to the extent He was able.

The Bábí Faith spread with amazing swiftness throughout Persia in such a way that the monarchy, which was closely aligned with the powers of the clergy, sensed a frantic need to react swiftly and ruthlessly to obliterate the Faith. By inciting uproar among the citizenry, the mullás encouraged attacks on the homes of the Bábís. During the two-year period from 1848–59, approximately twenty thousand Bábís were slaughtered, often by unspeakably hideous means. The heart-wrenching accounts of these attacks and the courage and heroism demonstrated by those Bábís who chose death rather than recant their beliefs can be found recounted in graphic detail in numerous sources.

The highlights of Bahá'u'lláh's part in these events is worth noting, though the complexity of His involvement is best recounted in Hasan Balyuzi's *Bahá'u'lláh: The King of Glory*, at present the most comprehensive biography of Bahá'u'lláh. In the summer of 1848 Bahá'u'lláh convened a conference of Bábí leaders and followers, ostensibly to consult on how to help rescue the Báb from imprisonment. In reality, the conference had a more subtle and profound purpose—to proclaim to the Bábís that the revelation of the Báb was not an attempt at reformation or purification of Islam, but a new independent revelation from God. In short, if they were to continue to be followers of the Báb, they should no longer consider themselves Muslims, but Bábís, and they should recognize the Báb as possessing a spiritual station on a par with that of Muḥammad.

In a symbolic gesture on this occasion, all were given new names or titles. At this time Mírzá Husayn-'Alí assumed the title "Bahá'u'lláh." This important conference also set in motion a series of events that would over the course of the following year result in the most grievous attacks on the Bábí communities. The most notable of these were the government siege of Fort Shaykh Ṭabarsí near Bárfurúsh (October, 1848–May,1849), the Zanján upheaval (May 13, 1850–January 1851), and the Nayríz upheaval (May 27, 1850–June 21, 1850). In July of 1850, the Báb Himself was executed.

As these persecutions spread throughout Persia, almost every Bábí leader of note was executed. Deranged by grief at the slaughter of friends and relatives, two young Bábís determined to take the life of the sháh. Though their plot was foolhardy and sternly discouraged by Bahá'u'lláh, the two approached the sháh intent on their purpose, but their weapon misfired. They were quickly seized, tortured, and executed.

While they confessed that they had no accomplices, the firestorm of persecution once again gained momentum throughout Persia, and being one of the few remaining Bábí leaders, Bahá'u'lláh Himself was arrested. In spite of His noble rank and respected character, He was placed in the infamous Siyáh-Chál, commonly known as the "Black

Pit." A subterranean dungeon formerly used as a water cistern, this foul smelling enclosure had neither light nor water. His neck in chains, His feet in stocks, Bahá'u'lláh was strung together in a row with eighty-one others, thirty-eight of whom were leading members of the Bábí community. Bahá'u'lláh's own description hints at the grievous conditions they endured:

> Upon Our arrival We were first conducted along a pitch-black corridor, from whence We descended three steep flights of stairs to the place of confinement assigned to Us. The dungeon was wrapped in thick darkness, and Our fellow prisoners numbered nearly a hundred and fifty souls: thieves, assassins and highwaymen. Though crowded, it had no other outlet than the passage by which We entered. No pen can depict that place, nor any tongue describe its loathsome smell. Most of these men had neither clothes nor bedding to lie on. God alone knoweth what befell Us in that most foul-smelling and gloomy place! (*Epistle to the Son of the Wolf*, p. 20)

On a daily basis, one Bábí prisoner would be selected, taken out to the courtyard, and executed. There was an air of expectation and celebration by the other Bábí prisoners as each one left, because Bahá'u'lláh would "comfort him with the assurance of an everlasting life in the world beyond":

> Soon after the martyrdom of each of these companions, We would be informed by the executioner, who had grown to be friendly to Us, of the circumstances of the death of his victim, and of the joy with which he had endured his sufferings to the very end. (Nabíl-i-A'ẓam, *The Dawn-Breakers*, p. 633).

It was clearly only a matter of time before Bahá'u'lláh Himself would be taken. Yet it was during this same period of imprisonment that Bahá'u'lláh received the signal that the time to initiate His own revelation had come. A vision in the form of the Maid of Heaven, a symbol of the Holy Spirit, visited Him and assured Him that He would be released, that He would unleash a revelation that would overpower all obstacles and that in time would transform the entirety of human civilization on earth. His own words taken from His Tablet to Násiri'd-Dín Sháh alluding to this turning point describe this "epiphany":

> O King! I was but a man like others, asleep upon My couch, when lo, the breezes of the All-Glorious were wafted over Me, and taught Me the knowledge of all that hath been. This thing is not from Me, but from One Who is Almighty and All-Knowing. And He bade Me lift up My voice between earth and heaven, and for this there befell Me what hath caused the tears of every man of understanding to flow. The learning current amongst men I studied not; their schools I entered not. Ask of the city wherein I dwelt, that thou mayest be well assured that I am not of them who speak falsely. This is but a leaf which the winds of the will of thy Lord, the Almighty, the All-Praised, have stirred. (*Summons of the Lord of Hosts*, pp. 147–48)

A TRANSFORMATION OR AN UNVEILING?

Having reviewed briefly some of the parallels in the lives of the Manifestations, focusing on Their assumption of titles as associated with the public declaration of Their station and missions, we can now approach a related but more crucial issue regarding Their ontology. At what would appear to be turning points in the lives of the Prophets, do

They undergo some change in Their essential nature, or is a previously concealed spiritual ascendancy suddenly unveiled?

Only a couple of these critical points of change are depicted with much detail or verifiable authenticity, and yet the point of beginning for each revelation seems to stem from a similar kind of experience. But because the terms used to depict these events are ambiguous, we are left to resolve the exact same problem that faced the ecclesiasts at the Synod of Nicaea: Are the Manifestations ordinary human beings who are transformed by God into representatives through whom He can communicate guidance to the rest of humankind, or are these Beings divine incarnations of the essence of God Who are able to take on human form? Or is there a third alternative? Could it be that the Manifestations are not ordinary human beings at all, but a distinct order of beings—Emissaries sent from the metaphysical realm, and yet essentially distinct from the Creator?

In the next two chapters we will focus on this crucial question of the ontology—the essential reality—of the Manifestations. Only after we have assessed the reality of these Beings can we hope to understand the plan or methodology by which the Creator has decided to educate us. Only by understanding the nature of the Prophets can we attain some comprehension of our own nature and purpose in fulfilling God's wish to be known.

7

THE EPIPHANY
OF THE PROPHETS

Briefly, the Holy Manifestations have ever been, and ever will be,
Luminous Realities; no change or variation takes place in Their
essence. Before declaring Their manifestation, They are silent and
quiet like a sleeper, and after Their manifestation, They speak
and are illuminated, like one who is awake.

—'Abdu'l-Bahá

From our discussion in the previous chapter, it is obvious that any attempt to understand the essential nature of the Manifestations of God must begin with an examination of what transpires when They undergo what appear to be transformative experiences. Whatever significance these profound events have for the Manifestations Themselves, these turning points seem to signify the beginning of Their active ministries.

THE EPIPHANY
The critical question that weighs heavily on our assessment of the nature of the Prophets is whether or not any substantive change takes place in the Prophets at the point of Their so-called epiphanies. If They are indeed transformed at this point, then do we infer that prior to this moment They are oblivious to the character, powers, and mission They are about to assume?

Whereas, if no fundamental change takes place in Their essential nature during this experience, then perhaps They already know They have a mission. And if They are already aware of Their destiny, then possibly the epiphany indicates that They are suddenly made aware of exactly what sort of task They must undertake. Still a third possibility is that They know from the very beginning of Their consciousness exactly who They are and what Their mission will be, but the vision or transformative experience is some sort of divine signal that the time has come for Them to reveal Their identity and inaugurate Their ministry.

Some anecdotal evidence we have already cited seems to indicate that the Manifestations may know who They are even in childhood. We have noted the story of Christ as a boy of twelve demonstrating what seems to be His inherent capacity and His awareness of His station. As we have also noted, this inference seems confirmed by parallel descriptions of childhood stories from the lives of Muḥammad, the Báb, and Bahá'u'lláh.

And yet clearly the accounts of the epiphanies in the lives of each Manifestation seem too similar and too dramatic not to indicate that something extremely significant is taking place. One obvious yet thoroughly strategic point we have failed to note about these seemingly transformative experiences is that we know about them *only* because the Manifestations have described them to Their followers. Because these are completely subjective experiences, nobody else could know about them unless the Prophets discussed what happened with others.

Nobody was with Moses when He saw the burning bush. No one witnessed the Holy Spirit descend like a dove when Christ was baptized.[1] No one was with Muḥammad when the Angel Gabriel appeared to Him. The Báb was alone when he experienced the dream-vision

---

1. As we will observe, in the gospel of John, John the Baptist is quoted as saying that he did witness the spirit descend.

of the martyred Imám Ḥusayn. No one in the Siyáh-Chál except Bahá'u'lláh saw the heavenly Maiden appear to Him and announce His station.

We must necessarily conclude, in other words, that the Prophets have some important reason for wanting us to know about these turning points in Their lives. Among the most obvious reasons is the strategic necessity for the Prophet to explain why He now possesses a station and power that He has not previously mentioned. If He did *not* give some dramatic explanation for how He is now able to produce a revelation direct from God, it is doubtful that many would pay any attention to His assertion, especially those who have been His friends, associates, and family. Indeed, as we will discover, the family of the Prophets are sometimes among the most vehement detractors of the Prophet.

MOSES AND THE BURNING BUSH

According to the accounts in both the Bible and the Qur'án, Moses encounters the Burning Bush on Mt. Horeb (also called Mt. Sinai) when He spies a light on the mountain. After He ascends, He sees the bush or tree that burns without becoming consumed. From the bush emanates the voice of God, revealing the name of God (Yahweh or Jehovah) to Moses, telling Him to deliver the Hebrew people from bondage in Egypt and bestowing various sensational powers upon the Him, such as the ability to change His rod into a serpent and to heal leprosy. In the Qur'án, Moses is exhorted to attempt to convince the Pharaoh to accept belief in God and then to free the Hebrews of his own accord.

CHRIST AND THE DOVE

The gospels speak of a spiritual experience occurring when Christ is anointed or baptized by John the Baptist. There is not much detail—

the "vision" is described simply in the three synoptic gospels as Christ's vision of the Holy Spirit descending upon Him "like a dove," though whether or not this is meant as a visual metaphor is not clear:

> And Jesus, when he was baptized, went up straightway out of the water: and, lo, the heavens were opened unto him, and he saw the Spirit of God descending like a dove, and lighting upon him: and lo a voice from heaven, saying, This is my beloved Son, in whom I am well pleased. (Matthew 2:16–17)

> And straightway coming up out of the water, He saw the heavens opened, and the Spirit like a dove descending upon Him, and there came a voice from heaven, saying, "Thou art my beloved Son, in whom I am well pleased." (Mark 1:10–11)

> Now when all the people were baptized, it came to pass, that Jesus also being baptized, and praying, the heaven was opened, and the Holy Ghost descended in a bodily shape like a dove upon Him, and a voice came from heaven, which said, "Thou art my beloved Son; in thee I am well pleased." (Luke 3:21–32)

He is never quoted as speaking directly about this experience Himself, even though there is obviously no other source from whom this subjective vision could have been narrated, except in the gospel of John. In this non-synoptic gospel, the epiphany is an external event and observable, at least for John the Baptist, who not only recognizes the station of Christ at first sight, but who also testifies that he himself saw the epiphany: "The next day John seeth Jesus coming unto him, and saith, Behold the Lamb of God, which taketh away the sin of the world. This is he of whom I said, After me cometh a man which is preferred before me: for he was before me. And I knew him not: but that he should be made manifest to Israel, therefore am I come baptizing with water. And John bare record, saying, 'I saw the Spirit descending from heaven like a dove, and it abode upon him'" (John 1:29–32).

MUḤAMMAD AND THE ANGEL GABRIEL

The appearance of the Angel Gabriel to Muḥammad in the cave while the Prophet is meditating is alluded to in the Qur'án, but the entire story derives primarily from ḥadíth. Furthermore, the Shí'ih version of the appearance is significantly different than the Sunni version. According to Shí'ih belief, Muḥammad expects the visitation, and He is thoroughly prepared to begin His ministry. However, according to Sunni belief, Muḥammad was so stunned and shaken by this event that he hurried home to be comforted by His wife Khadijah, who wrapped Him in a robe.

Obviously these distinctions are important because of the assumptions they imply about the station or ontology of the Prophet. If He is already aware that He is a Manifestation, then the appearance of the Angel Gabriel, while an important signal or turning point, would not have such an astounding or shocking effect as it would had He no idea that He was to be given such a mission, as is implied in the account of Moses.

THE BÁB AND THE MARTYRED IMÁM ḤUSAYN

As we noted in the previous chapter, the Báb describes in detail His dream-vision of the martyred Imám Ḥusayn in 1843. In this dramatic experience, the Báb visions Himself imbibing the blood that flows from the Imám's lacerated throat. He comments that "the mysteries of His Revelation were unfolded before My eyes in all their glory," but, like the description of Christ's anointing, the Báb Himself does not seem to place a great deal of emphasis on this turning point in His life. He does not allude to this epiphany as any sort of proof of His station or evidence of some newfound station or capacity.

BAHÁ'U'LLÁH AND THE VEILED MAIDEN

As we also noted in the previous chapter, Bahá'u'lláh in His tablet to Náṣiri'd-Dín Sháh speaks very specifically about the initial appearance of the Veiled Maiden to Him while He is imprisoned in the Siyáh-Chál. Furthermore, He alludes to this experience elaborately in several other later works. In His description, Bahá'u'lláh seems to portray a sudden transformation that includes a bestowal of knowledge and a capacity and assurance He did not have prior to this experience. Furthermore in *Epistle to the Son of the Wolf,* the last major work revealed by Bahá'u'lláh, a work which serves as a retrospective on His ministry, Bahá'u'lláh describes in dramatic sensual detail the subjective experience of these initial stirrings of the revelatory process:

> During the days I lay in the prison of Ṭihrán, though the galling weight of the chains and the stench-filled air allowed Me but little sleep, still in those infrequent moments of slumber I felt as if something flowed from the crown of My head over My breast, even as a mighty torrent that precipitateth itself upon the earth from the summit of a lofty mountain. Every limb of My body would, as a result, be set afire. At such moments My tongue recited what no man could bear to hear. (*Epistle to the Son of the Wolf,* p. 22)

Clearly this is the most elaborate and reliably authentic description of what the Manifestation experiences, or at least what Bahá'u'lláh experienced. From this recollection of the experience, we might infer two important features concerning the point when the ministry begins and where God communicates a revelation to humankind through His Intermediary.

First, the Manifestation may not be aware of the exact nature of His station prior to this epiphany. Second, the Manifestation is merely a conduit or mouthpiece through which God conveys new guidance to humankind, not the creative force behind the words He utters or the plan He unfolds.

In his commentary on Bahá'u'lláh's experience, Shoghi Effendi in *God Passes By* seems to confirm these two inferences when he compares the initial stirrings of the revelation of Bahá'u'lláh to the similar epiphanies experienced by Moses and Muḥammad:

> "One night in a dream," He Himself, calling to mind, in the evening of His life, the first stirrings of God's Revelation within His soul, has written, "these exalted words were heard on every side: 'Verily, We shall render Thee victorious by Thyself and by Thy pen. Grieve Thou not for that which hath befallen Thee, neither be Thou afraid, for Thou art in safety. Ere long will God raise up the treasures of the earth—men who will aid Thee through Thyself and through Thy Name, wherewith God hath revived the hearts of such as have recognized Him.'" In another passage He describes, briefly and graphically, the impact of the onrushing force of the Divine Summons upon His entire being—an experience vividly recalling the vision of God that caused Moses to fall in a swoon, and the voice of Gabriel which plunged Muhammad into such consternation that, hurrying to the shelter of His home, He bade His wife, Khadijih, envelop Him in His mantle. (*God Passes By*, p. 101)

Bahá'u'lláh recounts another exacting description of this experience in the Súrí-i-Haykal, (Súrih of the Temple), a major work revealed during His stay in Adrianople. We can cite here only a small portion of this first-person account because the assertions of the Maiden quoted by Bahá'u'lláh with which we end this excerpt go on to constitute the entirety of the remainder of this profound work (the next 50 pages) in which the Maiden speaks to Bahá'u'lláh as the "Living Temple" (p. 14), as the "Hand of God" (p. 27), as the "Pen" (p. 24), as the "Ancient Beauty" (p. 43), as the "Temple of Holiness" (pp. 49–50), as the "Temple of My Cause" (p. 66), and, finally, as the "Temple of Divine Revelation" (p. 80):

> While engulfed in tribulations I heard a most wondrous, a most sweet voice, calling above My head. Turning My face, I beheld a Maiden—the embodiment of the remembrance of the name of My Lord–suspended in the air before Me. So rejoiced was she in her very soul that her countenance shone with the ornament of the good pleasure of God, and her cheeks glowed with the brightness of the All-Merciful. Betwixt earth and heaven she was raising a call which captivated the hearts and minds of men. She was imparting to both My inward and outer being tidings which rejoiced My soul, and the souls of God's honored servants.
>
> Pointing with her finger unto My head, she addressed all who are in heaven and all who are on earth, saying: By God! This is the Best-Beloved of the worlds, and yet ye comprehend not. This is the Beauty of God amongst you, and the power of His sovereignty within you, could ye but understand. This is the Mystery of God and His Treasure, the Cause of God and His glory unto all who are in the kingdoms of Revelation and of creation, if ye be of them that perceive. This is He Whose Presence is the ardent desire of the denizens of the Realm of eternity, and of them that dwell within the Tabernacle of glory, and yet from His Beauty do ye turn aside.

O people of the Bayan![2] If ye aid Him not, God will assuredly assist Him with the powers of earth and heaven, and sustain Him with the hosts of the unseen through His command "Be," and it is! The day is approaching when God will have, by an act of His Will, raised up a race of men the nature of which is inscrutable to all save God, the All-Powerful, the Self-Subsisting. (*The Summons of the Lord of Hosts*, pp. 6–8).

WHAT REALLY HAPPENED IN THE SIYÁH-CHÁL?

As we have noted, some passages depicting the epiphany of the Prophets seem to indicate a transformation and not merely the point of announcement that a new revelation has begun. Some of the accounts imply that They are unaware of Their destiny and the lofty station to which They have now been appointed. These accounts by Bahá'u'lláh would certainly seem to confirm such an inference.

Fortunately, there are in the Bahá'í texts very explicit discussions of this event to clarify exactly what does take place, not only with Bahá'u'lláh, but with the epiphany of all the Manifestations. Perhaps more important, there are also unambiguous passages explicating the essential nature of the Manifestations in relation to Their "humanness"—explanations that provide additional clarity about what does and does not happen during these points in Their lives when They begin to receive a revelation direct from God.

As the primary objective of this entire study is to gain as much insight as we can into the purpose, nature, powers, and strategies

---

2. It was in Adrianople that Bahá'u'lláh instigated the official separation from His perfidious brother, Mírzá Yaḥyá. From this point on the followers of Bahá'u'lláh were alluded to as *Bahá'ís*, and Bahá'u'lláh refers to those who follow Mírzá Yaḥyá as "People of the Bayán" to indicate that they were disobeying the command of the Báb by refusing to become followers of "Him Whom God will make manifest"—Bahá'u'lláh.

of these specialized Emissaries from God, we have now arrived at a critical point—we must examine the fundamental parameters of the nature of the Manifestations. Let us set forth, therefore, some of these major parameters with appropriate candor.

First, the Bahá'í writings state that the Manifestations do not become essentially transformed. They are always aware of Their special station and mission. They are not ordinary human beings. They are endowed with Their special powers and occupy the station of Prophethood even prior to Their appearance in a temporal or human form. So what does occur in these ostensibly transformative moments when the revelatory process begins?

In the previous chapter, we examined Bahá'u'lláh's description of what happens to Him in the dark stench-filled prison known as the Siyáh-Chál, especially His statement in the opening passage in the Tablet to Násiri'd-Dín Sháh stating that before this epiphany, He was an ordinary human being sleeping on His "couch":

> O KING! I was but a man like others, asleep upon My couch, when lo, the breezes of the All-Glorious were wafted over Me, and taught Me the knowledge of all that hath been. (*Epistle to the Son of the Wolf*, p. 11)

Bahá'u'lláh's recounting of this same turning point at which His revelation begins is described slightly differently in another tablet to His followers:

> God is My witness, O people! I was asleep on My couch, when lo, the Breeze of God wafting over Me roused Me from My slumber. His quickening Spirit revived Me, and My tongue was unloosed to voice His Call. Accuse Me not of having transgressed against God. Behold Me, not with your eyes but with Mine. Thus ad-

monisheth you He Who is the Gracious, the All-Knowing. Think ye, O people, that I hold within My grasp the control of God's ultimate Will and Purpose? Far be it from Me to advance such claim. To this I testify before God, the Almighty, the Exalted, the All-Knowing, the All-Wise. (*Gleanings,* no. 41.1)

We also have the bounty of an authoritative third-person description of the significance of this event as portrayed by Shoghi Effendi who, in addition to alluding to this milestone, seems to provide a specific interpretation of what this event signified: "The circumstances in which the Vehicle of this newborn Revelation, following with such swiftness that of the Báb, received the first intimations of His sublime mission recall, and indeed surpass in poignancy the soul-shaking experience of Moses when confronted by the Burning Bush in the wilderness of Sinai" (*God Passes By,* p. 92). Shoghi Effendi goes on to compare this milestone in the life and ministry of Bahá'u'lláh to the similar epiphanies that occurred with other Manifestations.

TRADITIONAL INTERPRETATIONS OF EPIPHANY AND REVELATION

It is understandable that many infer from the first-person accounts of Bahá'u'lláh, and from the explanations of this event by Shoghi Effendi, that prior to this moment, Bahá'u'lláh was an ordinary human being. He may have been a very wonderful person, possibly even a stainless soul, but an otherwise normal human being who became suddenly transformed. He was, like the previous Manifestations, dramatically adorned with the mantle of Prophethood. Sometimes these interpretations further conclude that the once ordinary human being has now become transformed into another category of being, a divine Emissary, a conduit through which God can reveal specific guidance.

Some conclude that the actual words revealed by the Manifestations are likewise direct quotations by the Manifestations of what God tells Them to say. In short, these are not Their ideas or Their particular articulation of God's ideas—They merely repeat words They are told to utter. This understanding particularly applies to those occasions when a passage is preceded by the command "Say." The words that follow this command, it is inferred, are a direct quote from God. What is not clear is if such an interpretation means that all the other words revealed by the Prophet are simply a paraphrase of God's ideas.

This understanding is a standard interpretation of Muḥammad's revelation of the Qur'án. Many believe that the Angel Gabriel tells Muḥammad what to say, and whenever such "revelatory" experiences occur, Muḥammad stops, experiences some sort of trance, and begins uttering the words of God delivered to Him by Gabriel.

A REVELATION DIRECT FROM GOD

The term that Bahá'u'lláh uses to allude to the revelatory process— as opposed to other types of divine inspiration to which any spiritual individual may be receptive—is the phrase "a revelation direct from God." The context in which Bahá'u'lláh employs this phrase is in the Most Holy Book where He notes that anyone who claims to be a Manifestation before a full thousand years have passed is a "lying imposter": "Whoso layeth claim to a Revelation direct from God, ere the expiration of a full thousand years, such a man is assuredly a lying impostor" (Kitáb-i-Aqdas, ¶37).

Another interpretation inferred from both Bahá'u'lláh's account and Shoghi Effendi's description of the event is that while the Manifestation may be vaguely aware that He will have some special part to play in serving God—even as implied in the accounts of these Individuals during Their childhood—They are astounded and shocked that it is

They Who are to be the source through which an entirely new revelation or religion is revealed by God to the world. This inference might seem confirmed by the following assertion by Bahá'u'lláh: "Had the ultimate destiny of God's Faith been in Mine hands, I would have never consented, even though for one moment, to manifest Myself unto you, nor would I have allowed one word to fall from My lips. Of this God Himself is, verily, a witness" (*Gleanings,* no. 41.1).

Another term used by Shoghi Effendi in his assessment of the significance of this event that would also seem to confirm such an interpretation is the word "intimation." While the word has a fairly extensive range of possible meanings, the most common usage would seem to imply that at this point the Manifestation has the first sign or hint that He is the Manifestation, the One appointed to bring forth the revelation. If this is Shoghi Effendi's intended meaning, then he would seem to be confirming that prior to this "intimation," Bahá'u'lláh had no idea that He was the chosen One, the Manifestation of God Whose mission it now is to fulfill the prophecies of the past and to instigate a new religion.

Ostensibly corroborated by religious tradition, it is not infrequent that immediately prior to or immediately after this point, the Manifestation seeks some period of isolation, mediation, and reflection to prepare Himself for the rough path that lies ahead. For example, in the three Synoptic gospels, immediately after being anointed, Christ goes into the wilderness to confront Satan. The Bahá'í writings unambiguously deny the reality of Satan as an actual being or demigod (as depicted by literalist interpretations of this event). Instead, the Bahá'í texts assert that all allusions to "Satan" are actually references to the ego or to what 'Abdu'l-Bahá refers to as the "insistent self." Therefore, we might interpret Christ's "confrontation" with "Satan" as representing His determination to remove any remnant of self-interest or attachment to the things of this world before He sets forth to begin His ministry.

AN AUTHORITATIVE
EXPLICATION OF THE EPIPHANY

Fortunately, all ambiguity about what happens at these moments of "intimation" can be successfully, logically, and finally set aside by examining 'Abdu'l-Bahá's authoritative explication of the epiphany. His explanation is especially valuable when this detailed clarification is coupled with His other equally frank and logical explanations about the epiphanies and essential nature of all the Manifestations of God.

"ASLEEP UPON MY COUCH"

Obviously there was no couch in the vermin invested dungeon of the Siyáh-Chál (the "Black Pit"). Equally obvious is the fact that Bahá'u'lláh is employing an analogy to explain what He experiences as "the first intimations" of His revelation: He was *like* a man sleeping who suddenly became awake. 'Abdu'l-Bahá confirms this interpretation when He states that this is a common metaphor in Persian and Arabic: "For example, it is a Persian and Arabic expression to say that the earth was asleep, and the spring came, and it awoke; or the earth was dead, and the spring came, and it revived. These expressions are metaphors, allegories, mystic explanations in the world of signification" (*Some Answered Questions*, p. 84).

In interpreting Bahá'u'lláh's portrayal of this experience, 'Abdu'l-Bahá also explains that this description is intended to convey in sensibly comprehensible terms a spiritual experience or reality that we would not otherwise be able to grasp: "This is the state of manifestation: it is not sensible; it is an intellectual reality, exempt and freed from time, from past, present and future; it is an explanation, a simile, a metaphor and is not to be accepted literally; it is not a state that can be comprehended by man" (*Some Answered Questions*, p. 84).

'Abdu'l-Bahá explains further that this analogy is not in any way intended to imply that Bahá'u'lláh undergoes some ontological change—a transformation of His essential nature or being. Until this point of epiphany, He has kept Himself concealed or silent. Now He will speak or manifest His true identity: "Sleeping and waking is passing from one state to another. Sleeping is the condition of repose, and wakefulness is the condition of movement. Sleeping is the state of silence; wakefulness is the state of speech. Sleeping is the state of mystery; wakefulness is the state of manifestation" (*Some Answered Questions*, p. 84).

At the conclusion of his interpretation of what Bahá'u'lláh intends by His statement about this experience in the Siyáh-Chál, 'Abdu'l-Bahá gives a succinct axiom that is applicable to all the Manifestations of God: "Briefly, the Holy Manifestations have ever been, and ever will be, Luminous Realities; no change or variation takes place in Their essence. Before declaring Their manifestation, They are silent and quiet like a sleeper, and after Their manifestation, They speak and are illuminated, like one who is awake" (*Some Answered Questions*, p. 86).

THE CONCEPT OF "INTIMATION"

'Abdu'l-Bahá's logical and authoritative explanation demands that we reexamine and rethink what we might have assumed takes place when the Manifestations experience the beginning of the process by which They reveal the new "Book," the Word of God for the new revelation to set in motion a new dispensation. We are left to search for alternatives to the belief that the Manifestations become essentially transformed or undergo some fundamental change in being or station. This is further confirmed by a passage from the writings of the Báb cited by Bahá'u'lláh in *Epistle to the Son of the Wolf*:

> Whomsoever He ordaineth as a Prophet, he, verily, hath been
> a Prophet from the beginning that hath no beginning, and will

thus remain until the end that hath no end, inasmuch as this is an act of God. And whosoever is made a Vicegerent by Him, shall be a Vicegerent in all the worlds, for this is an act of God. For the will of God can in no wise be revealed except through His will, nor His wish be manifested save through His wish. He, verily, is the All-Conquering, the All-Powerful, the All-Highest. (*Epistle to the Son of the Wolf,* p. 155)

And yet we still have to understand what Shoghi Effendi intends by his allusion to the parallel dramatic events in the lives of the Manifestations as marking the beginning of Their revelation. Why is this experience so important to the Manifestations?

One solution to this dilemma resides in the circumstantial events pertaining to Bahá'u'lláh's description of the "station of distinction"—the fact that each Manifestation has a distinct soul, appears at a particular time in human history, and ministers to the particular exigencies of the age in which He appears:

[T]he station of distinction . . . pertaineth to the world of creation and to the limitations thereof. In this respect, each Manifestation of God hath a distinct individuality, a definitely prescribed mission, a predestined Revelation, and specially designated limitations. Each one of them is known by a different name, is characterized by a special attribute, fulfills a definite Mission, and is entrusted with a particular Revelation. Even as He saith: "Some of the Apostles We have caused to excel the others. To some God hath spoken, some He hath raised and exalted. And to Jesus, Son of Mary, We gave manifest signs, and We strengthened Him with the Holy Spirit." (Kitáb-i-Íqán, ¶191)

Thus the station of the Prophets is purposefully hidden and concealed from public knowledge until it is time for them to begin Their ministry. This concealment is a strategically important part of the methodology with which They educate humankind, as we will study in part 3, and it is also a means by which Their lives are protected until They are ready to confront the clergy and followers of the previous dispensation and, if necessary, to sacrifice Their lives in the process.

But there is another strategically important feature of there being a specific dramatic event associated with the unveiling of Their station and powers. They are, once They receive the divine signal to begin Their mission, in a position of having to announce that, in effect, yesterday They were merely ordinary human beings whereas today They are Manifestations of God with the power and authority to reveal the Word of God for a new age. They are now "suddenly," so it seems to those around Them, exemplary expressions of Godliness in human form and the fountainhead of spiritual guidance and divine authority. In other words, how are the Manifestations to explain to the world at large that They now possess a status and authority that they did not previously seem to have or assert?

Possibly such a stratagem might seem devious or deceptive, a sort of subterfuge. But clearly *some* explanation has to be given as to why They now openly make a such a claim.

ALWAYS AWARE OF THEIR STATION

So when does Their awareness of Their special ontology and mission begin? 'Abdu'l-Bahá observes that the Manifestations are aware of Their special station even in Their childhood: "Verily, from the beginning that Holy Reality (the Manifestation) is conscious of the secret of existence, and from the age of childhood signs of greatness appear and are visible in Him" (*Some Answered Questions*, p. 154). How, then, do we interpret Shoghi Effendi's statement that these subjective experiences are, indeed, the "first intimations" of the mission of the Manifestations? Does not the word *intimation* imply that this is Their first "hint" or "clue" that They are Manifestations?

The simple answer to this question is that the term *intimation* as utilized in this context does not mean what some may think it means. This may well be the first point at which They are given the signal to begin doing what They have always been aware They were going to do. We might understand the word *intimation* in terms of a runner who prepares for years to compete in the Olympics. There is no question in the mind of the athlete what He is training for or what the end result of that training will be. Nevertheless, when the moment finally does arrive and the gun fires to signal the start of the race, there is, we can be certain, a subjective experience unlike anything the runner has ever known before or imagined he or she might feel. However many times he or she may have practiced for this moment, reflected on this moment, imagined what it would feel like, once the race begins, an overwhelming confluence of emotions coarse through the being of the athlete.

Perhaps the runner may soon become accustomed to this new experience, this reality of being an Olympian. But the runner will always recall that singular moment when it first began and the myriad emotions associated with that first intimation that flooded their spirit with joy, excitement, trepidation, confirmation, and power, etc. Nevertheless, it was never a mystery what the runner was being trained to do.

While we certainly cannot presume to know what transpires in the consciousness of these incredible Beings, this perspective can assist us. If we consider that the word *intimation* in this context could refer to the concepts of "announcement," "communication," or "declaration," this expression could well be intended to imply both that this is the first announcement or manifestation of the Prophet's true identity to the world at large, or the announcement to the Prophet that it is time to begin.

8

HE IS THE BEGINNING
AND THE END

Know thou of a certainty that the Unseen can in no wise incarnate His Essence and reveal it unto men. He is, and hath ever been, immensely exalted beyond all that can either be recounted or perceived. From His retreat of glory His voice is ever proclaiming: "Verily, I am God; there is none other God besides Me, the All-Knowing, the All-Wise. I have manifested Myself unto men, and have sent down Him Who is the Day Spring of the signs of My Revelation. Through Him I have caused all creation to testify that there is none other God except Him, the Incomparable, the All-Informed, the All-Wise." He Who is everlastingly hidden from the eyes of men can never be known except through His Manifestation, and His Manifestation can adduce no greater proof of the truth of His Mission than the proof of His own Person.

—Bahá'u'lláh

If we assume that whatever the Manifestation is, He is this from the beginning, our question then becomes: What exactly is that station? Is the Manifestation an ordinary human being designated from birth to be a Prophet? Is the Manifestation another category of being who deigns to indulge in the human experience to bring us the divine guidance we need?

ORDINARY HUMAN BEINGS
VERSUS MANIFESTATIONS

The question of ontology—the essential nature or the "being" of the Manifestation—is at the heart of our entire study of these remarkable figures. These Beings are key to the Creator's wish to educate humankind on our planet, and, we might presume, on an infinite number of other planets as well. 'Abdu'l-Bahá provides key insight in the following passage in which he states that a being does not and cannot change its essential nature, even though there can be infinite change or refinement within a given category of being:

> Both before and after putting off this material form, there is progress in perfection but not in state. So beings are consummated in perfect man. There is no other being higher than a perfect man. But man when he has reached this state can still make progress in perfections but not in state because there is no state higher than that of a perfect man to which he can transfer himself. He only progresses in the state of humanity, for the human perfections are infinite. Thus, however learned a man may be, we can imagine one more learned.
>
> Hence, as the perfections of humanity are endless, man can also make progress in perfections after leaving this world. (*Some Answered Questions*, p. 238)

This much is clear, then—that we are capable in both this world and the next of infinite perfectibility or refinement without becoming something other than an ever-more-refined human soul. However, what 'Abdu'l-Bahá also makes clear in another passage on this same subject is that however refined we may become, we will never attain the station of the Manifestations of God:

A mineral, however far it may progress in the mineral kingdom, cannot gain the vegetable power. Also in a flower, however far it may progress in the vegetable kingdom, no power of the senses will appear. So this silver mineral cannot gain hearing or sight; it can only improve in its own condition and become a perfect mineral, but it cannot acquire the power of growth, or the power of sensation, or attain to life; it can only progress in its own condition.

For example, Peter cannot become Christ. All that he can do is, in the condition of servitude, to attain endless perfections; for every existing reality is capable of making progress. (*Some Answered Questions,* p. 231)

It is clear that 'Abdu'l-Bahá is alluding to two distinct categories of existence, a distinction that will become much more obvious in part 3 as we examine the extraordinary powers and capacities inherent in the nature of the Manifestations. But for now, let us content ourselves with observing the most fundamental difference between an ordinary human being and a Manifestation of God.

BEHOLD THE PERFECT MAN

Linguistically and logically, the term *perfect* does not admit degrees. If something is perfect, it has attained the epitome of its capacities. And yet in the previous passage, 'Abdu'l-Bahá seems to indicate that even a perfect man can make progress in degrees, though not in state. If this seems contradictory or confusing, it should, but if we examine further how this term is used in the context of the Bahá'í writings, the apparent contradiction quickly becomes resolved.

First of all, the term "perfect man" is used in two contexts in the Bahá'í writings. When written with uppercase letters, the term alludes exclusively to the Manifestations of God Who are, as we will study more extensively in the subsequent section, immaculate or flawless Beings. In the context of this usage, the term refers to the fact that the Manifestations exemplify or "manifest" the characteristics They exhort us to emulate. But while we should strive to acquire this same array of attributes, we will always be a work in progress, always striving to become more refined.

One statement used to designate this aspect of the ontology of the Manifestations is that They partake of the "The Most Great Infallibility." Here the term "infallible"—in addition to its obvious meaning of "being without error"—also connotes Their being "immaculate" or "sinless":

> Know thou that the term "Infallibility" hath numerous meanings and divers stations. In one sense it is applicable to the One Whom God hath made immune from error. Similarly it is applied to every soul whom God hath guarded against sin, transgression, rebellion, impiety, disbelief and the like. However, the Most Great Infallibility is confined to the One Whose station is immeasurably exalted beyond ordinances or prohibitions and is sanctified from errors and omissions. (Bahá'u'lláh, *Tablets of Bahá'u'lláh,* p. 108)

Therefore, in addition to implying that the Manifestation is without error in what He professes or asserts, the term *infallibility* as applied in the Bahá'í texts to the Prophets also implies that They are without imperfection in character—that They are immaculate or sinless.

'Abdu'l-Bahá reiterates this observation about how the Manifestations partake of "The Most Great Infallibility" by employing the analogy of the Manifestations to the sun. He says that Their perfection could no more be separated from Them than could the rays of the sun be separated from the sun itself. In short, it is the nature of the Manifestations that makes Them inherently distinct from ordinary mortals:

Essential infallibility is peculiar to the supreme Manifestation, for it is His essential requirement, and an essential requirement cannot be separated from the thing itself. The rays are the essential necessity of the sun and are inseparable from it. Knowledge is an essential necessity of God and is inseparable from Him. Power is an essential necessity of God and is inseparable from Him. If it could be separated from Him, He would not be God. If the rays could be separated from the sun, it would not be the sun. Therefore, if one imagines separation of the Most Great Infallibility from the supreme Manifestation, He would not be the supreme Manifestation, and He would lack the essential perfections. (*Some Answered Questions,* p. 171)

In this context, the term "Perfect Man" refers exclusively to the Manifestation: "The splendors of the perfections, bounties and attributes of God shine forth and radiate from the reality of the Perfect Man—that is to say, the Unique One, the supreme Manifestation of God" (*Some Answered Questions,* p. 221).

The term "perfect man," however, is also employed in the Bahá'í writings to designate a human being who may be sinless, but who does not partake of the "Most Great Infallibility." In these allusions, the Bahá'í writings refer to an ordinary human being who is not inherently perfect and who does not possess the same capacity or powers or station as does the Manifestation. Bahá'u'lláh states in the passage above that the term "infallible" can be "applied to every soul whom God hath guarded against sin" (*Tablets of Bahá'u'lláh,* p. 108). It is in this sense that Siyyid Káẓim observes that in religious history

[E]very hundred years there are a chosen few who spread and sow the precepts which explain that which is lawful and that which is unlawful; who tell of the things that were hidden during the hundred preceding years. In other words, in every century a learned and perfect man is found who causes the tree of religious law to revive and bloom; who regenerates its trunk to such an extent that at last the book of Creation comes to its end in a period of twelve hundred years. (Quoted in Nabíl-i-A'ẓam, *The Dawn-breakers,* p. 34)

Similarly, Bahá'u'lláh asserts in the Book of Certitude that prior to the appearance of each Manifestation a "perfect man" appears: "The sign of the invisible heaven must needs be revealed in the person of that perfect man who, before each Manifestation appeareth, educateth, and prepareth the souls of men for the advent of the divine Luminary, the Light of the unity of God amongst men" (Kitáb-i-Íqán, ¶73).

INFINITE PERFECTIBILITY REQUIRES CONTINUITY OF REVELATION

If we accept that there is a God who in His love and design for human education has sent us inherently perfect and learned Teachers from the realm of the spirit—the Messengers or Manifestations—it is unimaginable and totally illogical that this ongoing process would suddenly come to an end.

ENDLESS DEVELOPMENT

As noted above in the preceding passage from 'Abdu'l-Bahá about the human capacity for infinite refinement and development, if we are as human beings forever a work in progress, whether individually or collectively, then our need for further education and enlightenment must likewise be endless. And if our need for education is endless, then so must our eternal need for educators, for Beings more enlightened than we are.

Logically it is obvious that as individuals or as a body politic on planet Earth, we will never achieve a point of final or complete enlightenment. We will never become a finished product capable of no further improvement. Consequently, it necessarily follows that we will always need further Manifestations to bring further revelations. How could it be otherwise?

THE BEGINNING AND THE END

We have previously noted how the impact of the advent of a Manifestation is so profound that followers are tempted to assume that nothing similar could possibly occur again. This understandable inference is often compounded by the sometimes enigmatic statements Manifestations of the past made in explaining Their special status—that They are not ordinary human beings. They inherently and perfectly manifest all the attributes of God in the form of a human temple. They are the means by which we come to understand the nature of God and the means by which we can acquire "godliness" in our own character.

We have also noted that once a religion becomes stagnant over time and ceases adequately to encourage human development, its institutions may likewise become entrenched, implacable, and incapable of fostering the advancement of social and spiritual progress. As we have noted, the result is that the very force of religion, which is originally introduced to sustain the betterment of humankind, can become a source of conflict and human degradation.

Related to this need for appreciating the continuity of religion is the idea that each new revelation is correctly perceived as both the beginning and the end. It is the end—the objective and culmination—of all that has gone before, but it is the beginning of a new stage in human progress. For example, in the Christian scripture in the book of

Revelations, on four occasions the voice of the Lord says to John of Patmos that Christ is the "Alpha and Omega, the beginning and the end, the first and the last" (22:13).[1]

Since *alpha* and *omega* are the first and last letters of the classical Greek alphabet, they symbolize the "first" and the "last," or "the beginning and the end." So long as this attribute or station is applied to God the Creator, it makes perfect sense in various ways. God is the source of the beginning of creation, and yet, as we noted early in this study, as the object of our quest for knowledge and, subsequently, advancement and enlightenment, God is the "end" of all He has created. Or put in terms of our earlier discussion of the tradition of the Hidden Treasure, knowledge of God and the manifestation of His attributes is the sole objective of all creation.

The problem ensues when some read these passages as alluding exclusively to Christ. The result is two fundamental conclusions. Some believe these allusions to mean that Christ has always existed and always will exist because He is identical to God, the Father, in His essential nature. This is the conclusion of the Trinitarian doctrine. Others similarly interpret these passages to imply that the appearance of Christ is the single turning point in human history, that there will be no further revelations from God until the Second Coming, which, many Christians believe, is the very sequence of events that the Book of Revelations is portraying—the Last or Final judgment of humankind. It goes without saying, that either conclusion implies that Christianity is not only the endpoint of all previous revelations but also that the advent of Christ marks the end of God's revelation until the End Days when Christ will return to judge the world.

The concept of the beginning and the end, the first and the last, the seen and the hidden, is a major theme in the Bahá'í writings, especially

---

1. The other verses employing this same metaphor are Rev 1:8, 1:10, 21:6, and 22:13.

as the theme relates to the Manifestations. 'Abdu'l-Bahá alludes to the passage in the Book of Revelations and states that its meaning is that the station or ontology of the Manifestations never undergoes any change: ". . . Their heavenly condition embraces all things, knows all mysteries, discovers all signs, and rules over all things; before as well as after Their mission, it is the same. That is why Christ has said: 'I am Alpha and Omega, the first and the last'—that is to say, there has never been and never shall be any change and alteration in Me" (*Some Answered Questions*, p. 218).

Bahá'u'lláh gives a more complete explanation of this concept in terms of the continuity of revelation. In simple terms, Bahá'u'lláh explains that the terms "first and last," "beginning and end," and "seen and hidden" apply equally to all the Manifestations of God. Each Prophet is effectively the culmination or the end result of all the enlightenment and education that has derived from the previous revelations, and yet each Prophet is also the beginning of the next stage in the ongoing divine plan of God for humankind.

In an even lengthier and more abstruse explanation of this theme in the Book of Certitude, Bahá'u'lláh discusses in detail how these concepts apply to the spiritual concept of the unity of the Manifestations, not to any material conditions such as primacy or time. For example, in discussing the station of Essential Unity, Bahá'u'lláh notes that each of these peerless Beings manifests precisely the attributes of the same Essence (the Essential Reality of God), and Each sets forth precisely the same verities: that God is the source of all created things as well as the objective or end or goal of all creation:

Viewed in this light, they are all but Messengers of that ideal King, that unchangeable Essence. And were they all to proclaim: "I am the Seal of the Prophets," they verily utter but the truth, beyond the faintest shadow of doubt. For they are all but one person, one soul, one spirit, one being, one revelation. They are all the manifestation of the "Beginning" and the "End," the "First" and the "Last," the "Seen" and "Hidden"—all of which pertain to Him Who is the innermost Spirit of Spirits and eternal Essence of Essences. (Kitáb-i-Íqán, ¶196)

THE SEAL OF THE PROPHETS

Bahá'u'lláh's discourse on Muḥammad's assertion that He is the "seal of the Prophets" provides extensive and illuminating insight into this often misunderstood passage, as well as further enlightenment about the unity among the roles that the Manifestations play in progressive revelation itself.

Muḥammad states, "Muḥammad is not the father of any of your men, but (He is) the Messenger of Alláh, and the Seal of the Prophets, and Allah has full knowledge of all things" (33:40). The vast majority of Muslims interpret this verse to mean that there will be no further Messengers after Muḥammad. Most also interpret Muḥammad's allusion to His revelation as being complete and universal to mean that Islam and its practices represent the final assistance God will need to guide humankind. The next stage in religious history, most Muslims conclude, will be the Last Judgment and the Resurrection so often discussed throughout the Qur'án.

Bahá'u'lláh's response to these conclusions is that such interpretations are simply mistaken notions of what the term "seal" means in this passage and how it applies to all the Messengers, not merely to Muḥammad. He also condemns harshly those who have let this single word "seal" debar them from the truth about the continuity of God's plan, even as Muḥammad censures the concoction of the Trinitarian doctrine because it created chauvinism among the Christians and prevented them from recognizing Muḥammad. Bahá'u'lláh states, "[Y]et how many are those who, through failure to understand its meaning, have allowed the term 'Seal of the Prophets' to obscure their understanding, and deprive them of the grace of all His manifold bounties!" (Kitáb-i-Íqán, ¶176).

Bahá'u'lláh gives several alternative interpretations of Muḥammad's use of the term *seal*, one of the most pertinent being that at the time of appearance, each new Manifestation is the "seal" of the last Prophet, and that each new revelation is the consummation of all the previous revelations. Therefore, because human history is an endless continuum of evolutionary advancement, the appearance of a new Manifestation also represents a new beginning. It would be equally correct and logical to assert that each new Manifestation represents both the beginning and the end in relation to human history as an ongoing organic process.

What is more, since at His appearance each Manifestation represents as much as we are capable of understanding about God at that stage of human advancement, each Manifestation also represents the "seen"—the attributes of the Creator made perfectly manifest. However, because the essential reality of God will forever remain hidden from direct human understanding, the Manifestation also represents that which will forever remain hidden or "unseen." It is in this context that Bahá'u'lláh notes how the appearance of each successive Manifestation manifests the first and the last, the seen and the hidden:

> Even as in the "Beginning that hath no beginnings" the term "last" is truly applicable unto Him who is the Educator of the visible and of the invisible, in like manner, are the terms "first" and "last" applicable unto His Manifestations. They are at the same time the Exponents of both the "first" and the "last." Whilst established upon the seat of the "first," they occupy the throne of the "last." Were a discerning eye to be found, it will readily perceive that the exponents of the "first" and the "last," of the "manifest" and the "hidden," of the "beginning" and the

"seal" are none other than these holy Beings, these Essences of Detachment, these divine Souls. (Kitáb-i-Íqán, ¶174)

In the course of this same critical elucidation, Bahá'u'lláh points out that because each Manifestation comes for precisely the same purpose and represents the same truth (albeit articulated in different degrees or stages of completeness), there is no distinction among the Manifestations. Muḥammad asserts this same verity as follows

The Messenger believeth in what hath been revealed to him from his Lord, as do the men of faith. Each one (of them) believeth in Allah, His angels, His books, and His Messengers. "We make no distinction (they say) between one and another of His Messengers." And they say, "We hear, and we obey. (We seek) Thy forgiveness, Our Lord, and to Thee is the *end* of all journeys." (Qur'án 2:285)

It is in conjunction with this concept of "end" as referring to "objective" that Muḥammad in this passage states that God is the "object" or "end of all journeys." It is in this same framework that each Manifestation at the time of His appearance is the "end" or "objective" toward which all previous history has led humankind. Or to cite a useful analogy, every grade or level of our education is the end result of all our previous levels of study, and yet this new level is but the beginning point of all our subsequent study and progress.

THE "SEAL" OF A CYCLE

There is another and weightier sense in which Muḥammad can be considered the "end" or "seal" of all that precedes Him. The Bahá'í writings claim that the specific objective, mission, or assignment of the dispensation of Bahá'u'lláh is to bring together all the peoples of the world under the banner of one world Faith and a unified global polity. This is now possible because of all the preparation that has gone before. As a global community, we now find ourselves suddenly in desperate need of a global infrastructure to facilitate the newly emerged interdependence of all the nations and peoples that inhabit our small planet.

Knowing that this is the turning point human history has long awaited, both the Báb and Bahá'u'lláh describe this "Day of Days" as fulfilling all the eschatological allusions in previous scripture. According to the Bahá'í writings, the passages in the Qur'án referring to the Day of Resurrection and to the Day of Judgment have now been fulfilled with the appearance of the Báb and Bahá'u'lláh. These "Twin Manifestations" have ushered in the profound transformation and unification of our planet, the initial evidence of which is all the incredible global change and transformation that has occurred since the declaration of the Báb in 1844.

It is in this sense that the revelation of Muḥammad does indeed "seal up" the past by finishing all the preparation necessary for the advent of this Day of Days, this coalescence of the diverse peoples of the world into a global commonwealth established according to spiritual principles. As Bahá'u'lláh explains, this is the true meaning of the term "Day" as applied to the dispensations of the Prophets:

> It is evident that every age in which a Manifestation of God hath lived is divinely ordained, and may, in a sense, be characterized as God's appointed Day. This Day, however, is unique, and is to be distinguished from those that have preceded it. The designation "Seal of the Prophets" fully revealeth its high station. The Prophetic Cycle hath, verily, ended. The Eternal Truth is now come. He hath lifted up the Ensign of Power, and is now shedding upon the world the unclouded splendor of His Revelation. (*Gleanings,* no. 25.1)

So it is that the term "this Day" marks a specific turning point in human history, one appropriately designated as the "maturation of humankind." Yet this long-heralded "Day" is by no means an endpoint in the sense of the finality of human progress. Neither should this long-heralded transformation be considered the end of human history nor the end of our planet. Rather this Day of fulfillment is a maturation resulting from the culmination of eons of incremental advancement and preparation.

From this point forward, the Bahá'í writings affirm, there will be no need for vague allusions to the destiny of humankind, no need for "prophecy" in the sense that previous Manifestations had to make veiled allusions to a future that humanity could not possibly have conceived of at the time. Like pieces of a vast puzzle, the picture of what the unification of the human family really looks like can now be made plain.

Nevertheless, understood in the context of an endlessly perfectible social expression of divine principles, this age itself marks the time of maturation in the ascent of human society. It is the initial stage of all the progress that will follow—a turning point and the true beginning of a spectacular future for planet Earth and all those who will occupy it. We are witnessing, as it were, the embryonic formation of a global system that will rapidly evolve, first out of sheer necessity, then as a result of a collective will to embrace the healing remedy to universal ills that presently plague our planetary community.

THREE CONDITIONS OF THE REALITY OF THE MANIFESTATIONS

Closely related to the idea that each revelation, like a new day, is both an end and a beginning, is another essential realization about the ontology of the Prophets. The Manifestations frequently allude to Their awareness of one another and Their unity of purpose. In several instances, They seem to allude to having preexisted or having known each other prior to taking on Their human form. In other statements, the Manifestation may talk about assisting His followers after He has ascended to the spiritual realm. It is an essential point in coming to understand the ontology of the Prophets that we realize that each Manifestation exists in three distinct conditions, even while retaining the same essential reality.

As we have noted already, the doctrine of the trinity, though intended to make uniform the diverse concepts of the ontology of Christ (Christology), ended up causing doctrinal division within the Christian Church of the fourth century. The doctrine when interpreted literally totally perverts the teachings of Christ regarding His station in relation to God, as well as His relationship to all the Prophets that preceded Him and succeeded Him. However, in a poetic sense, the concept of the three conditions of the reality of the Manifestations are useful in discussing how these divine Teachers go about the task of assisting humankind.

THE PREEXISTENCE OF THE PROPHET

The first expression of the reality of the Manifestations relative to our understanding is Their existence in the metaphysical realm prior to their association with the human temple in this physical reality. But this preexistent state is not some amorphous condition. The Manifestations are, prior to assuming human form, cognitive Beings aware of Their station and active participants in the decision to undertake Their mission to assist humankind.

Shoghi Effendi makes it unmistakably clear, however, that preexistence is a condition confined to the Manifestations—ordinary human beings take their beginning when the soul or spirit emanates from the metaphysical realm during the process of conception: "The Prophets, *unlike us,* are preexistent. The soul of Christ existed in the spiritual world before His birth in this world. We cannot imagine what that world is like, so words are inadequate to picture His state of being" (Shoghi Effendi, *High Endeavors,* p. 71).

That this condition is one of wholeness and cognition is clear from other passages referring to this pre-incarnate reality. For example, many Christians are well aware of Christ's statement, "Before Abraham was, I am":

"Art thou greater than our father Abraham, which is dead? And the prophets are dead? Whom makest thou thyself?"

Jesus answered, "If I honour myself, My honour is nothing. It is my Father that honoureth me, of Whom ye say, that He is your God. Yet ye have not known Him, but I know Him. And if I should say I know Him not, I shall be a liar like unto you. But I know Him and keep His saying. Your father Abraham rejoiced to see my day, and He saw it, and was glad.

Then said the Jews unto Him, "Thou art not yet fifty years old, and hast thou seen Abraham?"

Jesus said unto them, "Verily, verily, I say unto you, before Abraham was, I am." (John 8:53–58).

Bahá'u'lláh refers to this same pre-incarnate condition in the Most Holy Book when He alludes to the "school of inner meaning." In this passage He affirms, "We, indeed, set foot within the School of inner meaning and explanation when all created things were unaware" (Kitáb-i-Aqdas, ¶175). In the continuation of this same discourse on the pre-incarnate state of the Manifestations, Bahá'u'lláh avows that He was well aware of what would be revealed well before the "people of the Bayán"[2] were born:

---

2. Those who continued to follow the Báb after the declaration of Bahá'u'lláh.

We saw the words sent down by Him Who is the All-Merciful, and We accepted the verses of God, the Help in Peril, the Self-Subsisting, which He presented unto Us, and hearkened unto that which He had solemnly affirmed in the Tablet. This we assuredly did behold. And We assented to His wish through Our behest, for truly We are potent to command.

O people of the Bayán! We, verily, set foot within the School of God when ye lay slumbering; and We perused the Tablet while ye were fast asleep. By the one true God! We read the Tablet ere it was revealed, while ye were unaware, and We had perfect knowledge of the Book when ye were yet unborn. (Kitáb-i-Aqdas, ¶175)

Perhaps the most amazing insight into the preexistent condition and the willful planning the Manifestations undertake prior to Their physical incarnation is derived from the fact that They are strategists for Their own revelation. For example, They choose the geographical location where They will appear. Shoghi Effendi in *The Advent of Divine Justice* states that the Manifestations purposefully choose to become manifest in places that are in a condition of moral depravity so that the light They bring forth might appear all the more bright because it emanates from such a spiritually desolate land: "To contend that the innate worthiness, the high moral standard, the political aptitude, and social attainments of any race or nation is the reason for the appearance in its midst of any of these Divine Luminaries would be an absolute perversion of historical facts, and would amount to a complete repudiation of the undoubted interpretation placed upon them, so clearly and emphatically, by both Bahá'u'lláh and 'Abdu'l-Bahá" (*The Advent of Divine Justice*, p. 17).

In a continuation of this same discussion, Shoghi Effendi observes that this has been the consistent motive of the appearance of every

Prophet: "For it is precisely under such circumstances, and by such means that the Prophets have, from time immemorial, chosen and were able to demonstrate their redemptive power to raise from the depths of abasement and of misery, the people of their own race and nation, empowering them to transmit in turn to other races and nations the saving grace and the energizing influence of their Revelation" (*The Advent of Divine Justice*, p. 17).

More specifically, Shoghi Effendi, Guardian of the Bahá'í Faith, states that the reason the Báb and Bahá'u'lláh chose Persia as the place of Their appearance was precisely Their desire to employ and demonstrate this same principle:

> In the light of this fundamental principle it should always be borne in mind, nor can it be sufficiently emphasized, that the primary reason why the Báb and Bahá'u'lláh chose to appear in Persia, and to make it the first repository of their Revelation, was because, of all the peoples and nations of the civilized world, that race and nation had, as so often depicted by 'Abdu'l-Bahá, sunk to such ignominious depths, and manifested so great a perversity, as to find no parallel among its contemporaries. (*The Advent of Divine Justice*, p. 17)

THE INCARNATE STAGE
OF THE MANIFESTATION

Naturally, we are most fully aware of the Manifestation when He appears in the second condition, the incarnate stage of His function as Intermediary or Emissary for God. Consequently, in the two remaining sections of this book, we will focus on how the Manifestations utilize Their earthly appearance to guide us. It is sufficient here to note that in this incarnate stage, the Manifestation first appears as if He were an ordinary human being among other human beings. He may possess an exemplary character, inherent wisdom, and extraordinary learning, but these characteristics will be discernible only to those who are spiritually perceptive. Physically, the Manifestation will not be remarkable. For example, Bahá'u'lláh's mother was concerned because her beloved son was quite small in stature:

> It is related that one day, when Mírzá Ḥusayn-'Alí was seven years old, as He was walking His parents were watching Him, and His mother remarked that He was a little short in stature. His father replied: "That matters not. Do you not know how intelligent He is and what a wonderful mind He has!" (H. M. Balyuzi, *Bahá'u'lláh: The King of Glory,* p. 19)

Obviously it is in the spiritual sense that the Manifestation is distinct from others, and that station is largely concealed until the appointed time of His revelation. Once He becomes manifest, He articulates the two categories of information which we have previously mentioned: a more expansive description of reality and a social regimen that includes a renewed or revised pattern of behavior to comply with the more advanced stage of human development.

In relation to the larger perspective, the Manifestation will mandate concepts about how the collectivity of humankind can construct a social edifice to befit the evolving spiritual and intellectual conditions of the body politic.

In this second incarnate stage, the Manifestation can correctly be said to represent the most complete expression of Godliness that we can comprehend during our own incarnate or associative stage of existence. The most complete statement of this relationship of the Manifestations to us has already been cited, but it bears repeating because of its focus on the full nature of Their ability to provide us with our source of information about the Creator:

> The essence of belief in Divine unity consisteth in regarding Him Who is the Manifestation of God and Him Who is the invisible, the inaccessible, the unknowable Essence as one and the same. By this is meant that whatever pertaineth to the former, all His acts and doings, whatever He ordaineth or forbiddeth, should be considered, in all their aspects, and under all circumstances, and without any reservation, as identical with the Will of God Himself. This is the loftiest station to which a true believer in the unity of God can ever hope to attain. Blessed is the man that reacheth this station, and is of them that are steadfast in their belief. (Bahá'u'lláh, *Gleanings*, no. 84.4)

To reiterate, our knowledge of God and of ourselves ultimately derives exclusively from the Manifestations. Without Their appearance, we would have no knowledge of God, even as Shoghi Effendi notes, "We find God only through the Intermediary of His Prophet. We see the Perfection of God in His Prophets. Time and space are physical things. God, the Creator is not in a 'place' as we conceive of place in physical terms. God is the Infinite Essence, the Creator. We cannot picture Him or His state; if we did, we would be His equals, not His Creatures. God is never flesh, but mirrored in the attributes of His Prophets, we see His Divine characteristics and perfections" (*High Endeavors*, p. 70).

Bahá'u'lláh discusses this same principle in a simple syllogism: "The source of all learning is the knowledge of God, exalted be His Glory, and this cannot be attained save through the knowledge of His Divine Manifestation" (*Tablets of Bahá'u'lláh*, p. 156).

THE POST-INCARNATE STAGE
OF THE MANIFESTATION

Finally, the Manifestation continues to guide His followers after His ascent to the realm of the spirit. Perhaps the most poignant statement about this continued relationship is found in Shoghi Effendi's allusion to the passing of Bahá'u'lláh: "the dissolution of the tabernacle wherein the soul of the Manifestation of God had chosen temporarily to abide signalized its release from the restrictions which an earthly life had, of necessity, imposed upon it. Its influence no longer circumscribed by any physical limitations, its radiance no longer beclouded by its human temple, that soul could henceforth energize the whole world to a degree unapproached at any stage in the course of its existence on this planet" (*God Passes By*, p. 244).

Obviously this continuation of guidance by the Manifestation in the metaphysical realm affects the success of plans set in motion by the teachings and institutions He established while on earth. Indeed, until the advent of the next "Day," the Manifestation will remain for us, His followers, the intermediary between us and God. Additionally, Shoghi Effendi states that even after we ourselves depart from this mortal stage of our existence: "We will have experience of God's spirit through His Prophets in the next world" because "God is too great for us to know without this Intermediary." He goes on to observe that the "Prophets know God, but how is more than our human minds can grasp." He concludes, that "we believe we attain in the next world to seeing the Prophets" (*High Endeavors*, p. 49).

As Bahá'u'lláh explains at length in the Book of Certitude, our spiritual proximity to the Manifestations of God is what is intended by the assurance that if we are faithful to the guidance bequeathed us by the Prophets, we will enter the "Presence of God": "Therefore, whosoever, and in whatever Dispensation, hath recognized and attained unto the presence of these glorious, these resplendent and most excellent Luminaries, hath verily attained unto the 'Presence of God' Himself, and entered the city of eternal and immortal life" (Kitáb-i-Íqán, ¶151).

PART 3

THE POWERS OF
THE PROPHETS OF GOD

The significance and essential purpose underlying these words is to reveal and demonstrate unto the pure in heart and the sanctified in spirit that they Who are the Luminaries of truth and the Mirrors reflecting the light of divine Unity, in whatever age and cycle they are sent down from their invisible habitations of ancient glory unto this world, to educate the souls of men and endue with grace all created things, are invariably endowed with an all-compelling power, and invested with invincible sovereignty. For these hidden Gems, these concealed and invisible Treasures, in themselves manifest and vindicate the reality of these holy words: "Verily God doeth whatsoever He willeth, and ordaineth whatsoever He pleaseth."

—Bahá'u'lláh

9

THE POWER OF REVELATION

In another passage He likewise saith: "And if ye be in doubt as to that which We have sent down to Our Servant, then produce a Surah like it, and summon your witnesses, beside God, if ye are men of truth." Behold, how lofty is the station, and how consummate the virtue, of these verses which He hath declared to be His surest testimony, His infallible proof, the evidence of His all-subduing power, and a revelation of the potency of His will. He, the divine King, hath proclaimed the undisputed supremacy of the verses of His Book over all things that testify to His truth. For compared with all other proofs and tokens, the divinely-revealed verses shine as the sun, whilst all others are as stars.

—Bahá'u'lláh

The accounts of God speaking to the Manifestations are portrayed as literal events in the Old Testament. We are asked to believe that an actual voice calls out from the heavens, or possibly from a burning bush, and is heard by the Prophets in audible tones so that, we must presume, anyone else in the same place at the time might also have heard the same words.

Christ alludes here and there to the fact that He says only what He is told to say, but He does not imply that He is hearing a literal voice or that He has no part to play in devising the words He speaks.

Muḥammad seems to make a distinction between His revealing the Word or the Book, and His speaking as an ordinary human being. In this sense, the words that were copied down as the súrihs by the companions of Muḥammad constitute the "Book" or the Word of God, and those statements of Muḥammad that were not explicitly dictated in this manner are referred to as ḥadíth or traditions, statements attributed to the Prophet, but not transcribed as part of the Qur'án.

The Báb was the first Manifestation to actually write down His revelation with His own hand, a rather remarkable feat considering He spent a majority of His ministry in secluded prisons. Yet Shoghi Effendi asserts that this "period of captivity, in a remote corner of the realm, far removed from the storm centers of Shíráz, Isfahán, and Ṭihrán, afforded Him the necessary leisure to launch upon His most monumental work, as well as to engage on other subsidiary compositions designed to unfold the whole range, and impart the full force, of His short-lived yet momentous Dispensation." As Shoghi Effendi further observes, even more remarkable than the mere fact of the revelation is the vastness and scope of His revelation, especially considering it was intended to endure but nine years:

> Alike in the magnitude of the writings emanating from His pen, and in the diversity of the subjects treated in those writings, His Revelation stands wholly unparalleled in the annals of any previous religion. He Himself affirms, while confined in Máh-Kú, that up to that time His writings, embracing highly diversified subjects, had amounted to more than five hundred thousand verses." (*God Passes By,* p. 22)

In the Book of Certitude, Bahá'u'lláh's apologia in defense of the Bábí Faith, Bahá'u'lláh observes the following about the scope of the Báb's revealed work: "the verses which have rained from this Cloud of divine mercy have been so abundant that none hath yet been able to estimate their number. A score of volumes are now available. How many still remain beyond our reach! How many have been plundered and have fallen into the hands of the enemy, the fate of which none knoweth" (Kitáb-i-Íqán, ¶240).

Bahá'u'lláh's own revelation exceeds that of the Báb in quantity of works and in scope of subjects, encompassing a variety of styles, subjects, and objectives. Some of this work was written in Bahá'u'lláh's own hand. Some of it was dictated to His eldest son, 'Abdu'l-Bahá, and later to Mirzá Áqá Ján, Bahá'u'lláh's principal amanuensis. Few works were written in Bahá'u'lláh's own hand after He was poisoned by His half-brother, Mírzá Yahyá, because His hand had a palpable tremor, as evidenced in the tablets that He did produce in His own hand after that time.

Regardless of how much or how little the individual Manifestations managed to reveal, according to the Bahá'í theory of the station and capacity of these specialized Emissaries, each was equally capable of producing whatever the age required and whatever the people of that time and place had the ability to comprehend and effectively utilize and implement. Therefore, distinctions of amount or complexity or efficacy are not indicative of distinction in station or capacity. Each is a divine physician charged with diagnosing and prescribing the remedy for the various ills afflicting humankind at the time of Their appearance.

TWO CATEGORIES OF REVEALED GUIDANCE

Whatever observations we might make about the distinctions among the revealed teachings of the various Manifestations, the most important generalization we can make is that each revelation invariably provides two broad categories of information for two distinct but complimentary and inextricably related purposes. The first category consists of information regarding the nature of reality, both physical and metaphysical. The second category consists of specific laws and guidance regarding personal comportment, social organization, and the administration of the affairs of the religion.

The Manifestations have not always made hard and fast distinctions between these two categories because of a very simple but extremely important fact regarding the mutuality and interdependence in the relationship between these two sorts of information. First of all, one aspect of guidance is not more important than the other. Second, all new knowledge relates to how that knowledge can be expressed in a more advanced form of action. Third, while the new knowledge has primacy in order (one cannot act out the new ideas without first understanding the ideas). These two categories are reciprocal stages of a single and integrated response. And yet one of the most crucial sources of conflict within a given dispensation or between various revelations is the distinction that followers and ecclesiasts have made between spiritual concepts (or faith) and the laws or regimen of action (or deeds) that are revealed by the Manifestation, then later interpreted and applied by those who attempt to sustain and promulgate the religion after His ascent. It is worthwhile to observe some examples of how this division emerges.

CHRISTIANITY

Certainly in Judaism, Christianity, and Islam, the emergence of schism between these twin aspects of relationship is of the utmost importance. For example, Christ (and later Paul) allude often to the fact that the Jewish Faith had lost its sense of spiritual insight and had become legalistic and materialistic in its attitude about spirituality. Paul's letters condemning the concept of salvation or justification through the "law"—his allusion to Judaic law—assume a gradually more central role in the long-term evolution of Christian doctrine.

Ultimately, the Christian view that faith is the sole avenue for personal salvation became the strategic theological impetus of the Protestant revolt against Catholic doctrine. This issue also caused early confrontations between Paul and James, whose well-known response to what was emerging as Pauline Christianity is that "faith without works is dead" (James 2:20).

Christ Himself is totally unambiguous about His own view regarding the inextricable link between knowledge (belief) and law (personal action). He states plainly that His followers must demonstrate the sincerity of their belief in Him by obedience to His new teachings regarding personal conduct:

"And every one that heareth these sayings of mine, and doeth them not, shall be likened unto a foolish man, which built his house upon the sand. And the rain descended, and the floods came, and the winds blew, and beat upon that house; and it fell: and great was the fall of it." And it came to pass, when Jesus had ended these sayings, the people were astonished at his doctrine. For he taught them as one having authority, and not as the scribes. (Matthew 7:26–29)

The problem of spirit and form became more pronounced after Christ's execution because He left no explicit design for His "church." Catholic belief accepts Christ's statement to Peter ("upon this rock I will build my church") as assigning Peter authority to establish a church. From the Catholic point of view, therefore, Peter was the first pope. What is problematic about this assertion is that Peter did not establish any well-defined institution as far as we know.

Most of the Protestant denominations of Christianity model their church structure and specific teachings around the guidance Paul gave in his letters to the congregations of Christian converts in Rome, Corinth, Thessalonica, Galatia, Ephesus, Philippi, Colossae, Thessalonica, and Jerusalem. Indeed, it is from these letters that Protestantism derives notions about the subservience of women and irrelevance of personal action or works to one's salvation.

ISLAM

There is no question that the Qur'án contains both spiritual guidance and personal and social laws. What it does not possess is the design for a religious institution to channel to the peoples of the world the teachings of Muḥammad. Consequently, at Muḥammad's death there was an explicit schism in the attempt to carry out the legacy He had bequeathed His followers and civilization in general.

According to the Shí'ih denomination of Islam, Muḥammad clearly indicated prior to His death that 'Alí, His cousin and son-in-law, was to become head of the Faith upon Muḥammad's death. Shí'ihs and Sunnis agree to the authenticity of the "Ḥadíth of the pond of Khumm" which states Muḥammad made this statement on March 10, 632 AD.

According to the Shí'ih interpretation of the ḥadíth or tradition of the "two weighty things" accepted as authentic by both major denominations, Muḥammad designated the sequence of His lineal descendants to be the successive leaders of Islam. According to this tradition, Muḥammad stated that He bequeathed to His followers both the Book (the Word of God or the Qur'án) and His family. He further cautioned that these two sources of guidance are inseparable and must forever be kept united.

According to the Sunni denomination of Islam, Abu Bakr was nominated for the leadership of the community by a group of Muslims as 'Alí and Muḥammad's family washed and prepared Muḥammad's body for burial. Consequently, from the Sunni perspective, Abu Bakr was made the first caliph, and, according to Sunni beliefs, he received the open support of 'Alí. In addition, much of the Sharia evolved from the extra-Qur'ánic sources of ḥadíth—collections of statements or deeds attributed to Muḥammad.

The end result of the schism that began precisely at Muḥammad's passing is that contemporary Islam is now divided and subdivided among various schools of belief. In addition, the schism between the essential spiritual principles and laws that are dominant themes of the Qur'án has been superseded globally by focus on what is perceived by fundamentalist Muslims to be the mandate to create a pan-Islamic super state. The main impetus for this movement is the belief, already cited previously, that Muḥammad was the last Manifestation from God and that Islam is, therefore, the last religion to be revealed by God and was intended by God to establish a worldwide theocracy.

THE BAHÁ'Í FAITH

Bahá'u'lláh is the first Manifestation to reveal a work that contains the explicit laws for His dispensation, together with the precise design for the religious institution that would implement these laws and have the authority and flexibility to create further law. Put in terms of utmost concision, with the Bahá'í revelation the twin aspects of revelation are permanently and inextricably bound together.

Bahá'u'lláh's revelation is extensive and complex, containing as it does literally hundreds of works of diverse length, style, and theme. Since it is the purpose of this revelation to provide guidance sufficient to minister the needs of all the peoples and cultures of the world, it is perfectly logical that this should be the case, and that access for every soul should be available. But at the heart and core of the revelation of Bahá'u'lláh are two principal works that specifically represent these twin categories of information—the new knowledge and the new law.

The Kitáb-i-Íqán (the Book of Certitude) is the main repository of the theological doctrine and spiritual insight articulated in full by

Bahá'u'lláh. This work sets forth a detailed explanation of progressive revelation, including a discussion about how this process has traditionally become diverted as the result of human misinterpretation of the holy text. In addition, this highly structured treatise discusses in exacting detail the ontology of the Manifestations and the nature of Their relationships with one another and with the Creator.

Bahá'u'lláh's Kitáb-i-Aqdas (the Most Holy Book) is the primary repository of the laws, ordinances, and exhortations of the Bahá'í dispensation. However, the work also establishes the exact succession of authority to be employed after the passing of Bahá'u'lláh. He designates 'Abdu'l-Bahá as the Center of the Covenant (head of the Bahá'í Faith), as infallible interpreter of the revelation of Bahá'u'lláh, and as exemplar of the Bahá'í teachings.

While the entirety of the administrative order created by Bahá'u'lláh was not completed until 1963 with the election of the first Universal House of Justice, the succession of authority after the passing of Bahá'u'lláh was firmly established in the authoritative texts of the Bahá'í Faith. The inseparability of the spiritual or humanitarian teachings from the laws and institutions is thus a major theme throughout the texts. One of the most cogent statements of this binding relationship occurs in the first sentence of Bahá'u'lláh's Most Holy Book where He asserts that the "twin duties" of recognizing the Prophet and being steadfast in obedience to His commandments are really two parts of a single process:

> The first duty prescribed by God for His servants is the recognition of Him Who is the Dayspring of His Revelation and the Fountain of His laws, Who representeth the Godhead in both the Kingdom of His Cause and the world of creation. Whoso achieveth this duty hath attained unto all good; and whoso is deprived thereof hath gone astray, though he be the author of

every righteous deed. It behooveth every one who reacheth this most sublime station, this summit of transcendent glory, to observe every ordinance of Him Who is the Desire of the world. These twin duties are inseparable. Neither is acceptable without the other. (Kitáb-i-Aqdas, ¶1)

An equally clear and powerful statement of this same principle appears in Shoghi Effendi's discussion of the unique features of the Bahá'í administrative order in his discourse *The World Order of Bahá'u'lláh:*

> It should be remembered by every follower of the Cause that the system of Bahá'í administration is not an innovation imposed arbitrarily upon the Bahá'ís of the world since the Master's passing, but derives its authority from the Will and Testament of 'Abdu'l-Bahá, is specifically prescribed in unnumbered Tablets, and rests in some of its essential features upon the explicit provisions of the Kitáb-i-Aqdas [The Most Holy Book]. It thus unifies and correlates the principles separately laid down by Bahá'u'lláh and 'Abdu'l-Bahá, and is indissolubly bound with the essential verities of the Faith. To dissociate the administrative principles of the Cause from the purely spiritual and humanitarian teachings would be tantamount to a mutilation of the body of the Cause, a separation that can only result in the disintegration of its component parts, and the extinction of the Faith itself. (*World Order of Bahá'u'lláh*, p. 5)

REVELATION AND THE BOOK

According to the Bahá'í authoritative texts, the first completely authentic or thoroughly reliable source we have for the revealed words of a Manifestation is the Qur'án. All the teachings of the Prophets prior to this are recollected accounts transcribed years after the Prophets passed away.

And yet even the Qur'án, while a thoroughly reliable recording of Muḥammad's words, is assembled as a collection of relatively independent and autonomously revealed observations. Each súrih is complete unto itself. It is in this sense that the Bahá'í revelation is the first instance in religious history on planet Earth where the Manifestation had the opportunity to design the entire canon of His revealed works.

THE BAHÁ'Í REVELATION

The Covenant of Bahá'u'lláh is established through documents explicitly defining the line of authority and the parameters of authority beginning with the Báb and succeeding through Bahá'u'lláh to the Universal House of Justice. However, it is extremely important for us to discuss what we mean by the concept of "revealed" words of the Manifestations— those teachings that constitute what we allude to variously as "the Word of God," "the Book," or simply the "Revelation."

A REVELATION DIRECT FROM GOD

As mentioned previously, in one of His exhortations to His followers in the Kitáb-i-Aqdas (the Most Holy Book), Bahá'u'lláh cautions that humanity need not look for the appearance of another Manifestation before a full thousand years have passed. Clearly He is not implying that there will not appear among us spiritually exemplary individuals to assist in guiding humankind toward its destiny—to fashion by degrees a global polity based on spiritual principles. What He does mean is explained by the precise language He chooses: "Whoso layeth claim to a Revelation direct from God, ere the expiration of a full thousand years, such a man is assuredly a lying impostor. We pray God that He may graciously assist him to retract and repudiate such claim. Should he repent, God will, no doubt, forgive him. If, however, he persisteth in his error, God will, assuredly, send down one who will deal mercilessly with him. Terrible, indeed, is God in punishing!" (Kitáb-i-Aqdas, ¶37)

Two things are worth noting about this specific prophetic warning. First, often in past scriptural prophecy, a day could symbolize a year, and a year could symbolize 365 years or possibly a century. Therefore, to be sure there is no mistaking His meaning, Bahá'u'lláh follows this statement with the explicit caveat: "Whosoever interpreteth this verse otherwise than its obvious meaning is deprived of the Spirit of God and of His mercy which encompasseth all created things." Furthermore, there is an authoritative note to this statement which observes:

> The intimation of His Revelation . . . in the Siyáh-Chál of Tehran, in October 1852, marks the birth of His Prophetic Mission and hence the commencement of the one thousand years or more that must elapse before the appearance of the next Manifestation of God. (Kitáb-i-Aqdas, p. 195, note 62)

REVELATION AS PROOF

From these passages it would seem that a "revelation direct from God" is the specialized process whereby God educates humankind by working through the Manifestations. But does this mean that the Manifestation is passive in this process? Is He simply the mouthpiece, the conduit for the words of God? Is the imperative "Say:" indeed the command from God, or from the Holy Spirit emanating from God, ordering the Manifestation to recite precisely the words that follow? If so, then does this mean these words are more literally or more accurately the words of God than the other words that constitute the Prophet's revelation? Is it not also possible, and even likely, that the command "Say" is a rhetorical device the Manifestation employs to demonstrate to His audience that everything He does and says is the principal means by which He is carrying out God's will?

In chapter 14 we will discuss more elaborately the creativity of the Manifestation in choosing the style of language with which He communicates the will of God to humankind for each particular stage in the educative process. For our present purpose, it is worth noting that while the general process is doubtless the same for each Manifestation, each employs a different dramatic account of it to His followers. Each account is tailored to accommodate what humankind is capable of comprehending at a given period and in a particular cultural context.

For example, the narratives about this process in the Old Testament seem at times to portray the Prophet as a bewildered or astounded human being Whom God tells in exacting terms exactly what to say and do. The dramatic episodes of Abraham and Isaac (or Ishmael) and of Moses and the burning bush represent possible examples of an anthropomorphic attempt by tribal historians to explain the otherwise unexplainable transformation of ordinary individuals into figures of authority capable of conveying the Word and guidance of God to humankind.

In the simplest sense, the power to reveal the Word of God is the greatest proof of the Prophet. The fact that They are able to utter scriptural passages without prior reflection, without further alteration, and without hesitation, is amazing evidence of Their station and power, especially for those who are privileged to witness this process. Even now, in our technologically advanced age, this capacity would be equally convincing.

Muḥammad alludes to this confirmation of His station in several verses. He declares that if anyone who hears Him doubts His authority or His station or if anyone questions whether or not He is truly receiving a revelation direct from God, let them reveal verses of equal rank and power. For example, in Súrih 17:88 Muḥammad says, "If the whole of mankind and Jinns were to gather together to produce the like of this Qur'án, they could not produce the like thereof, even if they backed up each other with help and support."

The Báb in His commentary on Muḥammad's Súrih of Joseph (Súrih 12) alludes to this same verse as He asserts His own authority as Revelator: "Verily, We made the revelation of verses to be a testimony for Our message unto you. Can ye produce a single letter to match these verses? Bring forth, then, your proofs, if ye be of those who can discern the one true God. I solemnly affirm before God, should all men and spirits combine to compose the like of one chapter of this Book, they would surely fail, even though they were to assist one another" (*Selections from the Writings of the Báb*, 2:4:1).

Bahá'u'lláh expresses the same idea in the Tablet of Aḥmad: "O people, if ye deny these verses, by what proof have ye believed in God? Produce it, O assemblage of false ones. Nay, by the One in Whose hand is my soul, they are not, and never shall be able to do this, even should they combine to assist one another" (*Bahá'í Prayers*, p. 210). But it is in another passage that Bahá'u'lláh sets forth axiomatically that the power of revelation is the clearest proof of the station of the Prophet other than His own person:

> Say: The first and foremost testimony establishing His truth is His own Self. Next to this testimony is His Revelation. For whoso faileth to recognize either the one or the other He hath established the words He hath revealed as proof of His reality and truth. This is, verily, an evidence of His tender mercy unto men. He hath endowed every soul with the capacity to recognize the signs of God. How could He, otherwise, have fulfilled His testimony unto men, if ye be of them that ponder His Cause in

their hearts. He will never deal unjustly with any one, neither will He task a soul beyond its power. He, verily, is the Compassionate, the All-Merciful. (*Gleanings*, no. 52.2)

THE REVELATION PROCESS IN DETAIL

According to scriptural accounts, Moses came down from the mountain and gave the law to His people as it had been given to Him by God. According to the gospel of John, Christ states, "I can of mine own self do nothing: as I hear, I judge: and my judgment is just; because I seek not mine own will, but the will of the Father which hath sent me" (John 5:30). In an even more subtle and encompassing statement about Himself as an Emissary of God, Christ establishes a syllogism of relationship for His followers: "All things are delivered unto me of my Father, and no man knoweth the Son, but the Father; neither knoweth any man the Father, save the Son, and he to whomsoever the Son will reveal Him" (Matthew 11:27). What the believers at the time did not seem to appreciate with sufficient clarity was that this logical relationship places Christ between the believers and God, but it makes Christ subordinate to God, not coequal, and not "partners" with God.

We have no information about what Christ looked like or felt like when He was delivering the "revealed" word of God, only His assurance that this process was occurring, whereas there are accounts of and hints about the revelation process in relation to Muḥammad. The various súrihs constitute the instances during which the "revelations" or "Signs of God" would come to Him, and He would pronounce them at whatever time and place these inspired revelatory thoughts would occur. To outward seeming they were transmitted by the angel Gabriel through Him. Besides the Sunni version of the initial revelation we have already mentioned—Muḥammad being so overwhelmed that He sought comfort from His wife—some accounts claim that these revelation experiences involved seizures.

The fact that these inspired statements seem to be delivered in the third-person through the intermediary of Gabriel commanding Muḥammad what to do and say had a tremendous importance in the context of the people Muḥammad was teaching. Two important objectives were accomplished by this dramatic portrayal of the revelation process.

First and foremost, it seemed emphatically obvious to the people who witnessed it that these words were from God because of the way they issued forth spontaneously from this flesh-and-bone human being before them. Secondly, instead of appearing as the immediate source of authoritative utterance as Christ had with His parables and sermons, Muḥammad effectively drew a distinction between His role as intermediary or Messenger and the station of God. This revelatory process undoubtedly countered any future danger that He, like Christ, would become deified or would be considered part of the same essence as God.

In the case of the revelations of the Báb and Bahá'u'lláh, we have reliable, extant manuscripts describing the revelatory process by first-hand observers. In the case of Bahá'u'lláh, we have a detailed portrayal of the process from the point when the utterance issues forth from the Manifestation to its final appearance in finished written form.

The account of the Báb revealing the opening sections of the Qayyúmu'l-Asmá' is a remarkably beautiful and enlightening narration bequeathed to us by the Báb's first follower, Mullá Ḥusayn:

> I sat spellbound by His utterance, oblivious of time and of those who awaited me. Suddenly the call of the *mu'adhdhin* summoning the faithful to their morning prayer, awakened me

from the state of ecstasy into which I seemed to have fallen. All the delights, all the ineffable glories, which the Almighty has recounted in His Book as the priceless possessions of the people of Paradise—these I seemed to be experiencing that night. Methinks I was in a place of which it could be truly said: "Therein no toil shall reach us, and therein no weariness shall touch us"; "No vain discourse shall they hear therein, nor any falsehood, but only the cry, 'Peace! Peace!'"; "Their cry therein shall be, 'Glory be to Thee, O God!' and their salutation therein, 'Peace!' And the close of their cry, 'Praise be to God, Lord of all creatures!'"[1]

Sleep had departed from me that night. I was enthralled by the music of that voice which rose and fell as He chanted; now swelling forth as He revealed verses of the Qayyúmu'l-Asmá', again acquiring ethereal, subtle harmonies as He uttered the prayers He was revealing. At the end of each invocation, He would repeat this verse: "Far from the glory of thy Lord, the All-Glorious, be that which His creatures affirm of Him! And peace be upon His Messengers! And praise be to God, the Lord of all beings!" [Qur'án 37:180] . . .

He then addressed me in these words: "O thou who art the first to believe in Me! Verily I say, I am the Báb, the Gate of God, and thou art the Bábu'l-Báb, the gate of that Gate." (Quoted in Nabíl-i-'Aẓam, *The Dawn-Breakers*, p. 62)

We have already alluded to the beginning of the revelatory process as it was received by Bahá'u'lláh in the Síyáh-Chál, but there also exists third-person accounts of the revelatory process when it involved transcribing or dictating the revealed word. Two of the most prominent ac-

---

1. These are citations from the Qur'án.

counts of this are recalled by Siyyid Asadu'lláh-i-Qumi as he observed this process in 1886 and by Tarazu'lláh Samandari as he observed the same process in 1892, the last year of Bahá'u'lláh's life.

According to these accounts, Bahá'u'lláh's primary amanuensis, Mirzá Áqá Ján, would be seated at a table with a large ink pot, about ten to twelve reed pens, and ten or more large sheets of paper in stacks. Mirzá Áqá Ján had developed his own special form of shorthand so that he could record the words of Bahá'u'lláh as they were revealed. According to the recollection of Siyyid Asadu'lláh-i-Qumi, Bahá'u'lláh would then speak without pause or correction, and the shrill scratching of the pens on the paper could be heard from twenty paces distance. Mirzá Áqá Ján would then transcribe the shorthand into exquisite calligraphy. When he was finished, he would show his work to Bahá'u'lláh, Who would correct any transcription errors Mirzá Áqá Ján had made.

Such is the heart of procedure of the revelation with every Manifestation. They pour forth the revealed word spontaneously without pause or correction, whether They are writing in Their own hand, or dictating to someone else. According to Siyyid Asadu'lláh-i-Qumi, "Such was the speed with which he used to write the revealed Word that the ink of the first word was scarcely yet dry when the whole page was finished. It seemed as if some one had dipped a lock of hair in the ink and applied it over the whole page. None of the words was written clearly and they were illegible to all except Mírzá Áqá Ján. But there were occasions when even he could not decipher the words and had to seek the help of Bahá'u'lláh" (quoted in Adib Taherzadeh, *The Revelation of Baha'u'llah*, vol. 1, p. 35).

The description of the same process by Tarazu'lláh Samandari as he observed it some six years later is much the same. He comments on the speed of revelation and the shorthand with which Mírzá Áqá Ján would record the words. However, he also comments on what distinguishes this process from any ordinary creative practice. He states that the "verses of God were revealed with great rapidity and without prior contemplation or meditation." He goes on to remark, "Thus the Word of God was revealed. The greatest proof of the authenticity of the Manifestations of God is the revelation of the words of God. No one else is capable of doing this. The holy Word revealed from the heaven of the Will of the All-Merciful first descends upon the pure and radiant heart of the Manifestation of God and then is spoken by Him" (quoted in Adib Taherzadeh, *The Revelation of Baha'u'lláh*, vol. 1, p. 36).

By this means Bahá'u'lláh penned or dictated hundreds of works. Some of them are relatively brief prayers or epistles, while others are book-length discourses on specific themes. The most important doctrinal work revealed by Bahá'u'lláh, the Book of Certitude, was revealed by Bahá'u'lláh without revision or change over the course of only two days and two nights.

10

THE CREATIVITY
OF THE PROPHETS

*O MY BROTHER! Hearken to the delightsome words of My
honeyed tongue, and quaff the stream of mystic holiness from My
sugar-shedding lips. Sow the seeds of My divine wisdom in the pure
soil of thy heart, and water them with the water of certitude, that
the hyacinths of My knowledge and wisdom may spring up fresh
and green in the sacred city of thy heart.*

—Bahá'u'lláh

As we discussed at length in the previous chapter, the Manifestations as
Emissaries of God testify over and over again that everything They do
and all that They ordain is derived not from Their own will, but from
the will of God working through Them. For example, immediately
prior to His arrest, Christ makes it clear that it was not His desire to
be crucified as a strategy for spreading His teachings. He was instead
acceding to the will of God: "And he was withdrawn from them about
a stone's cast, and kneeled down, and prayed, saying, 'Father, if thou
be willing, remove this cup from me: nevertheless not my will, but
Thine, be done'" (Luke 22: 41–42).

Similarly, Bahá'u'lláh observes that His return to Baghdad after His
two year retreat in the mountains of Kurdistán resulted from His as-
sent to the will of God, not from His personal desire:

The one object of Our retirement was to avoid becoming a subject of discord among the faithful, a source of disturbance unto
Our companions, the means of injury to any soul, or the cause
of sorrow to any heart. Beyond these, We cherished no other
intention, and apart from them, We had no end in view. And
yet, each person schemed after his own desire, and pursued his
own idle fancy, until the hour when, from the Mystic Source,
there came the summons bidding Us return whence We came.
Surrendering Our will to His, We submitted to His injunction.
(Kitáb-i-Íqán, ¶278)

These and similar statements by the Manifestations might understandably be taken to imply that They have no active or creative role to play
in what course of action They take or in what thoughts They reveal.
Their primary task, so it would seem, is to disregard Their own will or
desire, and comply with the will of God so that humankind will become enlightened and spiritualized. Or stated more accurately, Their
main objective is to so align Their own will with the will of God that
They are completely oblivious to self or self-interest.

It might seem quite logical, therefore, that the Manifestations have
some degree of free will in this arrangement. After all, it is possible,
albeit unlikely, that the Manifestation could choose *not* to do God's
will, even if, so far as we know, One never has refused to accede to the
demands of this difficult mission.

FREE WILL AND THE MANIFESTATION
Even if the Manifestations do have a certain degree of choice or free
will, should we attribute the creativity of Their appearance, teaching
techniques, and language to Them? If everything They do and say is
dictated by the will of God as communicated through the Holy Spirit,
then perhaps Their own part in this procedure is Their willingness to

obey the will of God and to submit to the humiliation, desecration, and cruelty that seems almost inevitably to be Their lot.

It is extremely important in our understanding of and relationship to these exalted Beings for us to know the full scope of Their powers. If we are wrong in our assumption, if They indeed do play some important part in fashioning what They say and do, then certainly we would want to become aware of this capacity.

While the Manifestations assert it is not Their personal decision to manifest Themselves, we have already established several proofs that the Manifestations do have free will in deciding whether or not They will accept this charge. The most obvious example of this power is exhibited in the passages above in which Christ in His prayer states that while He would rather not accept the "cup" of torture and crucifixion, He chooses to accede to the will of God. Likewise, Bahá'u'lláh states that were it solely a matter of doing what He would prefer, He would not return to Baghdad and face what He knows will be a life of tormenting trials and betrayals. He explicitly observes this fact about His destiny while traveling back to Baghdad. Bahá'u'lláh comments to Shaykh Sulṭán, who had come to retrieve Him, "that these last days of His retirement would be 'the only days of peace and tranquility' left to Him, 'days which will never again fall to My lot'" (quoted in Shoghi Effendi, God Passes By, p. 126).

The question then emerges as to how we know that there is a distinction between what They would do or could do and what God wills that They do? The answer is obvious. Since this is a completely internal matter, we become aware of it only because They want us to know it. After all, since Christ was alone as He prayed, how would we now be aware of what He prayed unless He told someone? In short, since each Manifestation is the exemplar of His own teachings, each wants us to become aware that we should attempt to respond in the same way to the challenges we face. We must try to distinguish between our own willfulness, and our joyful acquiescence to the will of God as revealed to us through the teachings and example of the Manifestations. Bahá'u'lláh states that "True liberty consisteth in man's submission unto My commandments, little as ye know it" (*Gleanings*, no. 159.4).

In other words, if the Manifestations are intensely aware from the beginning of Their mortal life that They have one purpose and one mission, we must seriously doubt that They are ever truly conflicted in Their choices. But inasmuch as we are exhorted to look to them for our example of Godliness expressed in terms of human performance and comportment, then They are, in effect, demonstrating how we should respond to analogous challenges. Consequently, if They really had no free will, if They were merely programmed to follow God's will, then Their example would not have the same effect or value for us.

CHRIST'S TEMPTATION IN THE WILDERNESS

One of the best examples of how the Manifestations use the incarnate phase of Their existence to teach us about free will in relation to the "insistent self" is conveyed through the story of Christ's confrontation with Satan immediately after He is anointed by John the Baptist. This story of the temptation must have some importance because it is narrated in each of the three Synoptic gospels (it is not found in John):[1]

And Jesus being full of the Holy Ghost, returned from Jordan and was led by the Spirit into the wilderness, Being forty days tempted of the devil. And in those days He did eat nothing, and

---

1. The episode appears in Matthew 4:1-11, in Mark 1:12-13, and in Luke 4:1-13.

when they were ended, He afterward hungered. And the devil said unto him, "If thou be the Son of God, command this stone that it be made bread."

And Jesus answered him, saying, "It is written, That man shall not live by bread alone, but by every word of God."

And the devil, taking him up into an high mountain, shewed unto him all the kingdoms of the world in a moment of time. And the devil said unto him, "All this power will I give thee, and the glory of them, for that is delivered unto me, and to whomsoever I will I give it. If thou therefore wilt worship me, all shall be thine!"

And Jesus answered and said unto him, "Get thee behind me, Satan, for it is written, 'Thou shalt worship the Lord thy God, and Him only shalt thou serve!'"

And he brought Him to Jerusalem, and set Him on a pinnacle of the temple, and said unto him, "If thou be the Son of God, cast thyself down from hence. For it is written, 'He shall give his angels charge over thee, to keep thee, and in their hands they shall bear thee up, lest at any time thou dash thy foot against a stone.'"

And Jesus answering said unto him, "It is said, 'Thou shalt not tempt the Lord thy God.'" And when the devil had ended all the temptation, he departed from Him for a season. (Luke 4:1–13)

From a traditional perspective, this story would seem to vindicate a belief that Satan is an actual being, even the same source of evil that appears in the Genesis account of the story of Adam and Eve. But the Bahá'í writings assert that there is no source of evil, no being from which emanates temptation for us to do things contrary to the will of God.

'Abdu'l-Bahá in a concise exegesis on the topic asserts that evil is essentially nonexistent. Rather, he asserts, evil is simply the result of the absence of goodness, in the same way that darkness is not a force, but the absence of the force of light.[2] Likewise, cold is not a force, but the absence of the force or energy of heat. These analogies by no means imply that the absence of these forces do not bring about important consequences. Their absence induces a profound effect. But the logical sense of this axiom is that evil has no essential reality. There is no demigod or spirit who is actively attempting to undermine goodness, nor is there any active force of evil at work in the universe, whether in the physical or the metaphysical aspects of reality.

Bahá'u'lláh explains that the Prophets have used the terms "Satan" and "Satanic" not as allusions to actual beings, and terms such as "heaven" and "hell" not as allusions to actual physical abodes. Rather, these terms function as metaphorical or symbolic methods by which the Manifestations can convey spiritual concepts and relationships. Bahá'u'lláh also observes that the use of this symbolic language has been effective in achieving this goal: "Even the materialists have testified in their writings to the wisdom of these divinely appointed Messengers, and have regarded the references made by the Prophets to Paradise, to hell fire, to future reward and punishment, to have been actuated by a desire to educate and uplift the souls of men" (*Gleanings*, no. 81.1).

SATAN AS THE "INSISTENT SELF"

The fact is that even if coldness is the absence of heat, and dark the absence of light, we still need to describe the effects of these conditions because they have a dramatic impact on our well-being. The use of

---

2. 'Abdu'l-Bahá's explanation can be found in *Some Answered Questions*, p. 263.

the term "Satan" or "Satanic" may be purely symbolic, but it is a very effective means of describing a subjective spiritual experience. After all, these are not imaginary conditions or easily defeated adversaries.

When we are tempted to become selfish, prideful, or power-seeking, it does indeed feel as if there is an active force within us urging us to sink to the depths of sensuality, cynicism, self-centeredness, and pessimism. Bahá'u'lláh Himself sometimes employs these terms to make a point about the process of individual and collective spiritual aspirations: "A world in which naught can be perceived save strife, quarrels and corruption is bound to become the seat of the throne, the very metropolis, of Satan" (*Tablets of Bahá'u'lláh*, p. 176).

The reality of Satan and the Satanic, however, is made absolutely plain in the Bahá'í texts. Satan is the "insistent self," the ego, and the Satanic is that which tempts us to place self-interest above all other concerns, whether in relation to family, to our fellow human beings, or even to God and His Manifestations so that we barter our spiritual values for whatever feels most existentially appealing or sensually delightful.

In alluding to those who attempted to undermine His revelation and take His life, Bahá'u'lláh says, "Observe, how those in whose midst the Satan of self had for years sown the seeds of malice and hate became so fused and blended through their allegiance to this wondrous and transcendent Revelation that it seemed as if they had sprung from the same loins" (Kitáb-i-Íqán, ¶118). Even more directly, 'Abdu'l-Bahá notes, "This lower nature in man is symbolized as Satan—the evil ego within us, not an evil personality outside" (*Promulgation of Universal Peace,* p. 287).

THE SYMBOLISM OF TEMPTATION

Shoghi Effendi was not a Manifestation. He certainly did not consider himself in any way equal to his beloved grandfather, 'Abdu'l-Bahá. In fact, it had been his cherished desire to become sufficiently educated so that he could serve as a secretary to 'Abdu'l-Bahá, which he did for a while.

When 'Abdu'l-Bahá died in 1921, Shoghi Effendi was in England studying at Oxford. Upon his return to the Holy Land, he discovered to his astonishment and shock that 'Abdu'l-Bahá had made him Guardian of the Bahá'í Faith. Shoghi Effendi was only twenty-four at the time. Added to the unfathomable sense of pain he felt at the loss of the beloved of his heart, Shoghi Effendi also found himself suddenly in charge of a religion that was just beginning to take root in the world and assume its rightful station as the source of reformation to usher in the transformation of human society.

Soon this burden so encumbered his mind and soul that he determined to take a leave of absence for two years, leaving the affairs of the Bahá'í Faith in the capable hands of his aunt Bahíyyíh Khánum, the sister of 'Abdu'l-Bahá who had selflessly devoted her entire life to serving her father, Bahá'u'lláh, and then her brother 'Abdu'l-Bahá. During this absence, Shoghi Effendi spent his time meditating, walking, and hiking through the Swiss Alps, and, according to his own words, coming to terms with his "self."

In a marvelous talk given by Leroy Ioas (a distinguished member of the Bahá'í community) in Johannesburg, South Africa, in 1958, just months after the unexpected death of Shoghi Effendi at age sixty, we find a poignant statement about how imperative Shoghi Effendi felt it was for him to come to terms with his new position and all it would require of him. Ioas quotes Shoghi Effendi as saying:

I had in mind that 'Abdu'l-Bahá would give me the honor of calling together the great conclave which would elect the universal House of Justice and I thought in His *Will and Testament* that that was probably what he was instructing be done. Instead of that, I found that I was appointed the Guardian of the Cause of God. I didn't want to be the Guardian of the Cause of God. In the first place, I didn't think I was worthy. In the next place, I didn't want to face these responsibilities. I didn't want to be the Guardian. I knew what it meant. I knew that my life as a human being was over. I didn't want it and I didn't want to face it.

You will remember I left the Holy Land and I went up into the mountains of Switzerland. And I fought with myself until I conquered myself. Then I came back and I turned myself over to God and I was the Guardian. Now Every Bahá'í in the world, every person in the world has to do exactly that same thing. (From an audio tape of the talk)

Is the story of Christ's temptation by Satan meant to be an allegory of the same process at work? Certainly as a Being of superior capacity and powers, the Manifestation could, theoretically, utilize those powers for self-interest rather than sacrificially for the salvation of humankind. As we will discover in the succeeding chapters, the Manifestation withholds Himself from revealing the full extent of His powers in order that He might be recognized for His spiritual comportment and not for sensational displays of power that we might regard as miracles.

We need not believe that Christ was seriously conflicted by the temptation to employ His powers for selfish ends, but we can believe that through this allegorical portrayal of an internal process, Christ is conveying to us for our benefit the fact that, even given His extraordinary powers and station, He must constantly maintain determination and vigilance to endure the daily ordeal that is His lot as God's vicegerent on earth.

This concept of will brings us one step closer to a more encompassing notion of the creative role the Manifestations play in carrying out Their mission. We have already observed in chapter 8 that, according to the Bahá'í texts, the Manifestations have a creative function in the incarnate stage of Their existence in deciding where They will appear and in what condition. Obviously these decisions are determined by what process They think will most effectively unleash the redemptive power of Their revelation. We have in the previous section concerning the nature of Their beings likewise observed that the Manifestations are not ordinary human beings. They are preexistent divine Emissaries, Whose entire presence among us is calculated to teach us.

The most expansive implication of this concept is that we can and should consider everything the Prophet does and says as worthy of our attention, as having some significance in teaching us, whether through example or through the various levels of meaning in Their utterances. Bahá'u'lláh articulates this fact with inescapable clarity: "all His acts and doings, whatever He ordaineth or forbiddeth, should be considered, in all their aspects, and under all circumstances, and without any reservation, as identical with the Will of God Himself" (*Gleanings*, no. 84.4).

If we accept this statement at face value, then we must also consider that the Manifestations are constantly aware that everything They do or say is an attempt to teach us, even if in some indirect and creative way. Insofar as the temptation of Christ is concerned, for example, the only way we could possibly know about this thoroughly personal and subjective experience is through Christ's own discussion—certainly no one saw the nonexistent demon take Christ on top of a mountain or building. Therefore, we must infer that, like Christ's parables, this story of the temptation by Satan has a purely spiritual or symbolic lesson to impart. And if, as the Bahá'í teachings affirm, Satan is but a metaphorical or symbolic representation of the ego or the insistent self, then we can conclude that Christ is illustrating what Shoghi Effendi states about his own struggle—that every person must face down the temptation to accede to the self and to self-interest and choose instead to live a life dedicated to the service of God and humanity.

CREATIVITY AND THE REVELATION

If the story of Christ's temptation is, in effect, a parable, not the literal truth, we might do well to consider what else the Prophets do and say that might also be contrived for our benefit or learning. That is, if *everything* They do and say is calculated to teach us something, we might wonder what other events in Their lives have a spiritual or symbolic meaning rather than literal importance.

The fact that the Manifestation may express an intense spiritual experience in terms of a physical analogy is not misrepresenting what takes place. We might more aptly think of this method as another sign of His creativity in providing us intellectual access to a process we might not otherwise be able to grasp. As it is, each of us must study the statements of the Prophets and decide for ourselves exactly what we think is taking place. But what is undeniably clear in the Bahá'í texts is that the specific language and guidance of each revelation results from the capacity of the Manifestations to craft God's will into a style and method appropriate to the people and age in which the Manifestation appears.

One explicit clue to the fact that the Manifestation employs creativity and artistic inventiveness in this revelatory process is made plain in Shoghi Effendi's statement about Bahá'u'lláh's genius in devising a plan for world polity. In commenting on the Most Holy Book, which contains the blueprint for a global society and the stipulations that will serve to uphold it, Shoghi Effendi says that the Most Holy Book, "whose provisions must remain inviolate for no less than a thousand years, and whose system will embrace the entire planet, may well be regarded as the brightest emanation of the mind of Bahá'u'lláh, as the Mother Book of His Dispensation, and the Charter of His New World Order" (*God Passes By,* p. 213).

Shoghi Effendi's allusion to this work as "the brightest emanation of the *mind* of Bahá'u'lláh" obviously implies that it is Bahá'u'lláh's creativity as author of the plan that is being praised, not Bahá'u'lláh's ability to transcribe words spoken to Him by an otherworldly source. This is an extremely important observation, for where Muḥammad, according to what we might infer from various ḥadíth, implied to those in His midst that the "Book" or Word of God coming through His mouth was not of His own devising, Shoghi Effendi implies here that the words of the Manifestation do indeed emanate from the creativity of the Manifestation's own mind and imagination.

This inference does not in any way counter the implications we may derive from previous descriptions of the revelatory process with past Manifestations. No doubt Muḥammad revealed a new súrih when the inspiration came to Him to do so. We can even assume that the general idea also came directly from the realm of the spirit, whether through the intermediary of Gabriel or even more directly as an idea emanating from the will of God. But the language of Muḥammad, the eloquence and choice of words appropriate to that time and that place and that people—these, we must conclude, were emanations from the mind of this incredible Being Whose every thought during His entire life was bent on this single purpose of functioning as an example of spiritual comportment and as a source for the latest chapter in the ongoing and ceaseless "Book" of God.

THE MANIFESTATION AS WORDSMITH

In the Hidden Words Bahá'u'lláh indicates that He has fashioned His revelation according to our limitations and capacities, not His own: "O Son of Beauty! By My spirit and by My favor! By My mercy and by My beauty! All that I have revealed unto thee with the tongue of power, and have written for thee with the pen of might, hath been in accordance with thy capacity and understanding, not with My state and the melody of My voice" (Arabic Hidden Word, no. 67).

Certainly this statement seems to be describing an artistic process by which the Manifestation is sensitive both to the quantity of information He can impart and to the "voice" or language He employs to express the new revelation. In this verse He also indicates that were He not to fashion the language to befit our capacity, we would be incapable of understanding the loftiness or complexity of the ideas He is articulating.

The Manifestation also fashions the style of His language to befit His audience. We have already remarked how Christ almost exclusively employs parables as an effective style for breaking through the literalism with which His Jewish audience discusses and considers questions of religion. Likewise, we have noted how Muḥammad employs a method whereby a voice of authority is suddenly channeled through Him. For the most part, He presents Himself as merely a means by which the otherwise imperceptible Word of God is made accessible to the believers.

THE ARTISTRY OF BAHÁ'U'LLÁH

Bahá'u'lláh states that He has purposefully restated every "theme" of His revelation in a variety of styles and levels of language so that no matter what the capacity of the reader, there will be some version of His teachings that can be understood: "We have variously and repeatedly set forth the meaning of every theme, that perchance every soul, whether high or low, may obtain, according to his measure and capacity, his share and portion thereof. Should he be unable to comprehend a certain argument, he may, thus, by referring unto another, attain his purpose. 'That all sorts of men may know where to quench their thirst'" (Kitáb-i-Íqán, ¶189).

In another verse Bahá'u'lláh assures us that He knew and understood what He was revealing to us before we were yet born (i.e., when

He was in His state of preexistence), but He has, for our benefit, fashioned this information into a language and into terms that are to our "measure" or capacity: "By the one true God! We read the Tablet ere it was revealed, while ye were unaware, and We had perfect knowledge of the Book when ye were yet unborn. These words are to your measure, not to God's. To this testifieth that which is enshrined within His knowledge, if ye be of them that comprehend; and to this the tongue of the Almighty doth bear witness, if ye be of those who understand. I swear by God, were We to lift the veil, ye would be dumbfounded" (Kitáb-i-Aqdas, ¶176).

THE CREATIVITY OF
BAHÁ'U'LLÁH'S GLOBAL PLAN

To conclude that the Manifestation is creative in His own right would hardly be an adequate plaudit for a Being whose capacities will forever remain far beyond the ken of human understanding. Nevertheless, as we will examine more fully in the final chapter about the suffering of the Prophets, it helps us identify with these divine Physicians when we come to realize that They are not simply spiritual automatons Who speak God's words at His bidding.

Even if we come to appreciate ever more completely the extent to which They willingly subject Themselves to the humiliation of assuming human form and undergoing the "human" mortal experience, we can never fully appreciate how carefully They must fashion everything They do and say to fulfill Their purpose of educating us. When we consider that every scintilla of what They do and endure and profess is carefully crafted to redound to our benefit and advancement, we begin to realize why we are duty bound to study Their lives. Only through recalling and recounting again and again the amazing experiences these Beings endure for us can we grasp even some minuscule degree of the love They must have for us and the untold debt of gratitude we owe Them. How can we possibly fathom what Bahá'u'lláh had to tolerate as He exhorted leaders of the world to heed His plainly rational and salutary call for peaceful cooperation, while He Himself was enduring exile, incarceration, execration, and humiliation at the hands of these same leaders?

It is not our intention here to discuss at length the genius of the overall plan of Bahá'u'lláh for creating a world polity. But we can hardly mention evidence of the personal creativity of the Manifestation in this Day without at least noting the ample tributes to the various dimensions of Bahá'u'lláh's plan as discussed in the works of Shoghi Effendi. In particular, the Guardian focuses on how Bahá'u'lláh's design of a world commonwealth employs the strongest elements from various forms of government while avoiding the pitfalls of each and not precisely emulating any of them:

> This new-born Administrative Order incorporates within its structure certain elements which are to be found in each of the three recognized forms of secular government, without being in any sense a mere replica of any one of them, and without introducing within its machinery any of the objectionable features which they inherently possess. It blends and harmonizes, as no government fashioned by mortal hands has as yet accomplished, the salutary truths which each of these systems undoubtedly contains without vitiating the integrity of those God-given verities on which it is ultimately founded. (*The World Order of Baha'u'llah,* p. 152)

In the final paragraphs of a collection of Shoghi Effendi's essays titled *The World Order of Bahá'u'lláh,* we discover the most weighty and profound allusion to the fact that it is the creative vision and wisdom of Bahá'u'lláh from which this world commonwealth draws both its ingenuity and power. In a truly magnificent poetic analogy, Shoghi

Effendi compares Bahá'u'lláh to a blacksmith or artisan, a master crafts-man Who has managed, through His own vision, creative design, and indomitable will, to forge together world governance from the "scat-tered and mutually destructive fragments" of our global community:

Not ours, the living witnesses of the all-subduing potency of His Faith, to question, for a moment, and however dark the mis-ery that enshrouds the world, the ability of Bahá'u'lláh to forge, with the hammer of His Will, and through the fire of tribula-tion, upon the anvil of this travailing age, and in the particular shape His mind has envisioned, these scattered and mutually destructive fragments into which a perverse world has fallen, into one single unit, solid and indivisible, able to execute His design for the children of men. (*The World Order of Baha'u'llah,* p. 123)

11

THE OMNISCIENCE
OF THE PROPHETS

*We make mention of you for the sake of God, and remind you of
His signs, and announce unto you the things ordained for such as
are nigh unto Him in the most sublime Paradise and the all-highest
Heaven, and I, verily, am the Announcer, the Omniscient.*
—Bahá'u'lláh

In chapter 9 we considered the unique capacity or gift of the Manifestations to receive a revelation direct from God, and in chapter 10 we
discussed evidence that They Themselves participate in this process by
functioning as the creative fashioners of Their own revelation. Clearly
all these discussions are indicative of a more general sort of distinction regarding the Manifestations—the superhuman knowledge They
must necessarily possess, a knowledge to which we alluded in part 2
when we discussed Their preexistence.

In this chapter we will consider a more comprehensive view of Their
knowledge to assess whether we are witnessing in These specialized
Emissaries a more intense or more advanced version of what we ourselves possess—merely different in degree—or whether the Manifestations possess a totally different category of information than that
which we can comprehend.

THE BOUNDARIES OF SCHOLARSHIP

Once again, we need to venture outside the parameters of traditional scholarship, particularly what have become the boundaries of contemporary scholarship which, by and large, adheres rather rigidly to materialist standards. Those academics in the field of religious studies, for example, are no longer much concerned with whether or not assertions about metaphysics might be correct or incorrect. Instead, contemporary studies tend to come from the perspective of a psychological and sociological examination of how humankind has created religion in a response to the need for a comforting mythic invention.

In general, the contemporary student of religion dare not broach the question of whether or not religion or religious philosophy might contain an accurate description of reality. The presumption is that because we are obliged to apply the standards of science to any claim to truth, either metaphysical reality exists, or it does not. If we can't prove objectively that it does, then we must presume it is totally theoretical. Furthermore, the presumption goes on, even if metaphysical reality does exist, it cannot possibly have an effect on material reality. And if the study of religion is focused on the origins of metaphysical reality in history and its influence on society, then whether or not its belief system is valid has little or no relevance to what we can observe scientifically and systematically.

LEARNING "CURRENT AMONGST MEN"

Clearly it would be erroneous to assume *a priori* that those claiming the station of Prophethood are possessed of a capacity and knowledge beyond the scope of the human mind. As Christ Himself notes, the standard by which one should measure the claims of such individuals is the fruit they bear. And among the foremost fruits of the Manifestation, indeed the most tangible evidence of Their station other than Their personhood, is the revelation—the utterance and guidance set forth in human language. The fact is that once the person of the Manifestation is no longer physically accessible, His words are the principal means by which we can know Him and become aware of His intentions for us.

It is only in this context that the often repeated disclaimers of Muḥammad, the Báb, and Bahá'u'lláh make much sense. Time and time again, these Prophets emphasize that They have not pursued "learning current amongst men," that They have not studied in any school, and that They have not been tutored by any other individual. Bahá'u'lláh even challenges those who might question the source of His eloquence to go to the places He has lived and discover whether or not His assertion is true.

This lack of external influence is a major proof that whatever comes from Their mouths or Their pens is from Their own minds. It is for this reason that in one of my own studies of the writings of Bahá'u'lláh entitled *The Ocean of His Words,* I emphasize the point that the ordinary standards of historical literary criticism are entirely inappropriate when approaching the work of Bahá'u'lláh, at least if we are to take Him at His word. And in order *not* to take Him at His word, we must discover proof or evidence that He did study at a school or under the tutelage of some learned figure.

Bahá'u'lláh is keenly aware of the contention between the standards of scholarship and the standards of assessing metaphysical or spiritual influence. After all, the major discoveries and studies that transformed contemporary science were taking place during His lifetime. Consequently, He employs the term "learning current amongst men" to designate the conclusions and methodology that was then prevalent within the academic communities, though His observations regarding them is no less applicable today. In short, rather than assuming that whatever He says must necessarily come from the influence of some school of thought to which He was subjected, we are challenged by Bahá'u'lláh to try to find any time in His life when such an occasion or opportunity could have presented itself.

It is in this vein that the Báb states, "God beareth Me witness, I was not a man of learning, for I was trained as a merchant. In the year sixty [1260/1844] God graciously infused my soul with the conclusive evidences and weighty knowledge which characterize Him Who is the Testimony of God—may peace be upon Him—until finally in that year I proclaimed God's hidden Cause and unveiled its well-guarded Pillar, in such wise that no one could refute it" (*Selections from the Writings of the Báb*, no. 1:4:7).

In His epistle to Náṣiri'd-Dín Sháh, Bahá'u'lláh similarly affirms, "The learning current amongst men I studied not; their schools I entered not. Ask of the city wherein I dwelt, that thou mayest be well assured that I am not of them who speak falsely. This is but a leaf which the winds of the will of thy Lord, the Almighty, the All-Praised, have stirred. Can it be still when the tempestuous winds are blowing? Nay, by Him Who is the Lord of all Names and Attributes! They move it as they list" (*The Summons of the Lord of Hosts*, p. 148).

Within the course of two consecutive pages in the Most Holy Book, Bahá'u'lláh addresses the "leaders of religion" with this same exhortation. First He asserts that they should not apply "such standards and sciences as are current amongst you" in evaluating the veracity of the "Book of God" because the book itself is the "unerring Balance," the standard by which everything else should be adjudged: "Say: O leaders of religion! Weigh not the Book of God with such standards and sciences as are current amongst you, for the Book itself is the unerring Balance established amongst men. In this most perfect Balance whatsoever the peoples and kindreds of the earth possess must be weighed, while the measure of its weight should be tested according to its own standard, did ye but know it" (Kitáb-i-Aqdas, ¶99).

He then more boldly challenges these same "leaders of religion" to replicate or equal the "utterance or wisdom" that issues forth from His pen: "O ye leaders of religion! Who is the man amongst you that can rival Me in vision or insight? Where is he to be found that dareth to claim to be My equal in utterance or wisdom? No, by My Lord, the All-Merciful! All on the earth shall pass away; and this is the face of your Lord, the Almighty, the Well-Beloved." He then reiterates the assertion He has made elsewhere—that the source of His knowledge and utterance is to be found nowhere but in His own mind: "We have not entered any school, nor read any of your dissertations. Incline your ears to the words of this unlettered One, wherewith He summoneth you unto God, the Ever-Abiding. Better is this for you than all the treasures of the earth, could ye but comprehend it" (Kitáb-i-Aqdas, ¶101, 104).

One final observation about Bahá'u'lláh's allusions to academic or scholarly learning among the clerics and the learned is well worth noting. On occasion in the Book of Certitude, and in later works as well, Bahá'u'lláh makes specific references to the works of others, especially ancient philosophers, poets, and even contemporary figures of authority. Certainly it would be logical to infer that however untutored He may have been in any formal sense, He must have had some degree of access to these works in order to make reference to the particular passages He cites.

Bahá'u'lláh's answer to this enigma, while startling, is expressed in frank and uncompromising terms. In the Tablet of Wisdom Bahá'u'lláh refers to some of the great thinkers of the past to demonstrate how each ultimately attributed his own wisdom to divine influence. Bahá'u'lláh then states that whenever He wishes access to some specific treatise or published work, the pages of that work appear before Him. This is the means, He asserts, by which He is able to cite passages from works to which He has never had physical access:

> Thou knowest full well that We perused not the books which men possess and We acquired not the learning current amongst them, and yet whenever We desire to quote the sayings of the learned and of the wise, presently there will appear before the face of thy Lord in the form of a tablet all that which hath appeared in the world and is revealed in the Holy Books and Scriptures. Thus do We set down in writing that which the eye perceiveth. Verily His knowledge encompasseth the earth and the heavens. (*Tablets of Bahá'u'lláh*, p. 149)

DISTINGUISHING TERMINOLOGY

We have in the previous two chapters discussed the process of revelation and the fact that the Manifestation plays an important creative role in both the language of the revelation and the ideas and plans that will serve to guide humanity for a given dispensation. Now we have further examined the claim of the Manifestations that, while divinely assisted and empowered, They possess a capacity that cannot be rivaled by mortal men, however learned and capable those men might be. This consideration quite logically and appropriately leads us to the matter of exactly how extraordinary Their knowledge is.

With regard to biblical passages, for example, one may examine this compendium of books assembled by early Christian scholars as being historical relics, divinely inspired writing, or, quite literally the Word of God. Naturally ascribing the latter epithet has become problematic to those who would view Genesis as a literal account of the geophysical beginnings of planet Earth, let alone the evolution of humankind through various stages of physical and social development. Equally troublesome to those who receive the Bible as infallible is the fact that the three Synoptic gospels differ slightly from the account of Christ in John.

As we have earlier noted, Christ indicates that His ideas and actions are divinely inspired by God and that He does as God guides Him to do. As we have also observed, similar claims are made by the Old Testament Prophets and by Muḥammad, the Báb, and Bahá'u'lláh, even though we have concluded that They play an extremely proactive and creative role in the process of carrying out the will of God.

The point is that we need to determine for the purposes of discussing intelligently the utterances of the Prophets the extent of Their personal knowledge as opposed to the information They receive directly from divine resources. Are these exalted Beings accurate but poetic, inspired but liable to error about mundane knowledge, infallible but not omniscient, presently omniscient but not prescient, or in possession of some combination of all these powers?

DIVINE INSPIRATION

The concept of divine inspiration has been used so widely and haphazardly that it probably lacks much weight or value in terms of defining a specific power or capacity. For example, those who do not accept the entirety of the Bible as being precisely "the Word of God," usually describe the authors of these various texts as divinely inspired. The Catholic Church will usually attribute the power of divine inspiration to most of those whom it officially canonizes as having been capable of performing some miraculous or superhuman feat.

The problem with this term and this concept is that it can be legitimately applied to such a broad range of meanings or processes. Most adherents of any monotheistic belief system affirm that the process of daily prayer and communion with God or with an intermediary—a Manifestation or a saint, for example—may result in a sense of personal resolve or guidance. Certainly this personal reflection or meditation can bring forth a sense of divine inspiration when one senses confirmation or the resolution of a problem.

The difference between this loose or wide-ranging concept of personal receptivity to metaphysical or spiritual influence—which may or may not be objectively accurate—and a "revelation direct from God," then, is not merely a matter of degree, but of certitude and clarity. We can never know for certain when we are acceding to our vain imaginings and when we are being precisely guided, although we may sense varying degrees of confirmation or conviction about our personal divine inspiration from moment to moment. Whereas figures who bring forth prophetic works, such as the Psalms of David or the Revelation of St. John the Divine, are thoroughly convinced of the veracity of the visions they set forth, and their visions eventually may seem to become vindicated by future events. For example, it seems fairly obvious that Psalm 22 is an explicit foreshadowing of the crucifixion of Christ, even alluding to such details as the soldiers gaming for His robe at the foot of the cross.

The divine inspiration of the Manifestation, however, assumes a different status or category of inspiration altogether. The claim of the Prophets is that every single utterance They categorize as being part of Their "revelation" is precisely and unambiguously the will of God set forth in human language. It is part of what Muḥammad alludes to as "the Book" of God, an ongoing and continuous sequence of guidance from God articulated through His Messengers. These words are distinguished, at least by the Manifestations, as being from a totally reliable divine source, as being authoritative, and as having binding power over Their followers.

THE MOST GREAT INFALLIBILITY

Possibly because of the confusion about the distinctive process that occurs when a Manifestation receives a revelation direct from God,

Bahá'u'lláh and 'Abdu'l-Bahá take great pains to clarify the distinction between any sort of vague usage of the term "divine inspiration" and "The Most Great Infallibility," a concept we have already discussed at some length.

This concept has been the subject of considerable discussion among Bahá'í scholars because the original term for "infallible" in Persian can also imply "sinless" or "immaculate." But the term is clarified by Bahá'u'lláh, 'Abdu'l-Bahá, and Shoghi Effendi to mean precisely infallible or "without error."

The concept of infallibility is defined in terms of two categories delineated by Bahá'u'lláh in the Tablet of Splendors and elucidated further by 'Abdu'l-Bahá in *Some Answered Questions* and in his Will and Testament. The first category is inherent infallibility, which pertains solely to the Manifestations of God. The second category is conferred infallibility, a power that can be conferred by God through the Manifestation on individuals or institutions.

According to the Bahá'í authoritative texts, Bahá'u'lláh, as a Manifestation of God, partakes of "the Most Great Infallibility," and is thus inherently without error in all that He says and in all that He decides. The following statement by Bahá'u'lláh in the Most Holy Book both confirms this theory and asserts that the infallibility of the Manifestations was not previously revealed, that it was "concealed ere now":

> He Who is the Dawning-place of God's Cause hath no partner in the Most Great infallibility. He it is Who, in the kingdom of creation, is the Manifestation of "He doeth whatsoever He willeth." God hath reserved this distinction unto His own Self, and ordained for none a share in so sublime and transcendent a station. This is the Decree of God, concealed ere now within the veil of impenetrable mystery. We have disclosed it in this Revelation, and have thereby rent asunder the veils of such as

have failed to recognize that which the Book of God set forth and who were numbered with the heedless. (Kitáb-i-Aqdas, ¶47)

This statement of "inherent" infallibility has an extremely important bearing on our discussion of the ontology of the Manifestations. In fact, given Their preexistence in the spiritual realm where, according to the Bahá'í writings, there are no limitations of space and time, it is logical that They would have a flawless and unfailing knowledge of reality.

Furthermore, we have already observed that physical reality is designed as a metaphorical expression of spiritual reality in order to teach us how to understand metaphysical reality by challenging us to penetrate these veils of concealment. Consequently, we can be certain that the Manifestations as Emissaries from the spiritual realm would understand perfectly how this teaching device works and how to expedite the advancement of human history.

CONFERRED INFALLIBILITY

As noted above, one of the powers of the Manifestation is to confer infallibility on another person or on an institution. According to Shí'ih and Bahá'í belief, Muḥammad confers infallibility on 'Alí and the successive twelve Imáms who were Muḥammad's lineal descendants. Bahá'u'lláh discusses this distinction between the two categories of infallibility by explaining the difference between the infallibility of Muḥammad and the infallibility conferred by Muḥammad upon the twelve Imáms:

In response to thy request the Pen of Glory hath graciously described the stations and grades of the Most Great Infallibility. The purpose is that all should know of a certainty that the Seal of the Prophets [Muḥammad]—may the souls of all else but Him be offered up for His sake—is without likeness, peer or partner in His Own station. The Holy Ones [the Imáms]—may the blessings of God be upon them—were created through the potency of His Word, and after Him they were the most learned and the most distinguished among the people and abide in the utmost station of servitude. (*Tablets of Bahá'u'lláh,* p. 123)

In this same tablet Bahá'u'lláh cites the Báb as having observed, "If the Seal of the Prophets had not uttered the word 'Successorship,' such a station would not have been created" (*Tablets of Bahá'u'lláh,* p. 123). In other words, it was exclusively the power of Muḥammad to ordain that the Imáms succeed Him and that they be endowed with the power of infallibility. Had He not chosen to confer this power, they would not have possessed it. And had they not possessed this authority, then the schism in Islam might not have been so fatal to its future ascendancy.

Insofar as successorship within the Bahá'í Faith is concerned, Bahá'u'lláh conferred infallibility on 'Abdu'l-Bahá, and 'Abdu'l-Bahá conferred infallibility on the Guardianship and on the Universal House of Justice through the power bestowed on him by Bahá'u'lláh. In discussing this concept of the distinction between inherent and conferred infallibility, 'Abdu'l-Bahá states, "To epitomize: essential infallibility belongs especially to the supreme Manifestations, and acquired infallibility is granted to every holy soul. For instance, the Universal House of Justice, if it be established under the necessary conditions—with members elected from all the people[1]—that House of Justice will be under the protection and the unerring guidance of God." In His *Will and Testament,* 'Abdu'l-Bahá states, "Whatsoever they [the Universal House of Justice] decide has the same effect as the

---

1. Universal suffrage as prescribed by Bahá'u'lláh and as elucidated by 'Abdu'l-Bahá and Shoghi Effendi.

Text itself." It is worth noting that 'Abdul-Bahá uses the term "acquired infallibility" here, though it is clear that he is referring to the same concept of "conferred infallibility." (*Some Answered Questions*, p. 172; *Will and Testament of 'Abdu'l-Bahá*, p. 20).

THE DISTINCTIVE NATURE OF INFALLIBILITY

Infallibility does not admit degrees. Something either complies with reality or it does not. A statement or a decision is either without error or it is not. A proposition cannot be mostly infallible or somewhat infallible.

The value of this observation, however obvious, relates to the above distinctions between inherent and conferred infallibility in a way that may not be so obvious. That is, while the spiritual and ontological station of the Prophets is distinct from the ontology of those upon whom the They may confer infallibility, the statements or decisions of these "lesser" beings is no less infallible even if their utterances are not derived from a "revelation direct from God."

It is precisely in this context that 'Abdu'l-Bahá observes that a decision of the Guardian or of the Universal House of Justice has "the same effect as the Text itself." It may not, however, have some of the other attributes of the revealed word. For example, the language of 'Abdu'l-Bahá, the Guardian, or the Universal House of Justice may not possess the multiple layers of meaning or the exalted beauty of the "revealed" word, but the authority or rank or effect of the decision is equally authoritative, infallible, and binding.

In this sense, were one to ask which Bahá'í law has more binding authority, a law of Bahá'u'lláh or a law created by the Universal House of Justice, the logical answer is inescapably clear—the two laws necessarily have equal weight or "effect." It is for this reason that in the Bahá'í Faith so much is made of the inextricable relationship between the revealed word and the administrative order. In the words of Shoghi Effendi, to dissever one from the other is "tantamount to a mutilation of the body of the Cause, a separation that can only result in the disintegration of its component parts, and the extinction of the Faith itself" (*World Order of Bahá'u'lláh*, p. 5).

INFALLIBILITY AND THE
STANDARDS OF SCIENCE

It is difficult for someone discussing these concepts from a materialist or traditional scientific orientation to accept as authoritative the assertion that, because of the revelatory process as created by God, the Manifestations are inherently infallible. The acceptance of this assertion is obviously contingent on one's willingness to accept the existence of a metaphysical reality, as well as the feasibility that there could be interpenetration between the metaphysical and physical realms of existence.

The Bahá'í texts repeatedly exhort anyone professing or desiring to profess belief in the Bahá'í revelation, or in any of the revelations of the past, to pursue such a quest with the same rigor and according to the same standards with which any good scientist goes about his or her study: "If religious beliefs and opinions are found contrary to the standards of science, they are mere superstitions and imaginations; for the antithesis of knowledge is ignorance, and the child of ignorance is superstition" (*Promulgation of Universal Peace*, p. 181).

Here again we see the important distinction between "faith" as it is understood and practiced by most religious traditions and how this term is conceived and practiced in the context of the Bahá'í Faith. Before one can accept the belief that the Manifestations are infallible, one must first come to the conclusion that such a Being could exist. And the only satisfactory way to prove this theory is to investigate the Manifestations firsthand. And the only means available for accomplishing this task is to study Their lives, Their revelations, Their promises, and Their guidance.

THE OMNISCIENCE OF
THE MANIFESTATIONS

If one finds it challenging to accept the belief that the Manifestations are inherently infallible, it may be much harder to accept a further assertion in the Bahá'í authoritative texts that the Manifestations are omniscient. According to Shoghi Effendi, the Prophets of God are "omniscient at will" (*Unfolding Destiny*, p. 449).

Shoghi Effendi makes this observation in passing as he describes his need for correct information in order to make correct decisions. He states that he "likes to be provided with facts by the friends, when they ask his advice, for although his decisions are infallibly guided by God, he is not, like the Prophet, omniscient at will, in spite of the fact that he often senses a situation or condition without having any detailed knowledge of it . . ." (*Unfolding Destiny*, p. 449).

One might assert that since the Latin roots of the word *omniscient* [*omni* "all" + *scient* "knowing"] mean "knowing everything," then there is nothing that the Manifestation does not know. This means that if we can discover one instance in which the Manifestation does not know something, we might refute this proposition. We can, for instance, assert that because the essence of God is, by definition, "essentially unknowable," then the Manifestations cannot know it. Therefore, have we discovered some limitation to their knowledge?

The response to this quandary is simple: Things are either capable of being known or they are not. If by definition something is "unknowable," then it cannot be known under any circumstances. Therefore, if we wish to be completely exact, we should state that the Manifestation can know everything that is capable of being known. Since the essence of God is in the category of "things that cannot be known," then the Manifestation's omniscience has not been compromised: "Magnified be Thy name, O Lord my God! Thou art He Whom all things worship and Who worshipeth no one, Who is the Lord of all things and is the vassal of none, Who knoweth all things and is known of none" (Bahá'u'lláh, *Prayers and Meditations,* p. 6).

THE BASIS FOR THE OMNISCIENCE OF THE MANIFESTATIONS

For those who have established a satisfactory basis for belief in the Manifestations, the surest testimony to Their omniscience is Their own assertion that They possess this power. In a most illuminating discussion about the divine process by which a new revelation infuses the entirety of the world with renewed vitality, Bahá'u'lláh states in unequivocal terms that one of His powers or attributes is omniscience: "In like manner, the moment the word expressing My attribute 'The Omniscient' issueth forth from My mouth, every created thing will, according to its capacity and limitations, be invested with the power to unfold the knowledge of the most marvelous sciences, and will be empowered to manifest them in the course of time at the bidding of Him Who is the Almighty, the All-Knowing" (*Gleanings,* no. 74.1).

Fortunately we also possess an explanation by 'Abdu'l-Bahá as to exactly why the Manifestations possess this inherent omniscience. In a weighty testimony regarding the distinctive nature of the spiritual reality of the Manifestations as compared to that of ordinary human beings, 'Abdu'l-Bahá compares our inherent knowledge of our own bodies to the Manifestation's inherent knowledge of reality itself.

'Abdu'l-Bahá states that our intuitive or inherent awareness of our bodies does not require effort because it is "an absolute gift" inasmuch as our "spirit" surrounds our body. By the same token, he continues, the Manifestation has inherent knowledge of reality itself because the essential reality of the Prophet (Their soul or spirit) surrounds reality: "Since the Sanctified Realities, the supreme Manifestations of God, surround the essence and qualities of the creatures, transcend and contain existing realities and understand all things, therefore, Their knowledge is divine knowledge, and not acquired—that is to say, it is a holy bounty; it is a divine revelation" (*Some Answered Questions,* p. 157).

12

THE OMNIPOTENCE
OF THE PROPHETS

*The Ancient Beauty hath consented to be bound with chains that
mankind may be released from its bondage, and hath accepted to
be made a prisoner within this most mighty Stronghold that
the whole world may attain unto true liberty.*

—Bahá'u'lláh

In an often cited passage referring to His incarceration in the barracks
prison in 'Akká, which He refers to as "The Most Great Prison," Bahá'-
u'lláh asserts that He "consented" to the imprisonment. This statement
seems to imply that there was some alternative available to Him, some
strategy by which He could have avoided the unspeakably grotesque
conditions He was made to endure. Further study of the life of Bahá'-
u'lláh and His successive imprisonments and exiles reveals that this
passage has a significantly more subtle and more profound implication.

THE EQUALITY OF THE PROPHETS
As we have observed repeatedly, all the Prophets are endowed with
the same capacity. They differ in how They express Their powers according to the exigencies of the Age in which They appear. Likewise,
the ultimate influence of the revelation a Manifestation reveals is con-

tingent on the place in history that it occupies relative to the overall progress of humankind, and to the collective response of humanity to the revelation.

It is in this light that Bahá'u'lláh in the Book of Certitude explains why some of the Manifestations seem to have a greater impact on human history than others. Citing a passage on this same theme from the Qur'án (2:253), Bahá'u'lláh establishes the underlying principle that all the Manifestations are equal in status and capacity and that to deny any one of them, or to prefer one over another, is to be in palpable error:

> These attributes of God are not and have never been vouch-safed specially unto certain Prophets, and withheld from others. Nay, all the Prophets of God, His well-favored, His holy, and chosen Messengers, are, without exception, the bearers of His names, and the embodiments of His attributes. They only differ in the intensity of their revelation, and the comparative potency of their light. Even as He hath revealed: "Some of the Apostles We have caused to excel the others." (Kitáb-i-Íqán, ¶110)

Bahá'u'lláh goes on to explain that the reason that not all the Prophets appear to possess the same capacity or attributes is that They manifest outwardly only those powers that are appropriate to the task at hand. They adapt a methodology consonant with the condition and capacity of those people to whom They appear. However, Bahá'u'lláh makes it quite clear that this distinction in no way implies that one Prophet possesses a power or capacity that another did not also have, should He have determined it appropriate to manifest it:

> That a certain attribute of God hath not been outwardly manifested by these Essences of Detachment doth in no wise imply that they Who are the Daysprings of God's attributes and the

Treasuries of His holy names did not actually possess it. Therefore, these illuminated Souls, these beauteous Countenances have, each and every one of them, been endowed with all the attributes of God, such as sovereignty, dominion, and the like, even though to outward seeming they be shorn of all earthly majesty. To every discerning eye this is evident and manifest; it requireth neither proof nor evidence. (Kitáb-i-Íqán, ¶110)

As we noted early on, the importance of this axiom regarding the station of the Manifestations is evident in the historical appearance of consistent religious conflict based primarily on the inability of followers to understand and accept it. Related to this failure to comprehend the essential equality and unity of the Prophets is a persistent erroneous assertion by followers of a new revelation that their religion must necessarily negate or debase the validity of the previous revelation. In addition, the followers often become so attached to the personality of a single Manifestation that they ignore or dispute the claims of the succeeding Prophet, even though their own religious history was begun under the oppression of this exact same attitude.

So not only do all the Manifestations occupy the same lofty station, even though They are distinct individual Beings, They all also possess identical powers and capacities—the power of revelation, the power of creativity, the power of omniscience, and, as we will now discuss, the unfettered power of power itself.

THE IMPORTANCE OF MIRACLES

One of the obvious distinctions among the Prophets is the manner in which each interacts with the immediate audience that He is teaching. Moses is best remembered by chroniclers for His ability to perform sensational or miraculous acts of power. He turns His staff into a serpent and then calls down the successive plagues upon Pharaoh and his people. He calls down the Angel of Death on the firstborn of those who are not passed over because they have not marked their doorposts with sheep's blood. He parts the Red Sea to escape Pharaoh's army. He ascends Mt. Sinai and comes down with the Ten Commandments dictated to Him directly by God. Later in the wilderness He brings forth manna from heaven and then water from a stone by tapping it with His staff.

Did these events really happen at all, or if they did, are they retrospective and anthropomorphic impositions on coincidental natural phenomena? Possibly the plagues or afflictions did happen, and possibly they happened during the same timeframe as the repeated requests of Moses that His people be released from bondage. Possibly some phenomenal weather or winds enabled the fleeing Hebrews to escape Pharaoh's army. But were these events actually caused by Moses' power to produce phenomenal intervention in physical reality, or are these simply examples of how oral historians try in retrospect to discern or interpret or impose some metaphysical cause-and-effect relationship on these events?

In the mid-1960s the "God is Dead" theology emerged among a group of radical theologians who asserted that the God of the Old Testament Who intervened so sensationally and directly in human affairs was apparently no longer at work. Many took the phrase at face-value and failed to appreciate what this theological perspective was intended to imply—that the God who directly intervenes in human history by parting a sea or bringing down the walls of Jericho with a trumpet blast or raising people from the dead, no longer seemed interested in manifesting Himself in such an overt and obvious way.

Interestingly, the portrayal of God as a father-figure in the teachings of Christ is less obvious and overt than the tribal-chieftain image of God in the Old Testament. Christ does seem to demonstrate ostensibly miraculous powers—the healing of the sick and the raising of the dead, not to mention having been born via the virgin birth and ascending bodily to heaven after His crucifixion—but the focus of Christ's teaching is sometimes overlooked. As we have noted, He sets forth His body of laws in the Sermon on the Mount as recapitulated in Matthew 5–7, and He produces a wealth of more abstruse teachings in almost sixty parables, some of which are brief analogies and others of which are lengthy and complex. Some of the parables He explicates or explains, while others He leaves to the believer to figure out independently, no doubt as a spiritual exercise. Many are extremely difficult and perplexing, the parable of the Vineyard being one of the more demanding.

The point is that the so-called miracles of Christ could well be seen as paling in comparison to the number and the importance of the spiritual teachings He revealed. In fact, He Himself seems clearly disturbed by those who would follow Him solely because He is capable of demonstrating what they perceive to be miraculous powers. For example, the multiplying of the loaves and fishes is the only miracle other than Christ's resurrection that is recounted in all four gospels, albeit with some differences in the telling. But while this act has obvious symbolic meanings (for example, that there is an endless supply of spiritual nourishment for all who desire it), the crowd witnessing and partaking of this miraculous feast are lost in the literal feat Christ has performed.

Consequently, according to the account in John, when Christ sees that the crowd wants to seize Him and crown Him king because of His powers, He flees their presence: "Then those men, when they had seen the miracle that Jesus did, said, 'This is of a truth that prophet that should come into the world.' When Jesus therefore perceived that they would come and take him by force, to make Him a king, he departed again into a mountain himself alone" (John 6:14–15).

When the people find Him in Capernaum the next day, He explains to them why He left them:

> Jesus answered them and said, "Verily, verily, I say unto you, Ye seek me, not because ye saw the miracles, but because ye did eat of the loaves, and were filled. Labour not for the meat which perisheth, but for that meat which endureth unto everlasting life, which the Son of man shall give unto you, for him hath God the Father sealed."
>
> Then said they unto Him, "What shall we do, that we might work the works of God?
>
> Jesus answered and said unto them, "This is the work of God, that ye believe on Him whom He hath sent." (John 6:26–9)

Christ does exhort His disciples simply to follow Him because of the works He does if they can not grasp the theological implications of His teachings. But this exhortation seems to refer to His comportment, His kindness, and to His exemplary conduct, and not to any miraculous acts they might believe He has performed.

Interestingly, while there are a number of miracles that could be cited regarding the early history of the Bahá'í Faith—for example, the events surrounding the martyrdom of the Báb—Bahá'u'lláh explicitly exhorts His followers not to recount to others what they might regard as miracles to prove the authenticity of His Cause: "We entreat Our loved ones not to besmirch the hem of Our raiment with the dust of falsehood, neither to allow references to what they have regarded as miracles and prodigies to debase Our rank and station, or to mar the purity and sanctity of Our name" (*Epistle to the Son of the Wolf*, p. 33).

He goes on to observe that people should turn to Him because He is a source of divine authority and has thus brought the remedy for those ills that presently afflict humankind, together with a blueprint for fashioning a just and spiritually based world order: "Gracious God! This is the day whereon the wise should seek the advice of this Wronged One, and ask Him Who is the Truth what things are conducive to the glory and tranquillity of men" (*Epistle to the Son of the Wolf*, p. 33).

In other words, this is the Day or the period in history when what is needed is not some brazen or sensational display of miraculous power, but rather the wisdom of a plan for global collective security and peace, the very thing that Bahá'u'lláh has brought. The elixir of this guidance, He seems to say, is ultimately far more miraculous, transformative, and astounding than any purely phenomenal event. Changing hearts and attitudes is demonstrative of a power far more subtle and constructive than any exhibition of raw force.

SYMBOLISM OF MIRACLES

The orally dictated poetry of the Old Testament is largely based on speculation about past historical events. More reliable, we can assume, is the recapitulation of these events by Christ, Muḥammad, the Báb, and Bahá'u'lláh. But let us assume for a moment that the miracles portrayed in the New Testament did occur literally rather than merely as symbolical statements of spiritual events. Let us assume that Christ did indeed heal the sick and raise the dead. Why would He consider these effective teaching devices?

'Abdu'l-Bahá discusses at some length the miracles associated with the Manifestations in relation to what probative value they have as proof of Their station. His general assessment is that the Prophets Themselves place little stock in them. 'Abdu'l-Bahá notes, "they are still only proofs and arguments for those who are present when they are performed, and not for those who are absent" (*Some Answered Questions*, p. 100). The true demonstration of the otherworldly power of the divine Beings, 'Abdu'l-Bahá goes on to explain, lies in Their ability to appear among us, single and alone, yet able to change the course of human history:

> But in the day of the Manifestation the people with insight see that all the conditions of the Manifestation are miracles, for They are superior to all others, and this alone is an absolute miracle. Recollect that Christ, solitary and alone, without a helper or protector, without armies and legions, and under the greatest oppression, uplifted the standard of God before all the people of the world, and withstood them, and finally conquered all, although outwardly He was crucified. Now this is a veritable miracle which can never be denied. There is no need of any other proof of the truth of Christ. (*Some Answered Questions*, p. 100)

This is the true demonstration of the superhuman or divine power of the Prophets, 'Abdu'l-Bahá goes on to explain, that They are able to induce a change in the immortal life of our souls. After all, he continues, if the Prophet gives physical sight to a blind man, the man will ultimately lose that sight when he dies. Similarly, if the Prophet brings a man's body back to life, the man is still going to die later on:

> The outward miracles have no importance for the people of Reality. If a blind man receives sight, for example, he will finally again become sightless, for he will die and be deprived of all his senses and powers. Therefore, causing the blind man to see is comparatively of little importance, for this faculty of sight will at last disappear. If the body of a dead person be resuscitated, of what use is it since the body will die again? But it is important to give perception and eternal life—that is, the spiritual and divine life. For this physical life is not immortal, and its existence is

equivalent to nonexistence. So it is that Christ said to one of His disciples: "Let the dead bury their dead;" for "That which is born of the flesh is flesh; and that which is born of the Spirit is spirit." (*Some Answered Questions,* p. 100)

'Abdu'l-Bahá makes an equally cogent and ironic observation regarding the belief in the literal physical resurrection of Christ followed by His physical ascent into Heaven. True, the body of Christ may have disappeared from the tomb, but of what possible spiritual meaning or value could that same body have in the limitless reaches of outer space, "a limitless area, void and empty, where innumerable stars and planets revolve" (*Some Answered Questions,* p. 103). Where would such a body reside and what use would it have to a being Who, like us, is essentially spiritual in nature?

The symbolic or true significance of the meaning of the "resurrection," 'Abdu'l-Bahá points out, is that the "body of believers" was as a thing quite dead, like a lifeless body:

The Cause of Christ was like a lifeless body; and when after three days the disciples became assured and steadfast, and began to serve the Cause of Christ, and resolved to spread the divine teachings, putting His counsels into practice, and arising to serve Him, the Reality of Christ became resplendent and His bounty appeared; His religion found life; His teachings and His admonitions became evident and visible. In other words, the Cause of Christ was like a lifeless body until the life and the bounty of the Holy Spirit surrounded it. (*Some Answered Questions,* p. 103)

The same concept of "resurrection" could be applied to the "miracle" that is the present-day Bahá'í Faith. In 1892 Bahá'u'lláh died as a prisoner of the Ottoman Empire. He was buried in a simple ceremony in a plain stone building the size of a normal room. Yet from His appearance and His revelation has evolved in the course of little more than a century the second most widespread religion in the world. All this has been accomplished without clergy and without the financial support of any external or vested interest. Logically, what, other than a metaphysical impetus or spiritual power, could account for this "miracle"?

It is in this sense and in the other "proofs" of the Prophets to which we have alluded—Their person and Their ability to produce spontaneously and without revision a revelation that transforms human society—that the true miracle of the appearance of these sanctified Emissaries is found. For even though They are clearly capable of performing acts that we might believe defy logical explanation, we can discern in Their person and actions the fruit of a true Prophet— demonstrations of spiritual power and ascendancy, not of material or political power. Of course, one organic and obvious influence Their advent and guidance ultimately introduces is the systematic elevation of social institutions and the incremental advancement of our collective learning and history.

THE LOGIC OF MIRACLES

As we mention in our discussion of the meaning of the temptation of Christ, at the heart of this episode immediately following the anointing of Christ by John the Baptist is the recounting of Christ's confrontation with "self-interest" so that He might fulfill His mission in complete servitude to God's plan for educating His creation. As we also mentioned in that brief exposition, implicit in this story is the fact that the Manifestation does indeed possess the power to do whatever He wishes, to possess whatever things or position He might desire. In such a context, then, it should not surprise us that the Manifestation can, when He deems it appropriate or necessary to do so, perform what we regard as miracles.

And yet a principal doctrine of the Bahá'í teachings is that there is no conflict or contradiction between science and religion. Or stated another way, there is no conflict between the laws that govern the physical dimension of reality and those laws that govern the spiritual dimension of creation.

The interplay or interpenetration between these two aspects or twin dimensions of reality is demonstrable, and, more to the point, quite logical. There have been several well-regarded studies demonstrating the reciprocity between these two aspects of reality. Among the most well-known studies are the several works by Larry Dossey about the effects of prayer, and the Princeton study of Jahn and Dunn about the effects of collective willpower as recorded in their book *Margins of Reality.*

The study of Jahn and Dunn is scientifically the more rigorous of the two, and I think we can derive from it an important insight into the logic of miracles. While proving in a replicable and empirically based study that human conscious thought can affect a material outcome, the authors do not conclude that this is evidence that the mind is a metaphysical reality. Nor do they conclude that the results of their experiments demonstrate evidence that there is a metaphysical reality or that spiritual forces can influence the outcome of physical events. Instead, as materialist scientists working in a materialist scientific milieu, they postulate that over time we will come to appreciate that this experiment, as well as their other experiments with simultaneous action at a distance, will be logically explained, most probably through quantum physics.

This same conclusion has been posited by scientists trying to explain the process of human consciousness and ideation created by the human brain. If one assumes *a priori* that there is no metaphysical aspect to the human reality—no "soul" or "spirit"—then one must naturally search elsewhere to explain all that the brain can do, including willpower, memory, and the ability to conceptualize an infinite array of abstract ideas.

While the law of parsimony would seem to dictate that the most "scientific" explanation for what the brain can do is that there is a non-physical or "metaphysical" source of the "self" or human consciousness, these scientist are at least forcing us to respond with an equally logical explanation. In short, because there is a metaphysical reality and interplay between the physical and metaphysical aspects of reality, we should conclude that this interplay is logical and capable of being rationally described or explained. For example, in time we may indeed discover how a metaphysical power—such as prayer—sets in motion certain phenomenal responses.

The fact is that logic and logical processes are inherent in all of creation, whether we are describing physical or metaphysical realities or relationships. The same axiom necessarily holds true for the inter-relationship between these dual expressions of reality. Indeed, what is occurring right this moment as you read these words is a perfect example of this axiom at work. From a Bahá'í perspective, our essential reality is our soul from which emanates our various human powers and capacities as expressions of the soul. These faculties include, but are not limited to, the power of self-consciousness, memory, will, ideation, and so on.

The physical apparatus that is our brain functions as an intermediary in this process, not as the ultimate origin of our uniquely human powers. The brain literally translates the metaphysical properties and powers of thought or will into biochemical impulses that in turn eventually trigger the physical sense of sight whereupon we read the words on this page. And because we have spent years training our conscious mind to understand what this otherwise meaningless array of signs and symbols represent, we can translate this configuration of physical lines into syntax and thought.

This thought has in fact been conveyed back from the eyes, to the brain, translated again into a complex of biochemical impulses, which are then understood by the metaphysical reality of the conscious mind, retained in the memory of that same consciousness, and then considered in light of previous understanding, knowledge, or recollected thought. Cutting to the chase, we are experiencing as we read these words an extremely intricate but quite logical sequence in which information is constantly flowing back and forth between our metaphysical self and the physical properties of this written page. Reflecting on this process allows us to appreciate that nothing can escape logic or logical relationships and that everything that we perceive to be a miracle ultimately has an underlying explanation.

It is not sufficient, then, to respond to doubters that the logical explanation for Christ's ability to heal the sick was that He was a Manifestation of God. This proposition may be entirely true and accurate, but it is insufficient because it does not attempt to explain all the logical processes by which His power is translated into physically medicinal effects. This is not to say we can presently understand that process or that we will ever be able to do so. We are simply acknowledging that a logical explanation exists and could potentially be articulated. Perhaps some future Manifestation will explain it to us.

As we have mentioned previously, the phenomena we now witness around us would appear as entirely miraculous to even the most ardent materialist of a century or two ago—a student meandering around a college campus with some strange object in his ear having a conversation with no visible human being in proximity; a voice emanating from a small map in a car, telling the driver where to go and even calling for help in the case of an accident; a person sitting down at a screen to have a conversation with the visual image of another human being who is on the other side of the earth; and on and on *ad infinitum*.

And if a miracle from a century ago is today's toy, what lies before us a century from now, or even next month?

MIRACLES AS PROCESSES
WE DON'T PRESENTLY UNDERSTAND

We apply the term *miracle* to an event, a power, or a process whose logic we do not presently comprehend. Therefore, when Bahá'u'lláh speaks of the power of what Shoghi Effendi refers to as the "creative word of God," we can either interpret His description as being hyperbolic or symbolic, or we can consider the possibility that the assertion is quite literally true but that it is alluding to a process that works at a level of reality we have yet to understand:

> Every word that proceedeth out of the mouth of God is endowed with such potency as can instill new life into every human frame, if ye be of them that comprehend this truth. All the wondrous works ye behold in this world have been manifested through the operation of His supreme and most exalted Will, His wondrous and inflexible Purpose. Through the mere revelation of the word "Fashioner," issuing forth from His lips and proclaiming His attribute to mankind, such power is released as can generate, through successive ages, all the manifold arts which the hands of man can produce. (*Gleanings,* no. 74.1)

And since the Manifestations are the Intermediaries through Whom the "creative word" is conveyed to us and by means of Whose command the power of that word is unleashed upon reality, we may find that a literal understanding of this passage is not at all beyond the realm of literal truth.

In fact, at the time Bahá'u'lláh was revealing this commentary on the power of the creative word, people could hardly have imagined or conceived of what miraculous changes would take place before the end of the century. Bahá'u'lláh Himself states this in this same discourse,

> This, verily, is a certain truth. No sooner is this resplendent word uttered, than its animating energies, stirring within all created things, give birth to the means and instruments whereby such arts can be produced and perfected. All the wondrous achievements ye now witness are the direct consequences of the Revelation of this Name. In the days to come, ye will, verily, behold things of which ye have never heard before. Thus hath it been decreed in the Tablets of God, and none can comprehend it except them whose sight is sharp. (*Gleanings,* no. 74.1)

So is there a logical explanation for how an ephemeral reality such as a "word" can have such an immense effect upon physical reality? Since this same passage is open to sundry interpretations, we probably shouldn't spend a great deal of time trying to investigate how such a process takes place. We would probably fare better to study its inner meaning or spiritual significance. Nevertheless, we can be certain that there is a precise process being described, that this process is alluding to a metaphysical influence on human society, and that however this process works, it has a logical basis that can and will be explained and understood.

THE THEORETICAL OMNIPOTENCE OF THE PROPHETS

There are several fairly simple syllogisms that lead us to the undeniable conclusion that the Prophets not only possess superhuman or otherworldly power but that They are also omnipotent. And while a logical proof alone does not give us much internal satisfaction with regard to our knowledge of the Prophets or our sense of intimacy with these Emissaries from God, such conclusions are certainly noteworthy and helpful in this process of understanding why They are worthy of our study.

PERFECT AND COMPLETE
MANIFESTATIONS OF GODLINESS

The idea that God has been made manifest in complete and perfect manner by each of the successive Prophets of God is hinted at by all the previous Manifestations, especially by Christ and even more completely by Muḥammad. But in the Book of Certitude, Bahá'u'lláh provides a complete elucidation of all aspects of this divine plan.

Clearly all the previous Manifestations are describing the same concept and are alluding to the same lofty spiritual Beings when They employ the terms Prophet, Son of God, Friend of God, or Messenger of God. Likewise, it is equally certain that the Manifestations are, one and all, describing the exact same process of the progressive enlightenment of human civilization through sequential and cyclical revelations, albeit in terms that accord with the capacity of those whom They have come to teach.

One enlightening distinction explained by Bahá'u'lláh regarding the term "Manifestation" (as opposed to more common epithets like "Messenger" or "Prophet") is that where one might regard a Prophet or Messenger or divinely inspired individual as doing the work of God, the term *manifest* carries with it the additional implication that a being is capable of demonstrating and expressing the nature, capacities, and powers of God. Put concisely, Bahá'u'lláh describes the Manifestations as capable of demonstrating and perfectly replicating *all* the various attributes of the Creator, including His powers. It is precisely in the context of this ontological description that Christ says that to see Him is to see God. Bahá'u'lláh states this verity with the following proposition:

Were any of the all-embracing Manifestations of God to declare: "I am God!" He verily speaketh the truth, and no doubt attacheth thereto. For it hath been repeatedly demonstrated that through their Revelation, their attributes and names, the Revelation of God, His name and His attributes, are made manifest in the world. Thus, He hath revealed: "Those shafts were God's, not Thine!" [Qur'án 8:17] And also He saith: "In truth, they who plighted fealty unto thee, really plighted that fealty unto God." [Qur'án 48:10] And were any of them to voice the utterance: "I am the Messenger of God," He also speaketh the truth, the indubitable truth. Even as He saith: "Muhammad is not the father of any man among you, but He is the Messenger of God." [Qur'án 33:40] Viewed in this light, they are all but Messengers of that ideal King, that unchangeable Essence. (Kitáb-i-Íqán, ¶196)

If we accept the premise underlying this passage as true, we come to the inevitable conclusion that the Manifestations of God are omnipotent at will, even as They are omniscient. For given the premise that "power" is an attribute of God, and given that the Manifestations manifest all the attributes of God perfectly, then we are forced to conclude that since the perfection of the attribute of power is omnipotence, the Manifestations must necessarily be omnipotent.

THE CONJOINING OF "B" AND "E"

A second proof of the omnipotence of the Prophets is more inferential but no less compelling. Throughout the Bahá'í writings, we find the statement that the Manifestations are the means by which the letters *b* and *e* have been "joined and knit together" (Bahá'u'lláh, *Prayers and Meditations,* p. 320). The meaning of this statement is less complicated or mystical than it might seem at first glance.

The word "Be!" as an imperative form of the verb "to be" is the creative word of God uttered by the Manifestation calling creation into being. In other languages, the translation will be rendered by dividing the same imperative into two parts. This passage and its explanation call to mind the first verse in the Gospel of John, which reads: "In the beginning was the Word, and the Word was with God, and the Word was God" (1:1), as well as the fourteenth verse of the same chapter which begins, "And the Word was made flesh, and dwelt among us." But this explanation should also remind us of the three stages of existence that apply to the life of the Manifestation. He preexists in the spiritual realm, becomes a perfect outward or sensually perceptible expression of the spiritual attributes of God, and then returns to the realm of the spirit where He continues to assist His followers.

In other words, the Manifestation joins or links together the dual aspects of the creative process—the knowledge or conception of an idea and the expression of that knowledge in action. Or to state this idea in terms of science and religion, the Manifestation is the means by which the dual expressions of reality are conjoined in our lives by enabling us to discern the reality of the divine as expressed in nature and by empowering our ability to express spiritual concepts in a regimen of daily action.

WHATSOEVER HE WILLETH

These are but two of the multiple possible meanings of this concept of how the Manifestation can be viewed as possessing and demonstrating the power to do whatsoever He wills in order to accomplish the work at hand. This is not to say that the Manifestation is the ultimate source of creation. The source of all reality is God, the Creator. The Manifestations channel or translate the creative power that emanates from God as the Holy Spirit into increments of enlightenment and guidance.

Consequently, as we have noted several times already, the Manifestations are the highest expression of God or Godliness to which we will ever be exposed, whether in this life or in the next. It is in this station of total servitude to God and to us that the Manifestations are emblems and expressions of the phrase "He doeth whatsoever He willeth and ordaineth whatsoever He pleaseth." For example, in abrogating one of the laws of the Báb, Bahá'u'lláh states, "God hath removed the restrictions on travel that had been imposed in the Bayán. He, verily, is the Unconstrained; He doeth as He pleaseth and ordaineth whatsoever He willeth (Kitáb-i-Aqdas, ¶65), implying quite obviously that His ordinances should be perceived as identical to the laws of God. In another similar passage, Bahá'u'lláh observers that our obedience to His guidance is required, even when we do not grasp the underlying logic and benefit inherent in whatsoever He ordains:

> Ponder thereon, if thou be of them that tread this path, that all thou didst ask of this lowly One may be made plain unto thee and that thou mayest abide within the tabernacle of this guidance. For He doeth whatsoever He willeth and ordaineth whatsoever He pleaseth. Nor shall He be asked of His doings, whilst all men will be asked of their every deed. (Bahá'u'lláh, *Gems of Divine Mysteries*, ¶86)

It is important to keep in mind as we ponder this lofty concept that the sole purpose of God in creating us and in having His Manifestations act on His behalf, is to assist us, to enlighten us, to prepare us for the continuation of our lives beyond our physical existence, and to advance human civilization so that earthly society gradually emulates the spiritual realm. In light of this underlying purpose in all that the Creator does and ordains through His Manifestations, we might find it useful when reading the following passages to reflect on the fact that even though They do whatsoever They wish and ordain whatsoever They please, it is always intended entirely for our own benefit and well-being:

> He is, in truth, the exponent of 'God doeth whatsoever He willeth' in the kingdom of creation. ('Abdu'l-Bahá, *Some Answered Questions*, p. 171)

> Thus the meaning of "He doeth whatsoever He willeth" is that if the Manifestation says something, or gives a command, or performs an action, and believers do not understand its wisdom, they still ought not to oppose it by a single thought, seeking to know why He spoke so, or why He did such a thing. ('Abdu'l-Bahá, *Some Answered Questions*, p. 173)

> O people of Tar! Give ear unto the Call of Him Who doeth whatsoever He willeth. In truth He remindeth you of that which will draw you nigh unto God, the Lord of the worlds. He hath turned His face towards you from the Prison of 'Akká and hath revealed for your sakes what will immortalize your memory and your names in the Book which cannot be effaced and remaineth unaffected by the doubts of the forward. (Bahá'u'lláh, *Tablets of Bahá'u'lláh*, p. 78).

Finally, we do well to conclude our examination of the power of the Prophets by citing a few of the instances in which Bahá'u'lláh seems to state point-blank that He, by the power of God working through Him, can indeed do whatever He wishes:

> Verily, such a man is blessed by the Concourse on high, and by them who dwell within the Tabernacle of Grandeur, who have

quaffed My sealed Wine in My Name, the *Omnipotent*, the All-Powerful. (*Tablets of Bahá'u'lláh*, p. 207)

It behoveth thee to turn thy gaze in all circumstances unto the One true God, and seek diligently to serve His Cause. Call thou to mind when thou wert in My company, within the Tabernacle of Glory, and didst hear from Me that which He Who conversed with God [Moses] heard upon the Sinai of divine knowledge. Thus did We graciously aid thee, enabled thee to recognize the truth and cautioned thee, that thou mightest render thanks unto thy bountiful Lord. Thou shouldst safeguard this sublime station through the potency of My Name, the *Omnipotent*, the Faithful. (*Tablets of Bahá'u'lláh*, p. 242)

How great is the blessedness that awaiteth the king who will arise to aid My Cause in My Kingdom, who will detach himself from all else but Me! Such a king is numbered with the companions of the Crimson Ark, the Ark which God hath prepared for the people of Bahá. All must glorify his name, must reverence his station, and aid him to unlock the cities with the keys of My Name, the *omnipotent* Protector of all that inhabit the visible and invisible kingdoms. (Kitáb-i-Aqdas, ¶84)

PART 4

THE METHODOLOGY OF THE PROPHETS OF GOD

Know verily that the purpose underlying all these symbolic terms and abstruse allusions, which emanate from the Revealers of God's holy Cause, hath been to test and prove the peoples of the world; that thereby the earth of the pure and illuminated hearts may be known from the perishable and barren soil. From time immemorial such hath been the way of God amidst His creatures, and to this testify the records of the sacred books.

—Bahá'u'lláh

13

THE PERSONHOOD
OF THE PROPHETS

*Say: Naught is seen in My temple but the Temple of God, and in My
beauty but His Beauty, and in My being but His Being, and in My
self but His Self, and in My movement but His Movement, and in
My acquiescence but His Acquiescence, and in My pen but His
Pen, the Mighty, the All-Praised. There hath not been in My soul
but the Truth, and in Myself naught could be seen but God.*

—Bahá'u'lláh

In this final section we will consider more specifically the strategy by
which the Prophets instruct us. Not surprisingly, we discover as we
survey the evidence of Their teaching technique that indirection and
subtlety is at the heart of Their method. All good teachers know the
value of the indirect technique, and the master teacher will employ a
variety of exercises by which the free will of the student is called upon.
The objective is that in the long run, the student will thirst for new
knowledge, will be trained in the use of specific tools that will enable
him to acquire that knowledge, and, finally, will be offered some form
of daily regimen so that the acquisition of that knowledge is completed
by applying the acquired wisdom to some pattern of action. The ultimate aim of all these strategies is that over time, the habituation of patterns of action will result in essential change to the human soul itself.

No other form of learning except this indirect technique, however overtly impressive, can bring about authentic learning. What so often passes for education consists mostly of the memorization and recitation of the learning of others. This practice may indeed have some limited value, but only if the student is also urged and assisted to comprehend and appreciate the inner meaning of that which he or she is required to commit to memory.

The four most critical instructional tools employed by the Manifestations are, not coincidentally, also the most potent proofs of Their station as Prophets: the person of the Prophet; the revelatory technique of the Prophet; the laws of the Prophet; and the constancy of the Prophet in the face of untold adversity, opposition, and suffering. In this last section we will explore why it is essential for us to understand how indirection is employed in each of these four aspects of Their teaching methodology.

In general, the four chapters in this concluding assessment of how God educates humanity through His Master Educators will help us appreciate more adequately the creativity and precision with which the Manifestations are able to inform and advance human society without ever becoming oppressive, dogmatic, or inflexible.

What is perhaps the most impressive feature of Their methodology is that They assist us in fashioning an ever more refined civilization without ever intervening directly or materially in human affairs. They neither seek nor accept political office nor any other sort of position of public prominence. They truly render unto Caesar the things that are Caesar's, and unto God that which is God's.

THE TEST OF THE PERSONHOOD OF THE PROPHETS

As we noted earlier, one of the foremost proofs of the station of the Prophet is the Prophet Himself. In addition to manifesting perfectly all the divine attributes, He also represents in His ordinary human behavior patterns of action and comportment that are intended to provide the people of a dispensation with a standard of behavior by which to gauge their own spiritual development. For while we will never attain the perfection of the Prophets, we can in any situation look to the example of how the Prophet responded in similar situations.

And yet there is also incredible indirection in this aspect of His teaching method, even as there is in the complexity of His language and laws. Among the most subtle features of the appearance of this force for social change in the form of an ordinary human being is the difficulty for the majority of people in recognizing the Prophet in the first place. For example, if a Manifestation were among us prior to the declaration of His mission, would we be able to pick Him out from among a group of ordinary human beings?

Certainly this is a question well worth our serious reflection. From a historical perspective we might wish to believe that we would be among those special few who see and immediately believe, who recognize the distinguishing characteristics of this divine Emissary, and who set aside all personal concerns to follow and obey Him. At the very least, we can hope we would *not* be among those so quickly swayed by their own ecclesiastical leaders to taunt and torture the Prophet and His followers.

THE TEST FOR THE "DIVINES"

The first subtle lesson that must be learned by anyone searching for the promised Manifestation is the very nature of that which is being sought. What will distinguish this Being from other human beings, even from impressive, sagacious, or extraordinary human beings? Will He be more appealing to the eye, overtly demonstrative in His wisdom, or apparent in some other outward aspect of His being? Will He be characterized by having a large following or by having a position of recognized spiritual authority or charisma?

Christ remarks succinctly that the Prophet will come like a thief in the night—at an unexpected time and in an inconspicuous guise. This first test is described by Bahá'u'lláh at some length in the Book of Certitude. Bahá'u'lláh characterizes it as the "judgment" that occurs each time a new Manifestation appears, a judgment that most clearly tests the followers of the previous Manifestation who must decide how to apply the standards of guidance bequeathed them, both by their own scripture and by the advice of their own religious leaders. For example, we are all familiar with the variety of sects and religious leaders who have for some time characterized particular contemporary events as heralding the Second Coming of Christ or the time of the End.

Bahá'u'lláh begins the Book of Certitude by noting that it is principally the inability of clerics to understand how to interpret scripture that has caused them so consistently to mislead those in their charge when a new Prophet appears. Citing a passage from the Qur'án about this pattern of response, Bahá'u'lláh observes, "Again, He saith: 'Say, O people of the Book! Why repel believers from the way of God?' [Qur'án 3:99] It is evident that by the 'people of the Book,' who have repelled their fellowmen from the straight path of God, is meant none other than the divines of that age . . ." (Kitáb-i-Íqán, ¶15).

Naturally the test of recognition is greater for those that possess spiritual status or occupy positions of religious authority vested in the previous revelation, because they have the most to lose when a new Manifestation appears. If they are indeed encountering the advent of a new revelation, then not only is their own status in question; so is the viability of the very religious institution they have served and to which they have devoted their vocations and their lives. In a spiritual sense, however, they have the most to gain should they be among those who have both the capacity to recognize the Manifestation and the courage to become a follower regardless of the personal consequences.

In the context of this conflicted mindset, the divines or clergy of a previous religion might have great difficulty in setting aside their bias to assess the claim of a humble carpenter's son to be the Messiah. The exact same test confronted the council assembled to examine the claims of the Báb in Tabríz in July of 1848. Having been brought from imprisonment in Máh-Kú to further imprisonment in Chihríq, the Báb was subsequently brought before an assemblage of governmental and ecclesiastical dignitaries. Shoghi Effendi in *God Passes By* describes the dramatic climax of this "examination" of the Báb:

> In the official residence, and in the presence, of the governor of Ádhirbáyján, Naṣiri'd-Dín Mírzá, the heir to the throne; under the presidency of Ḥájí Mullá Maḥmud, the Niẓámu'l-'Ulamá, the Prince's tutor; before the assembled ecclesiastical dignitaries of Tabríz, the leaders of the Shaykhi community, the Shaykhu'l-Islám, and the Imám-Jum'ih, the Báb, having seated Himself in the chief place which had been reserved for the Valí-'Ahd (the heir to the throne), gave, in ringing tones, His celebrated answer to the question put to Him by the President of that assembly. "I am," He exclaimed, "I am, I am the Promised One! I am the One Whose name you have for a thousand years invoked, at Whose mention you have risen, Whose advent you have longed to witness, and the hour of Whose Revelation you have prayed God to hasten. Verily, I say, it is incumbent upon the peoples of both the East and the West to obey My word, and to pledge allegiance to My person." (p. 21)

To outward seeming, here was a young prisoner of twenty-nine years of age, an unlearned and humble merchant. From the perspective of these officials, this young man had managed rapidly to acquire an enthusiastic following throughout Persia, and they wanted to know exactly who He thought He was and with what authority He had the audacity to stir up so much trouble.

The Báb's brazen claim astonished them into momentary silence. Such impudence from anyone—let alone from a young, untutored merchant claiming to be the Qá'im and the return of the Hidden Imám—was beyond the comprehension of these men so accustomed to obeisance on the part of any ordinary citizen appearing before them.

THE TEST FOR THE REST OF US

There is more to this episode. The daring and frank declaration by the Báb was followed by several exchanges in which He demonstrated His absolute fearlessness of their power and total disregard for His own well-being, as well as sufficient intelligence to respond appropriately to any query they put to Him.

But our objective here is not so much to impugn the blindness, duplicity, and oppression of those in power. The test or judgment upon the rank and file of humanity is no less important and certainly no less subtle. The appearance of the Prophet challenges us to perceive a spiritual power expressed through the vehicle of a Being Who, for all intents and purposes, appears among us as an ordinary human being.

After all, the Manifestation is born into this reality. He walks among us. He works. He eats. He sleeps. He gets sick. He falls prey to all the changes and chances that pester the rest of us and muddle our lives. And except for His prodigious knowledge and exemplary spiritual conduct, we may have no direct evidence that He is not simply a very nice neighbor, a reliable shepherd, a dutiful carpenter's son, a trusted trader, an honest merchant, etc.

As a result, the first followers are, more often than not, those who are sufficiently detached from the opinions of others or from some vested status in society. In the case of Christ, the first such individuals were three simple fisherman—Peter, James, and John. With Muḥammad, the first follower was his wife, the second His ten-year-old cousin 'Alí, followed by the meek, mostly disenfranchised people of Mecca who were without tribal protection. Many of the Báb's first followers were simple villagers throughout Persia, and it was largely these same souls who first declared their belief in Bahá'u'lláh.

WHY THE MEEK AND LOWLY?

According to Bahá'u'lláh in the Book of Certitude, another major technique by which the Manifestation uplifts society is the wisdom He demonstrates in selecting the first followers to Whom He reveals Himself.

One the one hand, they are most often not notables, not leading clerics or people in positions of secular authority. Neither are they mindless fanatics or lost and lawless souls who wish to rebel against the powers that be. They are meek but intelligent, kind and loyal citizens who have no intention or goal save their own spiritual edification and the well-being of their fellow human beings.

The character and quality of the first followers demonstrate to the rest of us that if the Manifestation is more interested in the character of a person than the social status of those He teaches, then He must have no ulterior motive. And if He attracts the best among us—the most exemplary souls—then there must be merit to His claims and His instruction.

Bahá'u'lláh describes this teaching technique as one of the first proofs of the capacity of the Manifestation to transform society—the fact that He uplifts and empowers those who have no aspirations to power, no personal agenda. He states, "Amongst the proofs demonstrating the truth of this Revelation [the Bábí Faith] is this, that in every age and Dispensation, whenever the invisible Essence was revealed in the person of His Manifestation, certain souls, obscure and detached from all worldly entanglements, would seek illumination from the Sun of Prophethood and Moon of divine guidance, and would attain unto the divine Presence." He goes on to recount the stellar quality of the first followers of the Báb, speaking particularly about Mullá Ḥusayn and Vaḥíd, who were men "of consummate learning" who "renounced, for the sake of the Beloved, the world and all that is therein" (Kitáb-i-Íqán, ¶246, 247).

Bahá'u'lláh also notes that the "divines of the age and those possessed of wealth, would scorn and scoff at these people" (Kitáb-i-Íqán, ¶246). In this vein Bahá'u'lláh cites a passage from the Qur'án in which Muḥammad likewise observes how those of prominence are usually veiled from the truth by virtue of their attachment to material signs of importance:

> Even as He hath revealed concerning them that erred: "Then said the chiefs of His people who believed not, 'We see in Thee but a man like ourselves; and we see not any who have followed Thee except our meanest ones of hasty judgment, nor see we any excellence in you above ourselves: nay, we deem you liars.'" They caviled at those holy Manifestations, and protested saying: "None hath followed you except the abject amongst us, those who are worthy of no attention." (Kitáb-i-Íqán, ¶246)

IF ONLY IT HAD WORKED!

When we review religious history in this fashion, we are naturally tempted to wonder how nice it might have been had the earliest believers been people of religious or secular rank, of political status and powerful influence. If only the leaders of the masses had passed this educational test, how different our history would be!

What if Pharaoh had recognized Moses' spiritual stature, released the Hebrews, or, better still, had become a believer along with the rest of his people? What if the Sanhedrin had recognized in Christ the fulfillment of the Messianic prophecies of their own scriptures? What if, accordingly, all the Judaic peoples had then become Christian? What if the Meccans had not warred against Muḥammad and His followers? What if the Grand Vizir to Muḥammad S͟háh had not deterred the Báb from complying with the king's request for an audience, and the king had become a Bábí, together with all of Persia? What if the kings and rulers to whom Bahá'u'lláh wrote eloquent epistles testifying to His station had accepted or even sincerely investigated His claims? Would not the world now be in a golden age of global peace?

Certainly we human beings have a degree of free will. Certainly each of these critical points in human history could have taken a different turn. And the fact is, according to Bahá'u'lláh, in the future, the transition from one dispensation to another will not meet with such turmoil and obstinacy. Bahá'u'lláh assures humanity that "This is the Day that shall not be followed by night . . ." (*The Summons of the Lord of Hosts,* p. 49)

Nevertheless according to Ṭarázu'lláh Samdandarí, 'Abdu'l-Bahá affirmed to him that it has always been the intent of God that the religion of the new Manifestation be spread "by the meek and lowly"[1] so that none may later claim that the emergence of the new Faith from obscurity to ascendancy resulted from any external influence or from any source other than its own inherent spiritual power.

WHY TEST US IN THE FIRST PLACE?

The fact that each of the revealed religions succeeded in spite of the opposition of the powerful and the failure of the generality of humankind to recognize the Manifestations in the initial stages of Their

---

1. This quote from 'Abdu'l-Bahá is from a transcript of notes taken from an interview with Ṭarázu'lláh Samdandarí.

revelations is in itself testimony and proof of the power latent within the revelations and the efficacy of the teaching techniques employed by the Manifestations. But we still might not understand why the Prophets must be so indirect, so disguised? What is the value of this test or judgment of our ability to recognize the new Manifestation? In secular educational systems, for example, the student is not challenged to search for who might be the next teacher.

THE EDUCATIONAL VALUE OF TESTING

For the wisest and best teachers, testing is neither a punishment nor an arbitrary obstacle. Useful testing is purposeful, instructional, and imaginative. When testing is cleverly conceived, it increases the student's resolve and induces thoughtful reflection about the principles underlying the problem at hand. For the master teacher, creative tests are a systematic method whereby the student is required to coalesce what has been learned, to reflect on that knowledge, and, afterwards, to demonstrate understanding by putting that knowledge into practice. As we have previously noted, the subsequent reciprocity between knowledge and action is also calculated to induce an escalation of both aspects of this process—acquiring greater increments of knowledge enhances the ability to express that knowledge in ever more expansive and creative forms of action, and so on.

As we noted in chapter 2, we are tested to recognize the beloved of our hearts, the Manifestation of God, so that we are prompted to become educated about the nature of that which we seek. Many commonplace analogies are capable of conveying the wisdom in this. For example, if we ask someone where to find a diamond, the person would most probably advise us to proceed to the nearest jewelry store. Likewise, once a religion is sufficiently established along with its institutions and places of worship, discovering the Manifestation becomes a lot easier. Indeed, many converts to the Bahá'í religion have come into the Faith as a result of visiting the Bahá'í Houses of Worship or the Bahá'í gardens on Mt. Carmel. Likewise, in the past the magnificent cathedrals and mosques have attracted seekers to Christianity and Islam.

But when the revelation of the Manifestation is incipient and largely concealed from obvious recognition, discovering the person of the Prophet would be tantamount to finding a diamond in the rough. Only an experienced gemologist would know likely places to find a diamond in its original condition, and even when the diamond is discovered, its character and magnificence remain concealed until its crude exterior has been removed, its surfaces have been finely polished, and it has been creatively cut so as to refract pure white light into an infinite array of colors. In other words, the inner brilliance and true character of the seemingly rough stone becomes apparent only after it has been thoroughly tested and tormented.

The test for one seeking diamonds, therefore, is to understand that this most exquisite and precious of jewels will be discovered only with great effort—digging through the dirt in the darkness of the bowels of earth, the most unlikely of places. The Manifestation of God for this day was chained and imprisoned in the filth and darkness of the Siyáh-Chál, then later in the putrid barracks in 'Akká. How can we expect that a king, a queen, a pope, a sulṭán, or any other figure of secular or religious prominence would have taken seriously letters penned by an unknown prisoner of the Ottoman Empire, regardless of how eloquent and remarkable the letters might have been?

WITHOUT TESTING, THERE CAN BE NO CERTITUDE

The converse of this axiom also reveals the wisdom in the Prophet's concealment. Let us presume that there is no concealment, no testing in this process. Let us presume that instead of veiled prophecies, abstract clues to character, and abstruse proofs of the advent of the new Manifestation, the guidance is without indirection or subtlety and that the directions for discovering the Manifestation are set forth in the most literal and ordinary terms.

Let us presume, for example, that instead of the clues surrounding the appearance of the "Comforter," Christ had simply stated that the next Manifestation would be born in the year 570 in Mecca and would belong to the Banu Hashim family. Who, can we assume, would have passed this "test"? Who would have shown up?

And if they did show up, why would they have shown up? And if they did recognize Muḥammad as fulfilling Christ's prophecy, would they actually agree to follow this simple leader of caravans, this un-learned merchant? Would they follow Him even if they were rich and powerful? And if they did agree to follow Him, what would be their motive for doing so? After receiving no material benefit, would they stay? And when the Prophet revealed laws they found contrary to their own teachings and their personal level of comfort, would they remain obedient? And if they were obedient and persecutions started, would they be steadfast? And if they were steadfast and faithful, would they begin to understand the basis for all their sacrifice?

Maybe the few who came for the right reason and who became confirmed in their belief would stick around in spite of all these tests. But we can be certain that over time most of those who showed up simply because they were told to be at a certain place at a certain time merely to discover a seemingly ordinary human being, would quickly lose interest. They would fail the test because they would not really understand the underlying and abiding rationale for their quest—to discover an Emissary from God providing them with personal and col-lective guidance capable of transforming them for eternity.

Surely this is the reason behind the concealment of the Prophets and Their refusal to use a sensational display of their power to attract a following. They want those who follow to be so desirous of spiritual development that they are willing to endure whatever obstacles come their way, and so pure of heart that they will know almost instantly the distinguishing character of the beloved. And while Bahá'u'lláh assures us that this is a day of recognition that will not be followed by the night of blindness, the same challenge will endure into the future—the test to recognize a Prophet of God in the guise of an ordinary human being, and the subsequent test to follow whatsoever He ordains.

THE TEST OF CIRCUMSTANTIAL PROBLEMS

As if the test of recognizing God made manifest in human form were not hard enough, Bahá'u'lláh explains that there is another more subtle test designed by the Creator regarding the social circumstances of the Prophet. As an example, Bahá'u'lláh cites the fact that Moses found it necessary to take the life of a man in defense of another and thus was reputed to be a murderer:

> And now ponder in thy heart the commotion which God stirreth up. Reflect upon the strange and manifold trials with which He doth test His servants. Consider how He hath suddenly chosen from among His servants, and entrusted with the exalted mission of divine guidance Him Who was known as guilty of homicide [Moses], Who, Himself, had acknowledged His cruelty, and Who for well-nigh thirty years had, in the eyes of the world, been reared in the home of Pharaoh and been nourished at his table. Was not God, the omnipotent King, able to withhold the hand of Moses from murder, so that manslaughter should not be attributed unto Him, causing bewilderment and aversion among the people? (Kitáb-i-Íqán, ¶58)

God was certainly capable of selecting someone who would not—in addition to the normal problems of becoming recognized as a Prophet—also be reputed to be a "murder." Similarly, Moses surely could have found some way of avoiding having to perform this act.

In this same discussion about these additional tests that God mandates, Bahá'u'lláh gives the example of the virgin birth of Christ. Bahá'u'lláh observes, as does Muḥammad in the Qur'án, that the virgin birth of Christ was not at the time a symbol of Mary's sanctity to those in her midst. It was in fact a rather wretched predicament for Mary, even as it was a severe test for others to believe that having a child born out of wedlock was somehow a spiritual proof of anything:

> Likewise, reflect upon the state and condition of Mary. So deep was the perplexity of that most beauteous countenance, so grievous her case, that she bitterly regretted she had ever been born. To this beareth witness the text of the sacred verse wherein it is mentioned that after Mary had given birth to Jesus, she bemoaned her plight and cried out: "O would that I had died ere this, and been a thing forgotten, forgotten quite!" . . . Reflect, what answer could Mary have given to the people around her? How could she claim that a Babe Whose father was unknown had been conceived of the Holy Ghost? (Kitáb-i-Íqán, ¶57)

Bahá'u'lláh explains that instead of perceiving this circumstance as a miraculous sign of Christ's identity as the Son of God, this miraculous sign became a "grievous test" for people to accept as the Messiah, one who "was known amongst the people as fatherless" (Kitáb-i-Íqán, ¶57)

Bahá'u'lláh concludes His discourse on this topic regarding circumstantial tests by noting in an ironic vein "how contrary are the ways of the Manifestations of God, as ordained by the King of creation, to the ways and desires of men!" He then observes that the more we come to study and comprehend the methods of these tests, these "divine mysteries" as He calls them, the more we will come to "grasp the purpose of God, the divine Charmer, the Best-Beloved" (Kitáb-i-Íqán, ¶61).

The epithet for God in this passage, "the divine Charmer," is of special note because it conveys so clearly a sense of God as being clever in the way He devises tests of a sort we least expect. Here again, we may call to mind the best qualities of the teachers we have had. Most likely they were animated, clever, and unpredictable. If they were truly inventive, they devised for us various indirect challenges that forced us to think for ourselves, to discover the difference between the obvious answer and the concealed or veiled key to a truth they were attempting to impart in a memorable way. And if we still recall these teachers and the methods they employed, then obviously this indirection and subtlety worked!

THE TEST OF HISTORICAL REFLECTION

Another test for those assessing the Bahá'í theory of the ontology of the Manifestations is found in the manner in which the chroniclers of the past religions describe events surrounding the lives of the Prophets of the more ancient religions. As we have mentioned, historians would sometimes attribute the punishment of a people to some sin committed by the Prophet.

'Abdu'l-Bahá devotes a chapter in *Some Answered Questions* to this very dilemma of how the Manifestations as perfect and immaculate Beings could conceivably commit a sin against God. His simple and logical explanation is that in every instance these passages are actually "directed to the people, through a wisdom which is absolute mercy, in order that the people may not be discouraged and disheartened." In other words, these reprimands "appear to be addressed to the Prophets; but though outwardly for the Prophets, they are in truth for the people and not for the Prophets" (p. 166).

'Abdu'l-Bahá notes that this same principle applies to those instances where, in Their own prayers, the Manifestations confess some inadequacy, even though They Themselves are freed from any flaws or error. This They do, 'Abdu'l-Bahá explains, as yet another indirect teaching technique—They are attempting to demonstrate to Their followers the prayerful and humble attitude that they must assume in their relationship with God: "How often the Prophets of God and His supreme Manifestations in Their prayers confess Their sins and faults! This is only to teach other men, to encourage and incite them to humility and meekness, and to induce them to confess their sins and faults. For these Holy Souls are pure from every sin and sanctified from faults." Appropriately, 'Abdu'l-Bahá concludes by observing that this process "will become evident and clear" to us once we have "diligently examined the Holy Books" for ourselves (*Some Answered Questions*, pp. 166, 169).

FASHIONING THE PERSONHOOD OF THE PROPHET—*THE SÚRIH OF THE TEMPLE*

As we will discuss in more detail in the final chapter, one of the foremost proofs of the Prophets' station is obvious to virtually anyone—Their constancy in the face of adversity. Logically, we must conclude that there is something credible about a decent person who willingly puts Himself in mortal danger for the sake of assisting humankind without the least possibility of any personal or material gain. Surely such a person is worthy of our attention and merits our examination of the veracity of any claims He might make regarding the reason for this personal sacrifice.

To conclude this examination of the personhood of the Prophet as one of the central teaching devices whereby God is made manifest among humankind, we would do well to study the Súrih of the Temple, in which Bahá'u'lláh portrays in a remarkably dramatic form the announcement by the "Maiden" to all creation of Bahá'u'lláh's station.

This tablet is among the most important and startling works of Bahá'u'lláh and was designated by Bahá'u'lláh as possessing a special status. Originally revealed during His stay in Adrianople (1864–68), the work depicts in vivid terms His spiritual experience during the first stirrings of His revelation while He was imprisoned in the Siyáh-Chál (1852). After His further exile to 'Akká, Bahá'u'lláh arranged for the Súrih of the Temple to be combined with five of His most potent and representative epistles to religious and political leaders of the world,[2] and then to be arranged calligraphically in the form of a Pentacle—a symbol of the human body.

This was among the first works that Bahá'u'lláh had published during the last years of His ministry. Toward the end of this work, the totality of which is some 134 pages in translation, Bahá'u'lláh appended the following:

> Thus have We built the Temple with the hands of power and might, could ye but know it. This is the Temple promised unto you in the Book. Draw ye nigh unto it. This is that which profiteth you, could ye but comprehend it. Be fair, O peoples of the earth! Which is preferable, this, or a temple which is built of clay? Set your faces towards it. Thus have ye been commanded by God, the Help in Peril, the Self-Subsisting. Follow ye His bidding, and praise ye God, your Lord, for that which He hath bestowed upon you. He, verily, is the Truth. No God is there but He. He revealeth what He pleaseth, through His words "Be and it is." (*The Summons of the Lord of Hosts,* p. 207)

---

2. The epistles penned to Pope Pius IX, Napoleon III, Czar Alexander II, Queen Victoria, and Náṣiri'd-Dín Sháh.

CONCEPTUAL STRUCTURE OF THE WORK

The relevance of the work to our analysis of how the personhood of the Manifestation both tests and confirms His station is fairly obvious. The Temple being built and adorned and fortified with powers and virtues represents the human guise or persona that the Manifestation of God will assume—the attributes of God will become made manifest in human form. Also obvious is the double entendre whereby the "Temple" is also the spiritual edifice wherein all who abide will be safe, secure, and enlightened.

Bahá'u'lláh's addition of five of His tablets to world religious and political leaders to the Súrih of the Temple itself has the effect of representing the challenge to all humankind to recognize in the form of a human temple the reality of Bahá'u'lláh as a Manifestation of God. These lengthy epistles, unlike the mystical tenor of the Súrih of the Temple itself, contain very explicit advice and very precise guidance about a course of action that the world's leaders should undertake to facilitate the advent of Bahá'u'lláh's vision for a world commonwealth of nations in which a permanent global peace will be secured.

Symbolically, the addition of these five tablets represents the five points of the pentacle, and can be interpreted as expressing the idea that the ultimate goal of human history is to bring about the kingdom of God in a human social structure of global proportions. These letters further emphasize the fact that this process can be completed only when the essential components of a world civilization are implemented by these same world leaders according to the advice and overall plan given by the Manifestation.

The Súrih of the Temple begins with a series of beatitudes in which Bahá'u'lláh praises God for having revealed verses through Him. Bahá'u'lláh also praises God for all the tribulation that "He hath destined to befall His Servant Who repaireth unto Him in His affliction and grief" (*The Summons of the Lord of Hosts,* p. 6). We will touch on the meaning of this enigmatic preamble in the last chapter about the suffering of the Prophet, but for now we should observe that following this praise is a first-person account by Bahá'u'lláh of His experience in the Siyáh-Chál where He was "engulfed in tribulations."

As we have already noted, during these first stirrings of His own revelation He describes beholding a Maiden[3] who embodies "the remembrance of the name of My Lord." Suspended in the air before Him, she begins "imparting to both My inward and outer being tidings which rejoiced My soul, and the souls of God's honored servants." She then points her finger at the head of Bahá'u'lláh and proceeds to address "all who are in heaven and all who are on earth" regarding the station of Bahá'u'lláh and the significance of what is about to take place in the course of human history. The remainder of this work consists of Bahá'u'lláh's depiction of the proclamation of the Veiled Maiden.

THE CENTRAL ALLEGORY

The heart of this extraordinary work is the allegory or analogy between the physical temple—or personage that is Bahá'u'lláh in human form—and the spiritual or intellectual significance of the "Temple" as representing a sanctuary for the worship and praise of God.

In beauteous poetic images, the Maiden addresses the Temple, adorns and praises the Temple, and in successive sections, exhorts the "Living Temple" to prepare itself for what it must endure and undertake. She exhorts the "Eyes of this Temple" not to look upon the heavens or the earth, "for We have created you to behold Our own Beauty." She exhorts the "Ears of this Temple" not to listen to any "idle clamor," but to "hearken unto the voice of your Lord." In similar fashion, the Maid

---

3. I have capitalized references to the Maiden because she effectively represents the Holy Spirit itself. Pronominal references to her in the text are likewise upper case.

speaks to the "Tongue of this Temple," the "Feet of this Temple," the "Breast of this Temple," and the "Inmost Heart of this Temple."

Interspersed among these exhortations is a passionate and authoritative summons to the peoples of the world and to their leaders to pay heed to this "Living Temple" and to the words He will utter. She affirms that this Temple is a perfect Manifestation of the divine beauty ("a mirror unto the kingdom of names").

The tablet concludes with the Maid commanding the Temple (Bahá'u'lláh) to "sound the trumpet" and to "raise the clarion call of Thy Lord," even as She cautions the people of the world to "take heed lest ye hesitate in recognizing this resplendent Beauty when once He hath appeared in the plenitude of His sovereign might and majesty":

> Hasten, then, to attain the living waters of His grace, and be not of the negligent. As to him who hesitateth, though it be for less than a moment, God shall verily bring his works to naught and return him to the seat of wrath; wretched indeed is the abode of them that tarry! (*The Summons of the Lord of Hosts*, p. 81)

14

THE LANGUAGE
OF THE PROPHETS

*The reading of the scriptures and holy books is for no other purpose
except to enable the reader to apprehend their meaning and unravel
their innermost mysteries. Otherwise reading, without
understanding, is of no abiding profit unto man.*

—Bahá'u'lláh

Just as the Manifestations Themselves appear among us disguised as
ordinary human beings, so the true meaning of Their language is likewise often veiled or concealed so that we are challenged to pierce the
literal or surface meaning to discern the heart and core of truth that
lies beneath.

But as with the concealment of the personhood of the Prophet, the
purpose in this indirection with regard to the language of the Manifestations is neither guile nor secrecy. The fact is that this educational
process forces us, the believers, to become adept students at thinking
for ourselves—a process that is tantamount to a definition of true
education. In this sense, obtaining the inner or spiritual meaning from
words of the Manifestation is an inseparable part of the meaning itself.

In learning how to read and understand the language of the Prophets,
we can begin to appreciate how authentic spiritual learning must tran-

scend some form of catechism or the mere memorization and recitation of verses: "The reading of the scriptures and holy books is for no other purpose except to enable the reader to apprehend their meaning and unravel their innermost mysteries. Otherwise reading, without understanding, is of no abiding profit unto man" (Bahá'u'lláh, Kitáb-i-Íqán, ¶185).

This axiom should not be taken to imply that reading or memorizing the "creative word" without understanding has *no* value—but it has a limited value, a value that does not endure and has no "abiding profit." Furthermore, since there are various degrees or levels of understanding, we are always exhorted to strive beyond whatever level of understanding we think we have presently achieved in order to attain an ever more lofty and expansive sense of what the Manifestation intends.

These observations do not imply that the language of the Manifestations is inevitably difficult in any ordinary sense. They do not usually employ esoteric jargon or an obscure literary technique. Bahá'u'lláh makes the revealing observation that our understanding of the words of the Manifestations is not dependent on intellectual acumen or any ordinary sort of learning, but rather on purity of motive and spiritual receptivity: "The understanding of His words and the comprehension of the utterances of the Birds of Heaven are in no wise dependent upon human learning. They depend solely upon purity of heart, chastity of soul, and freedom of spirit" (Kitáb-i-Íqán, ¶233).

HISTORICAL CONSEQUENCES OF WORD

Because of the historical failure on the part of followers and students of religion to comprehend this indirect process by which we gain understanding of the language of the Prophets, Bahá'u'lláh has made the symbolic nature of scripture a principal theme in His most important doctrinal work, the Book of Certitude.

He introduces this concept early on, but we might find it useful to examine one of His concluding statements about what He describes as the twofold nature of the language of the Manifestations. In His summary discourse on the language of the Manifestations, Bahá'u'lláh states that not everything the Manifestations reveal has some veiled or symbolic meaning. The laws, for example, are often straightforward and devoid of allusion. In this general sense, the Manifestations employ two broad categories or modes of language in Their utterance:

> It is evident unto thee that the Birds of Heaven and Doves of Eternity speak a twofold language. One language, the outward language, is devoid of allusions, is unconcealed and unveiled; that it may be a guiding lamp and a beaconing light whereby wayfarers may attain the heights of holiness, and seekers may advance into the realm of eternal reunion. Such are the unveiled traditions and the evident verses already mentioned. The other language is veiled and concealed, so that whatever lieth hidden in the heart of the malevolent may be made manifest and their innermost being be disclosed. (Kitáb-i-Íqán, ¶283)

Naturally it is the second category of language that causes confusion and consternation among the followers of a single revelation, as well as between the followers of diverse revelations. This conflict most often arises when statements that are intended to be metaphorical or symbolic are taken out of context and presumed to be literal.

For example, when Christ says to His disciples that when they see Him, they see God, some believers and ecclesiasts interpreted this statement literally. Consequently, a number of ecclesiasts in the evolving Christian institutions began to assert that Christ was God in the flesh.

It was this same sort of literalist interpretation that led the Jews who heard Christ's teachings to assume that His statement about being able to rebuild the Temple in three days referred to the physical edifice that was the Temple in Jerusalem. Therefore they mocked Him as He was dying on the cross. From their understanding, He did not have sufficient power to save Himself from a criminal's execution, let alone rebuild the Temple in three days.

Later Christian followers did not fair much better. They came to believe that Christ was alluding to His own body which, they inferred, had been physically resurrected and had ascended to a physical heaven in three days. Whereas a more useful figurative or symbolic meaning might allude to the three dispensations (the Day of Christ, the Day of Muḥammad, and the Day of the Báb) before the Day of Bahá'u'lláh would bring forth the righteousness of God in the social form of a global polity constructed on spiritual principles. Another aspect of such an inference would be that Christ is alluding to Bahá'u'lláh's Súrih of the Temple, a hallmark among the revealed works of Bahá'u'lláh. Thus the "Temple"—the physical expression of spiritual principles through three successive Manifestations and through three successive religious institutions—that would be torn asunder by the followers of three successive dispensations would, in the "Day of God," the "Day of Resurrection," become rebuilt in its fullness.

THE BOOK OF CERTITUDE AS
PRIMER ON SYMBOLIC LANGUAGE

In this same discussion Bahá'u'lláh observes that one of the educational purposes of this twofold language is to challenge the believers to learn how to discern which is which—whether or not the Manifestation is speaking literally or metaphorically.

By way of explaining this idea of language as an instructional tool, Bahá'u'lláh observes that some of the language is veiled so that "whatever lieth hidden in the heart of the malevolent may be made manifest and their innermost being be disclosed" (Kitáb-i-Íqán, ¶283). In other words, because some passages are open to interpretation, one will be inclined to find in them a meaning that best suits one's personal desires, thereby revealing one's private motives and inner character. Those who are in search of power or authority will interpret the text in such a way that it will redound to their own benefit. Those who sincerely are in search of spiritual enlightenment and transformation, however, will more likely understand the spiritual truth concealed in the garment of language.

In a demonstration of the critical nature of this indirect teaching method, Bahá'u'lláh devotes more than a hundred pages to analyzing three verses from Matthew (24:29–31) that allude to Christ's return. His stated purpose in this exercise is to demonstrate that a proper symbolic reading and interpretation of this scripture would have enabled Christians to recognize Muḥammad. To His most immediate audience, the learned Muslims, Bahá'u'lláh simultaneously reveals that this failure was not due to the corruption of the text in regard to Christian scripture, as Muslim clerics had claimed, but to their own inability to understand the symbolic and metaphorical expressions of Christ's words. Had they known how to read Christ's utterance in its poetic or symbolic meaning, the Muslim clerics could have demonstrated to Christians the proofs of the station of Muḥammad in the prophecies of Christ's own words.

Among the prominent symbolic terms Bahá'u'lláh elucidates from these three Christian verses are the precursive signs of the advent of the "Son of man": "the oppression of those days," the sun becoming "darkened," the "moon" failing to give light, the "stars" falling "from heaven," and the "earth" being "shaken." He subsequently explains in detail the meaning of each of these signs that herald the advent itself: "the tribes of the earth" shall "mourn," the "Son of man" will come "in the clouds of heaven with power and great glory," and "he shall send his angels with a great sound of a trumpet."

After explaining how all these symbolic and metaphorical terms are fulfilled with the advent of Muḥammad, Bahá'u'lláh explains that the same sort of symbolic terms from the Qur'án foretell and herald the advent of the Qá'im (the Báb). Bahá'u'lláh notes, however, that the vast majority of Muslim clerics have also interpreted their own scripture literally rather than symbolically, and Muḥammad's assertion that He is the "Seal of the Prophets" has been interpreted to mean that God would send no further revelation of any sort. Consequently, Bahá'u'lláh explains, most have deprived themselves of becoming capable of recognizing the Qá'im and benefitting from His revelation.

Thus history proceeded according to this ironic replication of the same fundamental error of spiritual leaders not being able to understand the "inner" or spiritual significance of the very scriptures they profess to revere.

FASHIONING LANGUAGE TO BEFIT THE REVELATION

While the language of the Manifestations may be twofold, the particular form that Their utterance takes depends entirely on the historical and cultural orientation of those peoples who will be the primary recipients of the revelation. As we have noted, Bahá'u'lláh employs a variety of styles and genres because His revelation is destined to unite all peoples. But the previous Manifestations fashioned their language and the style of presentation to the various circumstances surrounding both the appearance of the new "Book" and the character and capacity of the peoples the revelation would serve over the course of its duration. A brief examination of how the Manifestation fashions His utterance to befit the exigencies of His plan will help us appreciate the creativity and ingenuity with which the Prophets employ language to teach us.

THE LANGUAGE OF CHRIST

We find from the author of Matthew the following observation: "All these things spake Jesus unto the multitude in parables; and without a parable spake he not unto them that it might be fulfilled which was spoken by the prophet, saying, 'I will open my mouth in parables; I will utter things which have been kept secret from the foundation of the world'" (13:34–35).[1]

Two concepts are particularly noteworthy regarding this comment on the teaching style employed by Christ with regard to the form of discourse He chooses for His primary audience, the Jews of His day. First of all, the author of Matthew presumes that it is Christ's intention to fulfill past prophecies about His advent, and certainly Christ seems to confirm this speculation. In virtually everything Christ says, He interweaves verse upon verse from the Old Testament prophets and scriptures. Obviously Christ is well aware how these verses allude to Himself as the promised Messiah. Second, as Christ Himself explains to His disciples, His use of parables as the primary methodology with which to convey spiritual concepts to His audience has the explicit purpose of awakening them from spiritual lethargy by challenging the literalism of their understanding of scripture and spiritual concepts.

Therefore as the Jewish scholars listen to His words, they taunt him and attempt to trick Him with difficult questions derived from their own understanding, but it is readily apparent that the majority of them are totally incapable of discerning the spiritual significance or inner meaning of His responses, thereby fulfilling the prophecy in Isaiah (6:9–10):

And the disciples came, and said unto him, "Why speakest thou unto them in parables?" He answered and said unto them, "Because it is given unto you to know the mysteries of the kingdom of heaven, but to them it is not given. For whosoever hath, to

---

1. The "prophet" the author of Matthew is referring to is the author of Psalm 78, and the particular passage is the second verse.

him shall be given, and he shall have more abundance, but whosoever hath not, from him shall be taken away even that he hath. Therefore speak I to them in parables because they seeing see not, and hearing they hear not, neither do they understand. And in them is fulfilled the prophecy of Isaiah, which saith, 'By hearing ye shall hear, and shall not understand; and seeing ye shall see, and shall not perceive. For this people's heart is waxed gross, and their ears are dull of hearing, and their eyes they have closed; lest at any time they should see with their eyes and hear with their ears, and should understand with their heart, and should be converted, and I should heal them.'" (Matthew 13:13–15)

Christ then explains further why he employs parables as His principal teaching technique by explicating to them one of His more well-known parables, the parable of the sower. Christ explains that in this analogy, different types of soil are compared to the varying receptivity among those who receive the seeds, which are, in reality, the words of the Manifestation of God.

The point is that Christ consistently throughout His brief ministry employs one particular style of teaching with regard to His words or utterances—analogical or allegorical stories. Interestingly, while parables are an extremely effective way to explain complex abstract notions or metaphysical concepts, they can also be quite perplexing and difficult for someone accustomed to a literalistic approach to language. It is in this manner that parables may offer a major test of the spiritual capacities and sensibilities of the hearer.

One particular virtue of the parable is that it is capable of functioning on a variety of levels of meaning. For example, a young child could understand the fundamental meaning of the parable of the sower—how different types of soil represent different sorts of people, and how scattering seeds could represent words being spoken into the air to be received by different hearers. But on a higher level of applicability, one could apply the "soil" in this same analogy to characterize various intellectual attitudes or distinct types of personalities. Likewise, the outcome of the seeds or words being exposed to these different sorts of audiences could well be analyzed in terms of the way various people process language according to their character and background. One could further explicate the analogy in terms of the variety of plants that might emerge according to the nature of the soil and the type of seed sown, and the fruit that the plants might produce—the transformation resulting from the actions of those who receive the creative word into their hearts and minds.

Metaphors and various other forms of symbol and analogy are perhaps the most useful linguistic tool for teaching at every level, whether for a young child or for a graduate student. One of the reasons these linguistic puzzles are such a potent teaching tool is that they require the student to become actively involved in the process of gaining understanding. The teacher may provide hints or clues as to how the puzzle can be resolved, but ultimately the listeners or readers must exercise free will and personal effort in order to understand for themselves how the analogy works and how it can be applied to various levels of meaning.

THE LANGUAGE OF MUHAMMAD

The style of the Qur'án is quite different. Relatively speaking, it is more straightforward, even as Christ had told his disciples that the Comforter would tell them "plainly" of the Father: "These things have I spoken unto you in proverbs, but the time cometh, when I shall no more speak unto you in proverbs, but I shall shew you plainly of the Father" (John 16:25).

The Qur'án consists of segments (the súrihs), each of which is a separate session or revelatory experience as portrayed by Muhammad. The dramatic literary technique employed by Muhammad is to persuade His audience that at certain more or less arbitrary moments, the Angel Gabriel will suddenly utilize Him as the channel or vehicle through which to deliver the Word of God to humankind. As we noted earlier, these sessions or revelatory experiences would sometimes appear similar to a trance or seizure. No doubt this mystical process was impressive proof to the desert tribal people of Arabia, especially since the language that emerged from this "unlearned One" was more eloquent and more authoritative than anything they had ever heard in their native Arabic language.

Each súrih in the Qur'án has its own structure and theme. And while there are, in addition to the laws of the Qur'án, a series of major themes repeated throughout, we are hard put to discern in this remarkable revelation some formulaic order because Muḥammad Himself did not assemble the súrihs into their present order. It would not be incorrect, in other words, to assert that Muḥammad revealed one hundred and fourteen works of varying length and theme.

So it is that the major topics of the Qur'án are repeated throughout, like various colored threads interwoven through a vast tapestry. Among those we have already observed is the singularity or absolute sovereignty of God; the unity of purpose and the equality of station of all the Messengers (*Rasul*) of God; the continuity of the divine covenant beginning with Adam, rearticulated with Abraham, and fulfilled with Muḥammad; and obedience to the law of God as an integral and inseparable part of recognizing the Messenger.

This is not to say that there are no verses that are obscure or symbolic, that are not metaphorical or abstruse in the Qur'án. As the Báb and Bahá'u'lláh explain throughout Their own writings, in addition to the mysterious "disconnected letters" that appear at the beginning of certain súrihs, there are many passages in the Qur'án whose meaning is almost entirely indecipherable until they are explicated by the Báb and Bahá'u'lláh. And yet we should repeat what we have previously noted—

that the language of each revelation is carefully tailored to what will best communicate the Word of God to a particular audience at a particular historical period. The Báb observes, "These utterances are revealed according to your measure, not to God's, and unto this beareth witness that which is enshrined in the knowledge of God, did ye but know. Unto this testifieth He Who is the Mouthpiece of God, could ye but understand. By the righteousness of God! Were We to lift the veil ye would swoon away" (*Selections from the Writings of the Báb*, 1:2:4).

THE LANGUAGE OF
THE BÁB AND BAHÁ'U'LLÁH

The advent of the twin revelations of the Báb and Bahá'u'lláh inaugurates a new age in our collective religious and secular history on planet Earth, the arrival of the maturation of humankind. No longer will the spiritual transformation of our global society be accomplished piecemeal through a succession of Manifestations who, from a contemporary perspective, seem to have come arbitrarily, first to one place, then another, without any obvious rationale or connectedness that we can comprehend.

ACCESSIBLE LANGUAGE
FOR A GLOBAL REVELATION

As all the Prophets have incrementally tried to explain, all of the bits and pieces of past revelations are, when understood through the perspective of the concept of progressive revelation, necessary stages or ingredients of a divine plan of education whereby the human student body has been prepared for this, our graduation day. Now we are capable of "getting it"!

There is One God and one religion, the religion of God. It has been revealed in stages and in different places according to the needs and capacities of different people in different stages of social and spiritual evolution. Now we have emerged as a single people in a unified global society, the single proof of which (should any still be required) is that we are presently threatened with a variety of global crises which can only be resolved by concerted collective and collaborative action on the part of all the peoples and nations of the world.

Of course, graduation from one level of education means only that we are ready to enter the next more advanced stage of learning. In this sense, our "maturation" as a global society means we are ready to enter "college" where the nuts-and-bolts mode of our preparatory learning we have previously acquired will become assembled into a coherent program of more advanced enlightenment.

But as the Heralds of this new reality, the Báb and Bahá'u'lláh had before Them the most enormous and daunting undertaking that any Manifestations had ever faced before, or that any Manifestation will ever face again, at least on planet Earth—to bring together all the diverse peoples and cultures under the aegis of a single faith in a single community unified under the banner of justice and love, of sovereignty and reverence.

Naturally it is this task that underlies much of the guidance bequeathed by Bahá'u'lláh. Included in His plan for a unified global community are a global peace secured by a system of collective justice and a world peace-keeping force; a universal systems of weights, measures, and currency; a universal auxiliary language and script; global oversight of natural resources; universal compulsory education; and an economic system that, while encouraging individual initiative and rewarding excellence, would provide for the elimination of the vast extremes that presently exist between the exceptionally wealthy and the extremely poor.

Because Bahá'u'lláh's revelation contains the plan for human society as a whole, His blueprint for a world civilization is devoid of ritual and is carefully designed to be without cultural bias or orientation.

Every system and every practice of the Bahá'í religion—all its laws, administrative institutions, and spiritual practices—can be employed just as easily in one culture as it can in another.

TWIN TRUMPET CALLS

Even though the first followers of the Báb and Bahá'u'lláh were primarily Muslims living in various Middle Eastern cultures, the revelations of both Manifestations are vast and varied, both in literary style and subject. The themes range from matters of personal comportment to concerns as encompassing as constructing a world federation of governments. The language of both Manifestations is equally diverse in genre or literary forms, from simple prayers and jewel-like aphorisms to lengthy discourses and treatises.

Symbolically these twin revelations represent the twin trumpets foretold in the Qur'án, the first of which would awaken, astound, and dumbfound humanity, and the second of which would revive and unite all the diverse kindred of the earth, regardless of social or educational backgrounds or conditions. Bahá'u'lláh states:

> The summons and the message which We gave were never intended to reach or to benefit one land or one people only. Mankind in its entirety must firmly adhere to whatsoever hath been revealed and vouchsafed unto it. Then and only then will it attain unto true liberty. The whole earth is illuminated with the resplendent glory of God's Revelation. (*Tablets of Bahá'u'lláh,* p. 89)

At the heart of this task is a blueprint for how this structure can be created and sustained even while this same global commonwealth secures and maintains justice, universal suffrage, and individual rights and freedoms. The guidance for this process resides most obviously and prominently in His Most Holy Book, yet even a cursory overview of the variety of styles with which Bahá'u'lláh has spoken on behalf of God to the peoples of the world is sufficient to amaze even the most cynical among us.

THE REVELATION OF THE BÁB

Before we undertake a brief overview of how Bahá'u'lláh employs language and literary style to educate and unify all the peoples of the world, we must first acknowledge the rather astounding revelation of the Báb. For even though He was in strict confinement for six years of His seven-year ministry before His execution in 1850, the Báb revealed an amazingly vast repository of works that varied in style and tenor. In responding to a query addressed to the Báb as He was being examined by a panel of ecclesiastical dignitaries of Tabríz, the Báb affirmed that "His words constitute the most incontrovertible evidence of His mission." He subsequently "adduced verses from the Qur'án to establish the truth of His assertion, and claimed to be able to reveal, within the space of two days and two nights, verses equal to the whole of that Book" (Shoghi Effendi, *God Passes By,* p. 21).

THE SUPREME MYSTERY OF HIS REVELATION

Surely one of the great mysteries in the history of religion is the fact that the Báb states quite openly that His religion or dispensation is destined to endure but a brief period of time, nine years (1844–53), and yet He reveals such an abundance of work that we are only beginning to catalogue His writings.

As we have mentioned, no doubt because the Báb foreknew He would be deterred from conveying His revealed work to His followers, He beseeches the next Manifestation ("Him Whom God will manifest") to withhold overtly declaring His station until the year nineteen (1862). Nevertheless, volumes of the Báb's revelation have yet to be published in their original languages of Persian and Arabic, let alone translated and published in English and other languages. Furthermore, a number of works were lost or destroyed.

Because so many of the Bábí leaders were executed even before the Báb Himself was martyred, one of the major tasks that befell Bahá'u'lláh after His exile to Baghdad was to have the works of the Báb transcribed so that the Bábí community would have access to some of the writings of their own Faith. Effectively, even though Bahá'u'lláh had already experienced the first intimation of the beginning of His own revelation, He could hardly explain how he was fulfilling promises and prophecies of texts that the Bábís themselves had not yet had a chance to read. The result was that Bahá'u'lláh had to focus much of His attention during His ten-year exile in Baghdad to completing some portion of what the Báb Himself would have done had He not been executed and had the dissemination of His writings not been curtailed by religious and government authorities.

BAHÁ'U'LLÁH'S NINE STYLES FOR COMPLETENESS

Let us now complete our task of trying to capture a sense of the methodology by which the Manifestations use language as an essential tool for teaching us. Even a summary glance at the nature of the revelation of Bahá'u'lláh can provide us with wonderful evidence of how the Manifestation fashions His revelation to the exigencies of the age.

Bahá'u'lláh states in the Súrih of the Temple that His work appears in nine different modes or styles: "Say: We have revealed Our verses in nine different modes. Each one of them bespeaketh the sovereignty of God, the Help in Peril, the Self-Subsisting. A single one of them sufficeth for a proof unto all who are in the heavens and on the earth; yet the people, for the most part, persist in their heedlessness. Should it be Our wish, We would reveal them in countless other modes" (*The Summons of the Lord of Hosts*, p. 26).

Some have interpreted this literally as meaning that Bahá'u'lláh wrote in nine specific literary modes or genres. Since Bahá'u'lláh employs more than nine specific styles, there may be symbolic meaning to the statement as He Himself never explains what those nine "modes" are, nor does any other authoritative source.

The number nine in the Bahá'í writings symbolizes, among other things, the concept of "completion" or "perfection" or "sufficiency." It is in this sense, perhaps, that the two architectural constraints for a Bahá'í House of worship are that it contain nine entrances of equal stature and design as doorways to a central dome. The symbolic significance of this arrangement is that all the past world religions throughout history have been valid pathways to the same God.

As we have already discussed, the Bahá'í teachings recognize all world religions as having been sent from the same source to provide spiritual education and a gradually expanding understanding of the same God. Clearly there have been many more than nine revelations, but since the number nine symbolizes "perfection" or "sufficiency," this symbolic arrangement alludes to the fact that God will never leave humankind without a path, without sufficient guidance in the form of these divine Emissaries and the revelations They bring.

Possibly in this same vein, Bahá'u'lláh intends to imply that He has created a sufficiency of literary modes for every individual, regardless of intelligence or literary taste or preference. Certainly such seems to be the implication of the following statement of Bahá'u'lláh in the Book of Certitude:

> We have variously and repeatedly set forth the meaning of every theme, that perchance every soul, whether high or low, may obtain, according to his measure and capacity, his share and portion thereof. Should he be unable to comprehend a certain argument, he may, thus, by referring unto another, attain his purpose.

"That all sorts of men may know where to quench their thirst."
(Kitáb-i-Íqán, ¶189)

A SAMPLING OF PERFECTION

A single chapter such as this is hardly adequate to describe comprehensively the depth or breadth of the revelation of Bahá'u'lláh. As has already been noted, I have written a sort of introductory reader's guide to the nature of Bahá'u'lláh's revelatory works entitled *The Ocean of His Words*. Likewise, Adib Taherzadeh has produced *The Revelation of Bahá'u'lláh,* a most excellent four-volume introduction to the historical background for most of Bahá'u'lláh's major works. Valuable commentary on some of the major themes and literary features of the major works of Bahá'u'lláh has been authoritatively noted by Shoghi Effendi in his survey of Bahá'í history entitled *God Passes By*. Shoghi Effendi has likewise made helpful and enlightening observations in the context of his discussion of major themes of the works of Bahá'u'lláh that are collected in various publications, such as *The World Order of Bahá'u'lláh, The Promised Day is Come, The Advent of Divine Justice,* and *Bahá'í Administration*. In addition, Bahá'í historian Hasan Balyuzi composed what is presently now the most complete biography of Bahá'u'lláh, *Bahá'u'lláh: The King of Glory,* in which he also makes a number of valuable comments on and explications of some of the major works of Bahá'u'lláh.

In light of these studies, as well as countless other studies that have been made and that will in the future delve more deeply into the fathomless depths of the ocean of Bahá'u'lláh's words, we need do no more here than observe that the master Teacher for this age has bequeathed to us, His students, a repository of texts of such variety and inexhaustible delight, that we can quite easily spend our lifetime studying them. I myself have humbly spent more than fifty years immersed in these works without feeling the least bit competent to assert that I "have a handle" on Bahá'u'lláh's work. I feel I have done little more than scratch the surface.

GENERIC VARIETY

Suffice it to say that Bahá'u'lláh revealed literally hundreds of works. The most important of these have been translated into English, but hundreds more remain to be published in the original Persian and Arabic, let alone translated and published in English and other languages. The more varied categories of style and genre we encounter indeed do provide an enticing gateway to the most simple and sincere soul or to the most complex and astute scholar.

There are mystical treatises, such as the Seven Valleys and the Four Valleys. For the Persian Bahá'í, steeped in the poetic traditions of Rumí and other gifted masters, the figurative images, allusions, and symbols in these works are especially rich and instructive. Among earlier works of import is the beauteous collection of jewel-like poetry in the Persian and Arabic verses of the Hidden Words, a work in which Bahá'u'lláh has synthesized all the essential spiritual verities of past revelations, has "taken the inner essence" of each verity, and has "clothed it in the garment of brevity . . ." (the Hidden Words, p. 3).

Bahá'u'lláh has likewise bequeathed us doctrinal or philosophical essays, such as the Tablet of Wisdom and His principal doctrinal work the Book of Certitude. Shoghi Effendi describes this particular essay as "an *apologia* revealed in defense of the Bábí Revelation" (*God Passes By*, p. 172). He further describes this treatise as a "model of Persian prose, of a style at once original, chaste and vigorous, and remarkably lucid, both cogent in argument and matchless in its irresistible eloquence," a work which was penned in "fulfillment of the prophecy of the Báb, Who had specifically stated that the Promised One would complete the text of the unfinished Persian Bayán," and which set forth "the Grand Redemptive Scheme of God" (*God Passes By*, p. 139).

We have in this study had occasion to mention Bahá'u'lláh's use of allegory as employed in both the Súrih of the Temple and in the Tablet of the Holy Mariner. We have also discussed Bahá'u'lláh's book of laws, the Kitáb-i-Aqdas (the Most Holy Book), as well as His remarkable epistles to world leaders, including *The Book of My Covenant, The Epistle to the Son of the Wolf,* and various others.

But however abbreviated and inadequate our summary of the revelation of Bahá'u'lláh might be, we must make mention of the exquisite repository of prayers and meditations He revealed. There are prayers for healing, grief, marriage, children, and for the departed. There are supplications articulating for us every nuance of our inmost heart—our gratitude and praise, our fears, our longing to be faithful and constant, our pleas for help and forgiveness and understanding. Within these passages is the voice of God speaking to us personally, reassuring us, comforting us, empowering us, imploring us, and, perhaps most important of all, speaking on our behalf with a sensitivity and eloquence we could never hope to devise for ourselves.

It is needless to go on when the sense of our general conclusion is clear—that even to begin studying the works of Bahá'u'lláh is an awe-inspiring undertaking. And yet, as any student who has dared test these waters will readily attest, it is a venture of unspeakable and relentless joy. Whichever way one turns, there abide húrís waiting to be unveiled. With every glance we find ourselves engulfed in the melodies that could only descend from the authentic voice of God entrancing us, instructing us, exhorting us to strive ever more arduously to discover who we are by discerning the signs of divinity everywhere around us and, most powerfully of all, latent within our own being. At last, we are left speechless, except perhaps to exclaim, "No thing have I perceived, except that I perceived God within it, God before it, or God after it" (*Gleanings,* no. 90.2).

15

THE LAWS OF THE PROPHETS

Say: True liberty consisteth in man's submission unto My
commandments, little as ye know it. Were men to observe that which
We have sent down unto them from the Heaven of Revelation, they
would, of a certainty, attain unto perfect liberty.

—Bahá'u'lláh

It is a natural reflex for us to think of laws as restrictions. We grudgingly submit to them because we fear the consequences of disobedience, but usually we grumble at the limits they impose on our personal freedom. Of course, when we step back a little and consider what society would be like without laws, we quickly realize that any mental images of what delight we might derive from driving our cars as fast as we want, are instantly replaced by grotesque images of crashes, pillaging, plunder, and total chaos.

The fact is that without these troublesome laws, any personal freedom we thought we had would quickly vanish. All social systems would immediately degenerate, along with our personal supplies of electricity, water, sewage, and police protection. Without law, there can be no freedom, and yet as a society we strive for that sane balance between individual rights and freedoms and the necessity that we as a society deter individuals from infringing on the rights of others. There is, in short, a necessary reciprocity, a covenant, a social contract between the law-abiding citizen and the law-enforcing agencies employed by that same society to maintain law and order.

The laws of a healthy society thus emerge from the willing consent of the people and those who represent them in legislative agencies. But in the healthiest models of social order, there exists *not* an ever fluctuating balance between personal rights and freedoms and the necessary constraints that provide security for the social body politic, but rather a mutuality of interests. In the healthiest models of society there is a shared moral perspective where the well-being and felicity of the individual is totally consonant with the well-being and felicity of the social collective.

The present problem in contemporary society is that we no longer have a shared moral perspective about much of anything. For the most part, contemporary governance is based almost entirely on material-ist exigencies and very little on concepts of moral imperatives, such as the desire to instill virtue in our children or to construct a social milieu where our good character is valued more highly than our net worth. Clearly, the balance of law has shifted in favor of the rights of the individual over any sort of collective security or the protection of spiritual values.

Yet when a new Manifestation appears, He restructures the collec-tive moral perspective in terms of the altered exigencies in the social terrain. He redefines or re-describes and refines the moral portrait of the good person, the just citizen, the noble neighbor, the true friend. He re-envisions the roles and relationships of the healthy and felicitous family dwelling in the context of a redesigned community environ-ment. Moreover, in the case of Bahá'u'lláh, the entire global body politic wherein these redesigned communities exist is itself defined in such a manner that there is no longer an attempt to find that balance, to sacrifice either individual freedoms or the collective good to discern a comfort zone somewhere in the middle.

In the society Bahá'u'lláh has designed, there exists a mutuality of interests. The increased health and strength of the individual is integral to and inseparable from the prosperity and health of the body politic as a whole. In addition, the system of governance and laws and legislative tools that Bahá'u'lláh has devised is infinitely flexible and adaptable in its applicability, relying as it does on paradigms of governance rather than a vast or exacting canon of specific ordinances.

THE CONCEPT OF LAW AS FREEDOM

One of the foundational principles of Bahá'í law that distinguishes the governmental and civil systems envisioned by Bahá'u'lláh is that, when properly and justly devised, laws serve as sane and healthy guidance, as the path to the greatest degree of freedom—presuming that we understand our own nature and what best develops, sustains, and cultivates that nature. It is precisely in accord with this underlying concept of law that Bahá'u'lláh observes, "My commandments are the lamps of My loving providence among My servants, and the keys of My mercy for My creatures" (Kitáb-i-Aqdas, ¶3).

This sentiment contrasts markedly with the view that laws are created solely to forge some compromise between the public good and private freedom, a perilous conciliation created from the purely secular or materialist perspectives that create persistent and irreconcilable tension within the state. The offspring of this tension is a pendulum effect throughout the history of governance wherein there are periodic shifts from "conservative" to "liberal" orientations and agendas. At the forefront of the growing list of critical issues that hang in the balance as a result of these "swings" are matters of the right to life versus the right to abortion; the sacredness of life versus the right to euthanasia; the right to bear arms versus the need for gun control to assuage violence; the concept of a *laissez-faire* economy versus the concept of the need for stricter corporate regulations; and on and on.

SOCIAL LAW VERSUS RELIGIOUS LAW

In the West, we have come to think of laws derived from the Manifestations as dealing exclusively with private spiritual development and having very little to do with secular governance. We have ever more rigorously interpreted the concept of the separation of church and state as the separation of governance and morality or of education and virtue. In fact, we have come to associate all historical attempts to synthesize the secular and the sacred as oppressive and ultimately dysfunctional.

The term "theocracy" most immediately evokes images of the more fanatical Muslim sects and their suppression of women's rights and the freedom to choose a personal religion. For others, the concept of theocracy might call to mind the rigid constraints of the short-lived seventeenth century Puritan commonwealth in England under Cromwell, or else, even more grimly, the tyrannical domination of the Spanish Inquisition beginning in the late fifteenth century.

Of note is the fact that in American history the fear of such repression caused those who drafted the constitution of the United States to create safeguards against any single religion from holding sway. Clearly they did not envision that this doctrine would be taken to such an extreme that any semblance of worship or moral perspective would necessarily be extricated from all governmental and educational institutions in the name of preserving human rights.

Most likely, the founding fathers of the American democracy would have viewed the rulings of the modern era as anathema to the obligation of the state and its agencies to ensure that the freedom of worship is a part of all human activities, as long as there is no oppression and no perpetration of a single dogma. Neither, we must suspect, could these same intelligent young men have anticipated that any and all public expressions of shared religious or philosophical concepts would be at some point deemed antithetical to the public good.

In other words, our understandable fear wrought by the track record of previous theocratic regimes, once stated as a foundational legal principle, has had the deleterious effect of enabling the creation of a society in which morality itself is deemed antiquated and merely a private matter of personal choice that should not be broached in any public or governmental discourse. Yet, paradoxically, if social order itself is based on spiritual concepts of justice, of mutual respect, and of concern for one's fellow human beings, then morality or a moral code can hardly be considered alien to or dissevered from the law, from legislation, or from any well considered discourse about social order. Furthermore this relationship can ultimately never degenerate into a minimalistic afterthought. The very cornerstone of any attempt at a meaningful social contract is predicated on a panoply of assumptions about what it means to be human.

PERSONAL FREEDOM OF HABIT AND DISCIPLINE

On a personal level, we readily acknowledge that good habits instilled early in life—patterns of cleanliness, orderliness, good hygiene—are liberating, not confining. For someone who has not been so trained, an unfortunate amount of creative willpower will necessarily be devoted to undertaking the most menial types of chores, while the habituation of these same tasks into a daily routine that is undertaken instinctively and, therefore, somewhat effortlessly, liberates us to devote our creative energy and free will to more lofty and worthy challenges.

It seems to be an extended or more encompassing application of this same principle that Bahá'u'lláh notes when He asserts unambiguously that "True liberty consisteth in man's submission unto My commandments, little as ye know it" (*Gleanings,* no. 159.4). This paradox, of course, represents yet another instance of the indirect methodology of the Manifestations—that which might at first seem to be restricting our freedom, is, when understood in terms of one's loftier objectives as a human being, the surest path to true freedom.

One of the more obvious contemporary examples of this verity is drug addiction. From a secular perspective, one might argue that it should be left to the individual whether or not to imbibe alcohol or indulge in various other forms of recreational narcotics or hallucinogens. So long as one does not endanger others or infringe on the rights of others, how is society harmed by this and why should society have the right to prevent the individual from risking his or her own well-being? Yet Bahá'u'lláh forbids indulgence in both alcohol and drugs.

While we could argue that experience is the best teacher, and that if alcohol or drugs are indeed harmful, the individual will in time learn the lesson implicit in Bahá'u'lláh's statement about His laws being the surest path to true freedom. The problem is that experience is not always the wisest or kindest teacher, even if it is surely the most weighty or profound teacher. No one knows the lack of freedom incurred by drug abuse better than an addict, even as no one appreciates the preciousness of freedom more than a prisoner. And yet the value received from learning some lessons firsthand through personal experience is sometimes far outweighed by the cost to the individual of being forever enslaved by a relentless craving. Stated axiomatically, the indulgence in one sort of freedom has effectively obliterated the opportunity to enjoy a much more encompassing, beneficial, and rewarding sort of freedom. In these cases experience is best obtained vicariously or through faith rather than firsthand.

From this simple and obvious example we are able to understand the overarching principle behind Bahá'u'lláh's statement, whether or not we agree with it—that some lessons are best learned by taking the advice of someone we have come to respect and trust, someone we know has only our best interest at heart. In a healthy home, this advice should derive from capable parents. In a healthy society, deterrence derives from capable civil law created by well-intentioned legislators and other similarly motivated governmental agencies.

These are precisely the experiences and activities that Bahá'u'lláh and the previous Manifestations have interdicted. It is true that some of these laws change and evolve as social conditions change. The Mosaic dietary laws had obvious health benefits for the society living in that dispensation, benefits that they could not possibly have understood at the time. They did not have adequate scientific knowledge to appreciate the logic underlying these restrictions or this guidance in terms of human health. They were thus forced to follow these laws based on their reverence for divine authority, their "faith," and their "fear of God."

To offer an analogy—our own young children sometimes have to accept the ostensibly mindless explanation, "Because I said so!" For example, this is especially true on those occasions when there is no time to explain the underlying logic or health benefits of not playing in the street. Nevertheless, the child will reap the benefits of obedience to this guidance even if complicity results solely from fear of our authority.

There is a similar logic underlying all the laws of each Manifestation. Sometimes that logic will not be understood until much later. Sometimes that logic will not be understood at all during our lives on this plane of existence. But it is there all the same, and we do well to study these laws and attempt to discern the rationale behind them. Even when we don't fully understand the logic behind certain laws, we do well to follow them based on our belief that they emanate from a divine source and have been created and instigated solely for our benefit and not as arbitrary constraints on our freedom or as capricious tests of our obedience to authority.

Put more broadly, if there is, as we have previously noted in several instances, a precise and inextricable relationship between knowledge and action, between recognizing our essentially spiritual nature and expressing that recognition in appropriate patterns of action, then we can likewise begin to appreciate that divine law is created to educate and train us because it possesses a precisely similar reciprocal relationship in our daily life. Furthermore, as we will observe, this same principle holds true for those laws that prescribe for us some affirmative course of action, some systematic activity whose logic we may not immediately appreciate, as opposed to those laws that restrict us from some deleterious action.

THE DIVINE LOGIC OF LAW

The divine logic for every law of Bahá'u'lláh is to train us to be good people. Sometimes we can see that objective implicit in what we are told to avoid doing as well as in those actions we are exhorted to pursue. Ironically, sometimes we may think a law to be entirely devoted to our physical or social well-being, only to discover after some informative experience and reflection that the law imparts some important spiritual or intellectual instruction as well. The converse is equally true. We may comply with Bahá'u'lláh's laws regarding prayer or fasting or reading the creative word only to discover that these spiritual exercises also have a favorable effect on our physical health.

Naturally the concept of law as a means for attaining freedom depends entirely on how we define freedom. Bahá'u'lláh is quite clear that He is distinguishing between that freedom with which we can advance our spiritual development and enlightenment and that freedom that is mere license and, understandably, urges us toward licentiousness. The freedom Bahá'u'lláh is advocating sets in motion a process of empowerment in which our most lofty faculties and capacities are unleashed and our creativity and personal initiative is enabled.

The law of prayer provides us with a good example of how there is a greater logic underlying an activity that might seem to some to be better left to personal instincts or individual inclination. Bahá'u'lláh has ordained three daily obligatory prayers, any one of which we may choose. This law in no way implies that we cannot also say other prayers at any time we wish or as often as we want, including those supplications or "conversations" we devise spontaneously. These observations lead us to an obvious question: If compliance with this law is so simple and desirable, why make it obligatory?

While there are, no doubt, many equally valid and useful answers to this question, one of the more obvious ones derives from what we know about our inherent tendencies with regard to various emotional states of being. If left to our own promptings, we are inclined to resort to prayer in two antithetical conditions. We will probably feel like praying when we feel particularly good—in a state of joy, gratitude, and fulfillment. We will likewise resort to prayer when we are feeling disheartened, depressed, anxious, or fearful. And, indeed, Bahá'u'lláh has revealed remarkable prayers and meditations devoted to both of these extreme conditions.

The majority of the time, however, we may be in some emotional or mental state somewhere between these extremes. Consequently, Bahá'u'lláh has mandated prayer as daily discourse between our own consciousness and the divine realm as a source of essential spiritual nourishment. Without this sustenance, He affirms, we will not be able to live successfully, any more than we could survive in good physical health without daily increments of decent food.

This is a useful analogy to extend. We may feel quite hungry one day or during one part of the day, and not at all hungry on another day. But we know that it is best for us to eat regularly, to eat nutritious food, and to eat at specific times in moderate portions. All of our physical systems come to depend on this regular refueling. By analogy, if we pray only when we feel really bad or really good, we will obviously deprive ourselves of that regular communion with God that helps us sustain a proper condition of spiritual health and balance.

Moreover, constant communion helps keep us apprised of our present state of being.

Understanding this process of personal reflection and assessment that Bahá'u'lláh admonishes us to undergo on a daily basis can, once again, be explained well in terms of physical conditioning. If we have achieved a condition of good health, foods that lack nutrition or are actively injurious to our health will lack any serious appeal. But the converse of this axiom is also true. If we have become lax in our physical exercise and unmindful of what type of foods we eat or when we eat them, we may find that those foods that are beneficial for us lack appeal or even seem repugnant to us. Meanwhile, those foods that are actively injurious will suddenly become extremely appealing or even addictive.

Applying this principle to prayer, we can imagine that were we to rely solely on our own impulses or desires, we might find prayer unappealing if we have allowed ourselves to become spiritually negligent or disinterested in our progress as a human soul. Whereas if we maintain constant communion between our inmost self and the divine realm on a systematic basis, we are more likely to maintain a continuous state of spiritual strength adequate to sustain our daily need for a healthy outlook and intelligent choices. We will maintain the inner resources necessary to confront whatever challenges we face.

As anyone who is attentive to this law will readily attest, it is persistently common for one to begin a prayer out of a desire to be mindful and obedient, only to find within seconds of intoning the verses of Bahá'u'lláh's revelation that this practice has transformed reluctance or disinterest into a sincere communion characterized by inner peace and joy.

It is in this vein that we discover in a prayer revealed by the Báb the verity that had we not been trained by the Manifestation to pray and thereby to acknowledge our indebtedness to God, we would not have undertaken this practice. In other words, prayer is not an instinctive or intuitive practice until we become trained and encouraged directly by the Manifestations. Only gradually through the self-discipline exhorted by these Teachers does prayer and its benefits become an integral and indispensable part of our path to personal freedom:

> I have known Thee, O my God, by reason of Thy making Thyself known unto me, for hadst Thou not revealed Thyself unto me, I would not have known Thee. I worship Thee by virtue of Thy summoning me unto Thee, for had it not been for Thy summons I would not have worshipped Thee. (*Bahá'í Prayers,* p. 126)

LAW, ORDER, AND THE SOCIAL CONTRACT

Bahá'u'lláh, even more precisely than the Manifestations before Him, bequeaths as part of His guidance an explicit social contract between the believer and his family, between the family and the community, and between the community and the global commonwealth which will, we are assured, emerge in the near future.

Two laws of Bahá'u'lláh illustrate an important and logical link between the individual and the larger expressions of individual polity on a societal level. First, there is the law of Bahá'u'lláh that a Bahá'í must abide by the law of the land in which he or she resides. Naturally, in those countries where there is no blatant injustice built into the judicial or legislative system itself, this is not a terribly difficult law to follow. It implies nothing more than the goal of Bahá'ís becoming law-abiding and exemplary citizens, as well as spiritually enlightened and helpful members of the communities in which they live. Worldwide, this has become the case—the Bahá'ís are reputed to be peace-loving, accepting of all people and all religious faiths, and advocates of justice and security for all peoples.

But in those countries where the Bahá'í Faith itself is banned or where the rights of Bahá'ís are curtailed because of their beliefs, this law of obedience conjoins with another law of Bahá'u'lláh to test the individual Bahá'ís, the Bahá'í community as a whole, and, in the minds of those who do not understand the wisdom in this injunction, the wisdom of the law itself.

In the Muslim religion, there is the law or concept of *taqíyyih* or "dissembling." In essence, *taqíyyih* allows the believer to deny his or her faith in times of peril. Bahá'u'lláh explicitly abrogates this practice for all Bahá'ís, regardless of circumstance. The Bahá'í cannot recant or deny his beliefs, even if one's life is at stake and even if membership in the Faith is forbidden by law. The result of the confluence of these two laws has created great risk and notoriety for the Bahá'í community in those countries where the Bahá'í Faith is most vigorously persecuted—presently countries such as Iran and Egypt.

WHY COMPLY WITH UNJUST LAWS?

The spiritual or philosophical importance of this bond between the citizen and the government is illustrated in Plato's very powerful and dramatic dialogue, *The Crito*. In this work, the character of Socrates has been condemned to death unjustly. He is accused of "corrupting" the youth of Athens, the young intellectuals whom he has taught philosophical concepts of virtue. At the heart of this dramatic work is the argument about whether or not Socrates should escape from Athens and thereby avoid being executed. The dialogue is lengthy and complex, but it focuses on one central issue insofar as Socrates is concerned. By being raised in Athens and remaining in Athens, Socrates asserts that he has entered into a covenant with the city and its laws. He has honored its laws, obeyed them, and lived under their protection. If he now decides to vitiate that covenant by choosing not to obey a law simply because it has ruled against him, he would be setting an example that would serve to undermine respect for law in general.

Socrates' main point is that law and respect for law and obedience to law is the very heart and soul of social order. Destroying or undermining law, he argues, is to perpetrate a greater injustice than the injustice instigated by a single unjust decision. Had he deemed the law unjust, he could have attempted to have it changed. Had he deemed Athens a cruel and unjust place to live, he could have left early in his life. But having abided within Athens and having done his best to shape the thinking of its young citizens, he does not believe he can suddenly decide he will not be a law-abiding citizen, even if the law has condemned him.

This philosophical work of art by Plato, albeit based on the life of an actual heroic figure, might seem so contrived or theoretical as to be an unworthy contemporary example of how our individual lives presently relate to the social contract we have with the government of the land in which we live. But for those Bahá'ís presently condemned to prison and threatened with execution because of their religious beliefs, this argument and the philosophical principle it expresses is quite real and binding.

The divine logic supporting this response to injustice on the part of a government is that collective change and social reformation are ultimately more effective and more forceful when they take place gradually over time as a result of the obvious and abiding logic of justice. This response, the argument goes, will ultimately outweigh an ineffectual and unworkable system based on injustice. An unjust system will in time fall under the weight of its own flawed premise. To respond with rebellion or lawlessness, Plato argues, is simply to create further injustice. And certainly history has demonstrated that a government created by rebellion often falls prey to rebellion itself because of the precedent it has established for responding to dissatisfaction or injustice.

This is by no means to imply that in the system devised by Bahá'-u'lláh, injustice should be allowed to be perpetrated or prosper. One of the first and foremost principles operant in Bahá'u'lláh's design for a world commonwealth is the system of collective security whereby there is a world force to carry out the collective will of a world executive in such a way that injustice anywhere is the legitimate "business" of the world community. But until such remedial steps are executed, the citizen is bound to remain law-abiding.

Stated even more axiomatically, just laws in the context of a just system work effectively because they comply with reality. For example, Bahá'u'lláh states that prejudice should be eliminated. The basis for this mandate is that it complies with the reality that all human beings have a right to equal status because there is no race, nor any other discrete group of humankind, that is inherently superior to another. The law of Bahá'u'lláh forbidding prejudice is thus based on a moral principle, but the moral principle itself is based on reality, the facts of our existence. To disobey this law is not merely to incur the retribution of sovereign authority, but also to work at cross purposes in any attempt to create workable or realistic solutions to social dilemmas.

This relationship between law and logic abides with the guidance of all the Manifestations throughout human history. The laws of personal conduct and collective organization are, for the period in which the Manifestation appears, the most effective path to justice for everyone. Consequently, the most "freedom" that anyone can experience will be achieved by complying with the laws revealed by the current Manifestation, because for that particular time His laws will describe the most propitious method for complying with reality.

EVOLUTION VERSUS REVOLUTION

As we have repeatedly noted throughout this study, it is the principal thesis of Bahá'í theology that God has sent a sequence of Messengers from the very beginning of human history. A major corollary of this doctrine is that each Manifestation brings spiritual teachings and laws appropriate to the capacity and needs of the age and culture in which They appear. This concept of the incremental evolution of human civilization emanating from the advent of these sources of spiritual, intellectual, and social transformation is obviously distinct from any strictly materialist theory or the classic Hegelian model in which social change occurs as the result of conflict or the interaction of opposing forces.

This is not to say that conflict does not occur in social change—obviously it does. But from a Bahá'í perspective, conflict is not an essential ingredient in the process of human social advancement. As social conditions evolve, the reality of social structures and relationships also change. For one who recognizes this evolutionary advancement, change is not a source of conflict, and new paradigms of law and order are not necessarily antithetical to what has gone before. Both the change and the required alteration in laws and relationships to befit a changed society are natural, logical, and necessary parts of an evolutionary organic process.

Again, the example of the evolving individual in relation to parental law and changing modes of education helps illustrate the point. The rules that safeguard, guide, and educate a five-year-old must change radically over time or else what was once propitious and healthy guidance for this child will, if allowed to continue unaltered, become a source of impropriety and injustice for this same child. As the reality of the individual's capacities and knowledge and needs evolve, the type of guidance and education must accord with this changed reality.

When this process proceeds appropriately, there is no necessary conflict and no need for rebellion or antithesis. The child does not need to rebel against the parent to demand more freedom from the rigidity of past constraints or lead a coup to overthrow the third grade teacher to advance to the fourth grade. The wise parent, the wise teacher, the reality-based system will recognize in the gradual development of the child the readiness for changed laws and guidance.

AS THE CHILD GROWS, THE LAW RELENTS

With this simple overview of how law and social order must change to accord with an ever-advancing human condition, we can better appreciate the logic underlying all the spiritual guidance ordained by the Manifestations. As we have noted, these very same laws which serve for a time as the surest path to personal freedom and collective justice, can become, when imposed beyond the age or dispensation for which they were intended, a source of oppression and injustice.

This concept of the evolutionary nature of social change is at the heart of almost everything Christ says about the law, as well as His personal comportment in relation to the old law. As we have noted earlier, Paul seems to take issue with abiding by law (personal actions) as a means of attaining personal salvation, while James takes an opposing stand, arguing that one's faith or belief means little if it is not expressed in deeds. As we also noted, Christ is very explicit about the need to abide by the laws He has revealed, going so far as to say, "Whosoever therefore shall break one of these least commandments, and shall teach men so, he shall be called the least in the kingdom of heaven, but whosoever shall do and teach them, the same shall be called great in the kingdom of heaven" (Matthew 5:19).

And yet Christ seems to break the law of the Sabbath and completely abrogates the Mosaic tribal law of retribution: "Ye have heard that it hath been said, 'An eye for an eye, and a tooth for a tooth,' but I say unto you that ye resist not evil, but whosoever shall smite thee on thy right cheek, turn to him the other also" (Matthew 5:38–39). Doubtless from the perspective of the Jewish authorities and ecclesiasts, Christ's actions, attitude, and abrogation of laws they had long held sacred and binding seem antithetical to all they believe to be the "heaven" of their religion.

From the point of view of those in the midst of such a test or judgment, Christ may well have been perceived to be a social radical advocating rebellion against established law and social order. But from the perspective of progressive revelation, it was the purpose and objective of the followers of the previous Manifestation to recognize in Christ the fulfillment of their Messianic expectations. Indeed, this is the intended plan for the transition for every succeeding revelation—that there be no conflict, no rebellion against the old law, but recognition of the fulfillment and continuity of the law as it evolves to befit an enhanced capacity and a more complex and more sophisticated social contract, covenant, or plan.

It is precisely in this context that Christ says, "Think not that I am come to destroy the law, or the prophets. I am not come to destroy, but to fulfill. For verily I say unto you, till heaven and earth pass, one jot or one tittle shall in no wise pass from the law, till all be fulfilled" (Matthew 5:17–18). What else could He mean in this statement other than the idea that the law of God is not a series of separate or self-contained systems, but that it is one organic and continually evolving flow of guidance. In this sense, the law of God is like a river which, over time, may change direction or intensity, even while its source and purpose remains constant and changeless.

Each successive Manifestation must in turn decide how to update the laws and the social systems to implement these laws in compliance with the goals and objectives appropriate for the "Day" or dispensation of that revelation. Some laws He may keep. Others He may abrogate or alter. The point is that conflict arises not from any alteration in the purpose of divine revelation or the objective God has for the evolution of human social and spiritual development. Conflict arises exclusively as a result of the inability of humankind to discern the underlying unity and accord in the sequence of revelations and the continuity in the law as the means by which spiritual concepts are given social expression.

SOME UNIQUE PROPERTIES OF THE LAWS OF BAHÁ'U'LLÁH

With this attitude about the absolutely essential nature of law in our individual and collective lives, let us examine the genius underlying the laws and systems of justice established by Bahá'u'lláh. The subtlety of the legal systems Bahá'u'lláh has established is that they are not simply a mean between extremes, not some balancing act between a liberal and conservative approach to law, but an integrated and integrative system in which the health of the individual is consonant with the health of the whole.

One analogy that helps provide useful insight into this symbiotic relationship between the individual and society is the comparison of this mutuality of well-being created in Bahá'u'lláh's covenant to the relationship between a cell and the human body in which it resides. The cell might think its own security, health, and well-being autonomous and separable from the status of the body of which it is an integral part. In reality, however, the cell depends upon the overall health of the entire system for its own survival and perpetuity. Conversely, the body cannot afford to be negligent of the health and well-being of those individual cells of which it is composed. To ignore even the smallest and most discrete pathology at work anywhere in the body is to endanger the health and destiny of the entire body, as any oncologist will readily attest.

FLEXIBILITY AND JUSTICE IN RESPONSE TO LAW

Bahá'u'lláh has created legal systems rather than an exacting code of law, as the law applies to both the training and to the punishment of

302

individuals in society. One indication that Bahá'u'lláh's laws establish paradigms rather than codes is the fact that so many laws involve various levels or patterns of response rather than a single specific dictum.

For example, we have noted that Bahá'u'lláh makes daily prayer obligatory, but He reveals three different obligatory prayers for that purpose, each one distinctly different in tone and length. He then leaves it to the individual to decide which one to use, and there is no rank or preference in this. He further gives a number of exemptions from this obligation to accommodate the variety of conditions that might encumber one's ability to comply with this law.

While a number of laws offer various avenues of compliance, the abiding rationale for all variable responses would seem to lie in Bahá'u'lláh's demonstration of the fairness, justice, and educational function of law in general. For example, some laws involve a minimal standard coupled with a loftier alternative. Bahá'u'lláh establishes the minimum period of time a wife must wait after the absence of her husband when he fails to return after a promised time. Should her husband not return by the promised time, "it behooveth her to wait for a period of nine months, after which there is no impediment to her taking another husband; but should she wait longer, God, verily, loveth those women and men who show forth patience" (Kitáb-i-Aqdas, ¶67).

Perhaps one of the clearest examples of the fairness and flexibility demonstrated in Bahá'u'lláh's laws is the commandment that His followers "allow no trace of dirt to be seen upon your garments." He goes so far as to state that should the "garb of anyone be visibly sullied, his prayers shall not ascend to God, and the celestial Concourse will turn away from him." And yet, in the midst of discussing this apparently severe consequence for being unmindful of cleanliness, proper decorum, and comportment, Bahá'u'lláh states, "Whoso falleth short of this standard with good reason shall incur no blame. God, verily is the Forgiving, the Merciful." The overall implication of this command would thus seem to be that God's justice considers every deed according to individual motive and the circumstances pertaining to all our actions. (Kitáb-i-Aqdas, ¶74, 76)

FLEXIBILITY IN RESPONSE TO VIOLATIONS OF LAW

In general, we can infer from Bahá'u'lláh's Most Holy Book that all religious law, whether personal and private or civil and public, has as its animating purpose the education of the human soul: "Throughout, it is the relationship of the individual soul to God and the fulfillment of its spiritual destiny that is the ultimate aim of the laws of religion" (the Universal House of Justice, quoted in Kitáb-i-Aqdas, p. 4). It might seem logical, therefore, that penology as a process of punishing an individual for violation of law, would primarily concern those laws that overtly affect the public good, those laws that protect the rights of the citizenry.

But the laws of Bahá'u'lláh do not make any rigid distinction between civil or secular law and religious or sacred law. The reason for this, of course, is that a spiritually based society, essentially theocratic in form, makes no such distinction—all Bahá'í law presumes a coherent relationship between both aspects of our existence, the social/physical and the private/spiritual.

Bahá'u'lláh states throughout His writings that justice and order (as well as individual training) derive from the application of the twin stimuli of reward and punishment: "That which traineth the world is Justice, for it is upheld by two pillars, reward and punishment. These two pillars are the sources of life to the world." Bahá'u'lláh goes on to remark in this same passage that the application of this remedy to the human body politic is, in this day, the responsibility of the Universal House of Justice: "Inasmuch as for each day there is a new problem and for every problem an expedient solution, such affairs should be referred to the House of Justice that the members thereof may act according to the needs and requirements of the time" (*Tablets of Bahá'u'lláh*, p. 27).

The overriding concept we derive from this very brief assessment of the laws and the punishment for violation of law as devised by Bahá'u'lláh is that all legislation and judicial processes are devised to bring about justice at every level of society. In the application of justice, there must necessarily be the sufficient flexibility provided to the judicial bodies so that they are not bound or constrained by case law. Rather the exigencies of each situation dictate the appropriate response.

The essential purpose of penology in Bahá'í law is neither retribution nor retaliation, but training and deterrence: "Man has not the right to take vengeance, but the community has the right to punish the criminal; and this punishment is intended to warn and to prevent so that no other person will dare to commit a like crime" ('Abdu'l-Bahá, *Some Answered Questions*, p. 268).

What is obvious about law as devised in the context of society as designed by Bahá'u'lláh is that there is no need to find the right balance between what is beneficial to the individual versus what is beneficial to the community. Bahá'í law takes into account that both the individual and society have a future existence far beyond the moment and far beyond even a span of years. Therefore, on the face of it, one might view the possibility of capital punishment for a crime as regressive compared to Christ's admonition to His followers to "turn the other cheek." But in explaining Christ's teaching, 'Abdu'l-Bahá observes:

Thus when Christ said: "Whosoever shall smite thee on the right cheek, turn to him the left one also" (Matt 5:39) it was for the purpose of teaching men not to take personal revenge. He did not mean that, if a wolf should fall upon a flock of sheep and wish to destroy it, the wolf should be encouraged to do so. . . .

To recapitulate: the constitution of the communities depends upon justice, not upon forgiveness. Then what Christ meant by forgiveness and pardon is not that, when nations attack you, burn your homes, plunder your goods, assault your wives, children and relatives, and violate your honor, you should be submissive in the presence of these tyrannical foes and allow them to perform all their cruelties and oppressions. No, the words of Christ refer to the conduct of two individuals toward each other: if one person assaults another, the injured one should forgive him. But the communities must protect the rights of man. (*Some Answered Questions*, p. 269)

It is only in the light of the total plan of God in creating a spiritual society that we appreciate the wisdom and logic underlying His guidance. As He confirms time and again, the purpose of His laws is to train and prepare us as individuals for the continuation of our lives beyond our physical experience, and as a society for an ever more advanced and refined expression of spiritual reality expressed in terms of a global commonwealth.

Once we begin to comprehend this abiding principle, we can then begin to appreciate why Bahá'u'lláh portrays the gift of His guidance as a precious blessing and not as the restriction of our freedom: "Think not that We have revealed unto you a mere code of laws. Nay, rather, We have unsealed the choice Wine with the fingers of might and power. To this beareth witness that which the Pen of Revelation hath revealed. Meditate upon this, O men of insight!" (Kitáb-i-Aqdas, ¶5)

16

THE SUFFERING
OF THE PROPHETS

Thou seest Thy dear One, O my God, lying at the mercy of Thine enemies, and hearest the voice of His lamentation from the midst of such of Thy creatures as have dealt wickedly in Thy sight. He it is, O my Lord, through Whose name Thou didst beautify Thy Tablets, and for Whose greater glory Thou didst send down the Bayán, and at Whose separation from Thee Thou didst weep continually. Look Thou, then, upon His loneliness, O my God, and behold Him fallen into the hands of them that have disbelieved in Thy signs, have turned their backs upon Thee, and have forgotten the wonders of Thy mercy.

—Bahá'u'lláh

We have already discussed the method by which the Manifestations employ indirection when They appear among us in the guise of ordinary human beings. To a certain extent, Their willing submission to whatever suffering and humiliation the powers that be inflict upon Them is but another facet of this concealment. Their feigned powerlessness or veiled powers would seem to deny any claim They might make to a station of divine authority or sovereignty. What is equally apparent, however, is that without complete assurance of Their own continuity after death and of the worthiness of the Cause for which

They give Their lives, They would be completely foolish to make such sacrifices, especially given the fact that none of Them endure on earth long enough to witness the fruition of Their efforts.

THEIR SUFFERING IS OUR TEST

The submission of the Manifestations to suffering is perhaps the most weighty test or judgment for those in Their midst, especially for those who are expecting some overt or sensational signs of Their ascendancy, such as the exercise of miraculous superior power over temporal authority or over oppressive circumstances.

As we noted earlier in this study, it is only years later in retrospect, after the impact of Their advent has been fully acknowledged and accepted, that this same acquiescence and suffering become regarded as confirmation of Their station rather than as signs of weakness. It is only later on that Their suffering becomes for Their followers a hallmark of Their devotion and a major proof of Their station.

What is historically remarkable is that this suffering is not an occasional thing. It was not unfortunate misunderstandings that led to the execution of Christ or the Báb. Every single Manifestation has endured exactly the same wretched treatment: "Since the Seal of the Prophets (Muḥammad)—may all else but Him be His sacrifice—and before Him the Spirit of God (Jesus), as far back as the First Manifestation, all have at the time of Their appearance suffered grievously. Some were held to be possessed, others were called impostors, and were treated in a manner that the pen is ashamed to describe" (Bahá'u'lláh, *Epistle to the Son of the Wolf*, p. 92).

Since it is clear from all we have examined thus far that the Manifestations willingly undergo these trials—this torture, rejection, and sometimes even execution—it is important that we understand and appreciate the wisdom inherent in Their consent to endure such humiliation. If They are our perfect Teachers, what exactly do They plan for us to learn from Their suffering? Were it not important for us to reflect on This enigma, to discover what lessons we are meant to learn from what They willingly endure, They surely would not submit Themselves to such agony, nor would They Themselves speak so openly and pointedly about the irony of these conditions.

THE EXAMPLE OF CHRIST

Clearly one of the most important lessons we learn from reflecting on the dire circumstances the Prophets endure is that in the long run, They prevail. From a historical perspective, Their teachings, Their impact on society, and even Their personal sacrifice are understood as expressions of power, not weakness. Indeed, it would not be incorrect to assert that the visceral image of Christ's martyrdom is the single most galvanizing force among the diverse sects of the Christian religion. Whatever doctrinal issues may cause consternation or discord, virtually all Christians recognize both the literal and the figurative significance of this act of atonement. In fact many sects ignore most of the laws and other teachings of Christ altogether and view His final "passion" as the focal point of belief. For many, Christianity would not be Christianity without the cross.

We have earlier noted Christ's discussion of how the Jewish people rejected some of the previous prophets who were sent to them. Christ reprimands the Jews, saying, "O Jerusalem, Jerusalem, thou that killest the prophets, and stonest them which are sent unto thee" (Matt 23:37). Here He is referring to the stoning of the prophet Zacharias. As we have also noted, Christ Himself was well aware of the fate ordained for Him, though He willingly submits to the will of God and nobly and humbly endures the chastening and the crucifixion.

As the lashed and bleeding Christ is presented to the raucous crowd just prior to execution, Pontius Pilate announces, *"Ecce Homo!"*— "Behold the man!" As Prefect of Judaea, Pontius Pilate offers the people of Jerusalem one last opportunity to save the Savior, to recognize their true King standing before them bleeding from His crown of thorns. The Sanhedrin may have condemned the "King of the Jews," but the Roman Prefect, finding no fault in Him, washes his hands in a symbolic gesture—he will have no part in this. He leaves it to the rabble of townspeople to decide who should be saved from the cross that day.

Heedless of their own Messiah, they instantly choose Barabbas, the notorious mischief-maker. Thereby do they seal the fate of the Son of Man, and simultaneously deprive themselves of the Anointed One sent by God for their edification and salvation.

As we reflect on this ironic circumstance we do well to recall once more Christ's temptation in the wilderness, the temptation to save Himself. Like those who see Him so abased, we, too, may well wonder why, as He is nailed to the cross, the Manifestation of God makes no attempt to demonstrate to these dim souls His true power. We, like Socrates' friends, might wish to urge Him to escape, even as does the thief on the cross beside Him, even as do the mocking priests standing beneath Him, "wagging their heads, and saying, 'Ah, thou that destroyest the temple, and buildest it in three days, save Thyself, and come down from the cross!' Likewise also the chief priests mocking said among themselves with the scribes, 'He saved others; Himself he cannot save! Let Christ the King of Israel descend now from the cross that we may see and believe!'" (Mark 15:29–32).

But it is not for them that Christ rejects their devilish temptation, and it is not due to a lack of power to perform such a miraculous feat. It is for those who will come after, those who will discern beneath His outward humiliation and seeming powerlessness that He ignores the taunting crowd, forgives their ignorance, quotes to them the prophecy of this event from their own scriptures, then turns His face heavenward, His work on earth completed, and bids them farewell: "Father, into thy hands I commend my spirit" (Luke 23:46).

To outward seeming, Christ has been killed and His religion is doomed, consisting as it then did of a handful of disorganized and disheartened disciples. But the future impact of His advent would have it otherwise. Just three hundred years later, that same cross became the symbol of victory over death, and the Christian religion had spread throughout the Mediterranean so thoroughly and powerfully that it was chosen by the Emperor Constantine to be the state religion of the Roman Empire.

THE EMERGENCE OF ISLAM

Often in the Qur'án, Muhammad reminds His followers of the fate that the previous Messengers of God have had to endure: "We gave Moses the Book and followed him up with a succession of Messengers; We gave Jesus the son of Mary clear (Signs) and strengthened him with the holy spirit. Is it that whenever there comes to you a Messenger with what ye yourselves desire not, ye are puffed up with pride? Some ye called impostors, and others ye slay!" (2:87).

Muhammad stresses this theme because He and His followers endure this same sort of rejection and persecution, even as Bahá'u'lláh observes, "For this reason did Muhammad cry out: 'No Prophet of God hath suffered such harm as I have suffered.' And in the Qur'án are recorded all the calumnies and reproaches uttered against Him, as well as all the afflictions which He suffered" (*Gleanings*, no. 8.9).

Yet, as with the religion of Christ, after the death of Muhammad the Muslim religion spread rapidly throughout Arabia, the whole of North Africa, the Middle East, and into Eastern and Western Europe. Regarding this transformation of civilization wrought by the advent of this apparently unlearned individual appearing in the midst of isolated tribal peoples, Bahá'u'lláh remarks, "Consider, how great is the change today! Behold, how many are the Sovereigns who bow the knee before His name! How numerous the nations and kingdoms who have sought the shelter of His shadow, who bear allegiance to His Faith, and pride themselves therein! From the pulpit-top there ascendeth today the words of praise which, in utter lowliness, glorify His blessed name; and from the heights of minarets there resoundeth the call that summoneth the concourse of His people to adore Him" (*Gleanings*, no. 8.10).

THE SUFFERING OF THE BÁB

As we have noted, the concealment and suffering of the Báb is perhaps the most dramatic story among the lives of all the Manifestations. From the very outset of the declaration of His station as Qá'im, He was cast into prison where He was held captive until His execution. And yet, because in this concealment and oppression He perceived the will of God at work, His own depiction of these circumstances contains only praise of God for providing Him the opportunity, the comfort, and the power He needed to make of His imprisonment a means whereby He could conquer the hearts of humanity.

In a prayer revealed after a year of being incarcerated in the prison of Chihríq, the Báb reflects on His dire circumstances as if God had caused Him to dwell in a palatial mansion or in the loftiest realm of paradise. He recounts not the horrors of these dismal prison abodes, but the "blessings Thou has vouchsafed unto Me":

> Thus I departed therefrom by Thy leave, spending six months in the land of Sád [Iṣfáhán] and seven months in the First Mountain [the prison of Máh-kú], where Thou didst rain down upon Me that which beseemeth the glory of Thy heavenly blessings and befitteth the sublimity of Thy gracious gifts and favors. Now, in My thirtieth year, Thou beholdest Me, O My God, in this Grievous Mountain [Chihríq] where I have dwelt for one whole year.

Praise be unto Thee, O My Lord, for all times, heretofore and hereafter; and thanks be unto Thee, O My God, under all conditions, whether of the past or the future. The gifts Thou hast bestowed upon Me have reached their fullest measure and the blessings Thou hast vouchsafed unto Me have attained their consummation. Naught do I now witness but the manifold evidences of Thy grace and loving-kindness, Thy bounty and gracious favors, Thy generosity and loftiness, Thy sovereignty and might, Thy splendor and Thy glory, and that which befitteth the holy court of Thy transcendent dominion and majesty and beseemeth the glorious precincts of Thine eternity and exaltation. (*Selections from the Writings of the Báb*, 7:12:1–2)

In His last major work, *Epistle to the Son of the Wolf*, Bahá'u'lláh notes the incredible irony of the treatment of the Báb, given the fact that for twelve hundred years the Muslims had invoked the return of the promised Qá'im, only to imprison and execute Him when He appeared in their midst: "For twelve hundred years they have cried 'O Qá'im!,' until in the end all pronounced the sentence of His death, and caused Him to suffer martyrdom, notwithstanding their belief in, and their acceptance and acknowledgment of, the True One—exalted be His glory—and of the Seal of the Prophets, and of the Chosen Ones" (p. 163).

Finally, after the miracle witnessed by thousands in which the Báb suddenly disappeared amid the smoke from the gunpowder of seven hundred rifles aimed at His heart, the Báb was again suspended by ropes from a pillar on the barracks. Like Christ, He was now ready to depart. Having issued final instructions to His secretary, the Báb, Who was to be executed alongside a young follower named Anis, issued a forewarning to the crowd as a parting gesture. He told them that in time they would recall this event with the same sad ironic retrospection with which history regards the suffering of all the Prophets of God:

> "O wayward generation!" were the last words of the Báb to the gazing multitude, as the regiment prepared to fire its volley, "Had you believed in Me every one of you would have followed the example of this youth, who stood in rank above most of you, and would have willingly sacrificed himself in My path. The day will come when you will have recognized Me; that day I shall have ceased to be with you." (Shoghi Effendi, *God Passes By* p. 53)

BAHÁ'U'LLÁH, "THIS WRONGED ONE"

Because Bahá'u'lláh lived to age seventy-five, His suffering was long-lived, relentless, and various. Though briefly enduring false imprisonment for supposed connection with the murder of the uncle of Ṭáhirih, the first truly severe treatment of Bahá'u'lláh occurred in 1848 when He was en route to assist the besieged Bábís at their makeshift fort at the shrine of Shaykh Ṭabarsí. On this occasion He was arrested in the town of Ámul, reviled by crowds, and then bastinadoed:

> It was for the sake of those same defenders, whom He had intended to join, that He suffered His second imprisonment, this time in the masjid of Ámul to which He was led, amidst the tumult raised by no less than four thousand spectators,—for their sake that He was bastinadoed in the namáz-khánih of the mujtahid of that town until His feet bled, and later confined in the private residence of its governor; for their sake that He was bitterly denounced by the leading mullá, and insulted by the mob who, besieging the governor's residence, pelted Him with stones, and hurled in His face the foulest invectives. (Shoghi Effendi, *God Passes By,* p. 68)

Perhaps the most egregious physical suffering Bahá'u'lláh was made to endure occurred in 1852 after two young Bábís, crazed from witnessing the slaughter of their friends and family, made an attempt on the life of Náṣiri'd-Dín Sháh. By this time, most of the other Bábí leaders had been executed. As one of the few surviving acknowledged leaders of the religion, Bahá'u'lláh was immediately arrested and sentenced to imprisonment in the notorious Siyáh-Chál without light or sanitation, His neck in chains and His feet in fetters.

After four months in these excruciating conditions, Bahá'u'lláh was spared from execution and released because of the intervention of the Russian minister. But He was then forced to walk in the dead of winter over the mountains and into exile in the city of Baghdad, where He would spend the next ten years rebuilding the tattered Bábí community, transcribing the works of the Báb, and preparing the Bábís for the disclosure of His own revelation.

As if the persecution of government and clerical authorities was not enough, Bahá'u'lláh had to endure for the next fifteen years (1853–68) the persistent betrayal and affliction of His own half-brother, Mírzá Yaḥyá. When everything Bahá'u'lláh attempted to do by way of assisting the Bábí community in Baghdad was portrayed by Mírzá Yaḥyá as an attempt to usurp Yaḥyá's station as nominal leader of the same community, Bahá'u'lláh left Baghdad for a two-year sojourn. He wandered about in the guise of a dervish throughout the mountains of Kurdistan, and returned only after Mírzá Yaḥyá himself pleaded for His return and assistance.

For the following eight years, Bahá'u'lláh trained the Bábís in the teachings of the Báb and helped turn them into a respected community of exemplary citizens. Naturally this remarkable transformation attracted the attention of the townspeople and the Muslim clerics. Gradually, visitors traveled from near and far to Baghdad to meet Bahá'u'lláh and to benefit from His wisdom.

As this attention escalated, the clerics became increasingly agitated by the influence and by the mounting following Bahá'u'lláh was gaining. Soon they instigated a barrage of petitions to the Persian king, Náṣiri'd-Dín Sháh, requesting that Bahá'u'lláh be exiled further away from their midst so that they could resume the status and authority they believed Bahá'u'lláh was appropriating from them.

The further exile to Constantinople in 1863 and then to Adrianople four months later culminated in the grievous and pernicious attempts by Mírzá Yaḥyá (at the instigation of Siyyid Muḥammad of Iṣfáhán) to disrupt His influence among the Bábís and to have Bahá'u'lláh arrested or murdered. The ignominy, shame, and anguish this rebellion caused Bahá'u'lláh by one He had raised as if he were His own son caused Bahá'u'lláh to describe this excruciating time as "the Days of Stress," a period which culminated in His official separation from Mírzá Yaḥyá and those whom He henceforth alluded to as the "people of the Bayán."

This turmoil attracted the attention of government authorities and precipitated yet another exile and a more intense and more heinous imprisonment, this time in the fowl and sparse barracks cell in the prison city of 'Akká. In the confines of this wretched abode, Bahá'u'lláh would next endure the grievous loss of His beloved son, Mírzá Mihdí, titled "The Purest Branch," who fell through a skylight in the prison while pacing the roof during his devotions.

In time Bahá'u'lláh would be released from strict confinement, though He remained under house arrest until June of 1877 when He was allowed to reside outside the city walls. For the rest of His days, however, He would officially remain a prisoner of the Ottoman government, and He would never escape the persistent machinations of members of His own family who plotted against Him and who, after His passing, attempted to destroy His covenant by diverting the explicit provision of His will—that 'Abdu'l-Bahá, "The Most Great Branch," would become the head of the Bahá'í Faith.

This, then, is the context in which we can come to appreciate why, in so many of His epistles and prayers, He alludes to Himself as "this Wronged One." He is hardly being self-pitying nor pleading for some felicitous change in His circumstance. Like the Báb before Him, Bahá'u'lláh repeatedly praises God for having bestowed upon Him the honor of being His Emissary and Manifestation:

> My God, my Master, my Highest Hope, and the Goal of my desire! Thou seest and hearest the sighing of this wronged One, from this darksome well which the vain imaginations of Thine adversaries have built, and from this blind pit which the idle fancies of the wicked among Thy creatures have digged. By Thy Beauty, O Thou Whose glory is uncovered to the face of men! I am not impatient in the troubles that touch me in my love for Thee, neither in the adversities which I suffer in Thy path. Nay, I have, by Thy power, chosen them for mine own self, and I glory in them amongst such of Thy creatures as enjoy near access to Thee, and those of Thy servants that are wholly devoted to Thy Self. (*Prayers and Meditations,* p. 278)

This remarkably moving conversation between Bahá'u'lláh and God emphasizes yet again the Manifestation's willingness to accede to all the suffering that befalls Him in the course of His ultimately glorious mission. Bahá'u'lláh also goes on to remark that it is His suffering and the attempt of adversaries to "put out that light" that ultimately demonstrates the ascendancy of the divine will of God at work in human history. In an incredibly poignant passage, Bahá'u'lláh describes what He senses the Báb is saying to Him from the spiritual realm:

Thou seest, therefore, O Thou Beloved of the world, Him Who is dear to Thee in the clutches of such as have denied Thee, and beholdest Thy heart's desire under the swords of the ungodly. Methinks He [the Báb], from His most exalted station, saith unto me: "Would that my soul, O Prisoner, could be a ransom for Thy captivity, and my being, O wronged One, be sacrificed for the adversities Thou didst suffer! Thou art He through Whose captivity the standards of Thine almighty power were hoisted, and the day-star of Thy revelation shone forth above the horizon of tribulation, in such wise that all created things bowed down before the greatness of Thy majesty.

"The more they strove to hinder Thee from remembering Thy God and from extolling His virtues, the more passionately didst Thou glorify Him and the more loudly didst Thou call upon Him. And every time the veils of the perverse came in between Thee and Thy servants, Thou didst shed the splendors of the light of Thy countenance out of the heaven of Thy grace. Thou art, in very truth, the Self-Subsisting as testified by the tongue of God, the All-Glorious, the one alone Beloved; and Thou art the Desire of the world as attested by what hath flowed down from the Pen of Him Who hath announced unto Thy servants Thy hidden Name, and adorned the entire creation with the ornament of Thy love, the Most Precious, the Most Exalted." (*Bahá'í Prayers,* p. 40).

Finally, Bahá'u'lláh early on acknowledges that He is totally impervious to the injury inflicted on Him by those who would harm His person or attempt to quench the light of His revelation. The only grief that can assail Him and the only force that can deter the advancement of His Cause, He observes, is the actions of those who bear His name but who act in a manner that besmirches the hem of His robe.

THE AFTERMATH

After the death of Bahá'u'lláh, various members of His family, including some of His own sons, contested His will and rebelled relentlessly against the authority of 'Abdu'l-Bahá. The extent of their perfidy is almost unthinkable, including as it did the stealing of the seal rings of Bahá'u'lláh, the refusal to allow 'Abdu'l-Bahá to visit the tomb of Bahá'u'lláh, complaining to government officials about 'Abdu'l-Bahá's claim to authority, and asserting that Mírzá Muḥammad 'Alí ('Abdu'l-Bahá's half-brother, titled "The Greater Branch") was the rightful heir to Bahá'u'lláh's authority and legacy. It was not until 1918 when the British general Allenby liberated 'Akká from Turkish rule that 'Abdu'l-Bahá was finally safe—the Turkish commander had stated that were he to be victorious, 'Abdu'l-Bahá and his family would be crucified on Mt. Carmel.[1]

Now, a little more than ninety years later, the religion that was ostensibly on the verge of extinction, whose designated leader had barely escaped crucifixion, has spread to the extent that it is currently the second most widespread religion in the world. The Bahá'í Faith has acquired a following of over six million strong and its beauteous World Center is spread across the face of the same Mt. Carmel where 'Abdu'l-Bahá was to be executed. Equally ironic, the Bahá'í *qiblih* (the Point of Adoration) and principal place of pilgrimage for the Bahá'í world is the Shrine of Bahá'u'lláh, a simple burial place just outside 'Akká where He died while still a prisoner of the Ottoman Empire in 1892.

The global administrative order designed by Bahá'u'lláh is now a reality. In fact, according to Shoghi Effendi, the present-day structure of the Bahá'í Faith is the most reliable foreshadowing of the worldwide institutions that will over the course of time form the basis for a

---

1. See Lady Blomfield, *The Chosen Highway*, p. 220.

world commonwealth. Ironically, during His own lifetime Bahá'u'lláh exhorted the religious and political rulers of the day to begin constructing the foundation for the very same edifice. The circuitous and arduous route we must now take to achieve this same objective derives from the blatant refusal of those same leaders to heed Bahá'u'lláh's advice.

LESSONS THEIR SUFFERING CAN TEACH US

The Prophets willingly submit to whatever harm or repudiation besets Them or afflicts Their earthly lives because They are completely aware that this concealment of Their true power and authority is strategically beneficial in the long run. They are fully aware that Their suffering will help bring to fruition the ultimate success of the truth and enlightenment They bring us.

But other than the obvious demonstration of Their willingness to endure hardship because of Their unconditional love for us, we still might want to know the logical basis for this course of action. What exactly does Their suffering teach us and *how* does it make us free? What is the strategic purpose in Their humiliation, bondage, and execration?

SUFFERING AND CONCEALMENT

We have already noted that the concealment of the identity of the Manifestation is a crucial strategy in their educational method. We are exhorted to recognize spiritual power and its ascendancy in the midst of temporal powers that determine what happens to these immaculate Beings. Consequently, in the same way that They withhold themselves from demonstrating Their station through acts of crass sensationalism or public miracles, they feign physical powerlessness as a part of that same test. After all, it is one thing to endure adversity nobly and heroically—many soldiers in warfare are called upon to summon the courage to endure such physical sacrifice. But to endure torture and deprivation and sacrifice when at any moment one could instantly extricate himself from such treatment is something significantly more astounding.

It might be sufficient that They are simply exemplary spiritual beings—They never sin, never hurt others, are ever seemly and refined in everything They do and say. They allow no vestige of human frailty or physical discomfiture to mar Their display of virtue. They are, as we have said before, Godliness expressed as best it can be in human form.

Certainly it is impressive enough to be sinless, refined, and Godly even when life is good and when we are surrounded by friends and loved ones. However it is an entirely more exalted accomplishment to remain exemplary when we are tested severely, not once or twice, but constantly and in ever increasing degrees and in ever more devious ways: physical confinement and torture, public humiliation and desecration, subterfuge and rebellion, the merciless slaughter of followers and companions.

The capacity of the Manifestations to maintain undeviating Godliness no matter how severe the circumstances They encounter is the standard They invariably act out for us. As They Themselves testify, no force on earth can assuage Their confidence, deter Their reliance on God, or forestall Their determination to fulfill Their destiny to advance the enlightenment of humanity. Bahá'u'lláh states in a passage referring to the horrific circumstances surrounding the life of the Báb that the constancy of the Prophet in the face of adversity is one of the most weighty testimonies and proofs of His station.

Alluding to the constancy of the Báb, Bahá'u'lláh says,

Another proof and evidence of the truth of this Revelation, which amongst all other proofs shineth as the sun, is the constancy of the eternal Beauty in proclaiming the Faith of God. Though young and tender of age, and though the Cause He revealed was contrary to the desire of all the peoples of earth, both high and low, rich and poor, exalted and abased, king and subject, yet He arose and steadfastly proclaimed it. All have known and heard this. He was afraid of no one; He was regardless of consequences. Could such a thing be made manifest except through the power of a divine Revelation, and the potency of God's invincible Will? (Kitáb-i-Íqán, ¶257)

A few passages later, Bahá'u'lláh alludes to verses in the Qayyúmu'l-Asmá', in which the Báb prophesies His own martyrdom. In another passage the Báb actually states that He "craved martyrdom," causing Bahá'u'lláh to observe, "Could the Revealer of such utterance be regarded as walking any way but the way of God, and as having yearned for aught else except His good-pleasure?" (Kitáb-i-Íqán, ¶260).

THE ABASEMENT OF BEING HUMAN

What may well be the most significant suffering the Manifestations endure is probably not what would most quickly come to mind. We think of Their suffering, and we immediately think of physical torture or martyrdom. Yet there is a subtle aspect to what They endure that might go completely unnoticed by us, were it not for information we have established in our study about the preexistence of these Beings.

If what we have presented is valid, then the Manifestations do dwell in the metaphysical realm prior to their incarnation. Doubtless They are content there. They foreknow that They will dwell among us, and that many people will deride them and torture them while They abide humiliation and withhold using Their inherent powers to defeat Their adversaries.

They submit to this task because it is the desire of God that They sacrifice comfort, ease, and the blessedness of a heavenly existence in order to assist human beings in a systematic fashion. Yet They state that They are pleased and grateful beyond measure to have the honor of serving God and serving us. They also state very pointedly, however, that this mission is painful, lonely, and hard.

Of course, we cannot know what it would feel like to be a Manifestation anticipating such a demeaning and perilous undertaking. We can suppose that such critical service would be thrilling in its own way. Yet certainly we can imagine the utter frustration These exalted Beings must feel in our presence, trying so carefully to teach and guide us without being too heavy-handed in their technique.

As we have discussed earlier, being a parent is our best chance to experience anything like the emotions that the Prophets must necessarily endure to fulfill Their charge. For me it calls to mind once again the poem I cited in the first chapter, a work by Bahá'í poet Robert E. Hayden called "Those Winter Sundays."

The poem is cast as a recollection by the speaker of his father, a menial laborer who hauled a coal cart through the icy streets of Detroit in the winter. He remembers in particular how this lowly and humble man never failed to make sure that his only son would be dressed and ready for church every Sunday morning. In the final lines the speaker, now with a child of his own, realizes how little he understood in childhood about the unspeakable pain of ingratitude that the dutiful and caring parent must endure to express love, sometimes in the most unexpected and unheralded ways:

Those Winter Sundays
Sundays too my father got up early
And put his clothes on in the blueblack cold,
then with cracked hands that ached
from labor in the weekday weather made
banked fires blaze. No one ever thanked him.
I'd wake and hear the cold splintering, breaking.

When the rooms were warm, he'd call,
and slowly I would rise and dress,
fearing the chronic angers of that house,
Speaking indifferently to him,
who had driven out the cold
and polished my good shoes as well.
What did I know, what did I know
of love's austere and lonely offices?

In this same vein, we cannot possibly appreciate the sacrifice the Manifestation makes to show His love for us. Surely becoming one among us and withholding all He would so love to tell us must incur the most profound suffering of all. The austerity of His "lonely" office is compounded not only because He must lower Himself to our level and be careful not to teach us more than we can handle, but also because the Manifestation knows ahead of time that His sacrificial efforts will at first be largely rejected, and, even more unfortunately, be rejected by the very ones who have grounds to know better, who have a basis for understanding, and who have every reason to embrace Him as fulfilling their long-held expectations.

In alluding to the conflicts Bahá'u'lláh foreknew would arise among His followers after His passing, He bequeaths this poignant and comforting testimony in His Most Holy Book: "Say: Let not your hearts be perturbed, O people, when the glory of My Presence is withdrawn, and the ocean of My utterance is stilled. In My presence amongst you there is a wisdom, and in My absence there is yet another, inscrutable to all but God, the Incomparable, the All-Knowing. Verily, We behold you from Our realm of glory, and shall aid whosoever will arise for the triumph of Our Cause with the hosts of the Concourse on high and a company of Our favored angels" (Bahá'u'lláh, Kitáb-i-Aqdas, ¶53).

CONCLUSION

Though we must bring to a close this present effort at understanding the process by which God educates us, we should in no wise conclude that we have done much more than make a rather crude beginning at trying to comprehend God's divine plan.

Neither should we for a minute think we have nothing further to study or understand about the plan of God or the Manifestations. For if we as individuals possess the capacity for infinite progress, and if the global society on planet Earth is likewise capable of infinite refinement, then we are forced to conclude that the educational process promoting this advancement is likewise infinitely variable and infinitely beyond any final or complete comprehension on our part.

Additionally, our study should lead us inexorably to the conclusion that we will never have any definitive sense of the nature of the Teachers employed by the Creator to carry out His ongoing plan. And yet our effort to make a start has hardly resulted from hubris or vanity.

We have established with some degree of certitude, after all, a number of critically important features of how this process works. Furthermore, we have established a number of useful, logical, and penetrating truths about the purpose, nature, powers, and methodology of these otherworldly Teachers who appear among us to implement God's educational plan.

Possibly the most crucial information we have gained from this lengthy assessment is that the Manifestations of God are not ordinary human beings who become transformed or inspired. The Prophets of God throughout our collective history are of a higher order of existence than are we, and the love, appreciation, and gratitude we owe them is beyond the power of our eloquence.

Where we strive to emulate the example They establish in our minds and hearts, They appear before us already perfected. Where we strive to understand as much as we can about the reality the Creator has fashioned for our enlightenment—both its physical and metaphysical properties—these specialized Teachers have at Their disposal an inherent knowledge of the totality of reality. Finally, where we are commanded to strive to know and to worship God, the Manifestations are the only means by which we can fulfill this divine mandate.

Recognizing Them and becoming obedient to Their guidance is the method by which we can know our Creator and establish our love relationship with Him inasmuch as His Messengers, His Vicegerents, His Emissaries, His Mirrors, are effectively the Face of God among us.

EPILOGUE:
BAHÁ'U'LLÁH'S EXPLANATION
OF GOD'S METHODOLOGY

All praise to the unity of God, and all honor to Him, the sovereign Lord, the incomparable and all-glorious Ruler of the universe, Who, out of utter nothingness, hath created the reality of all things, Who, from naught, hath brought into being the most refined and subtle elements of His creation, and Who, rescuing His creatures from the abasement of remoteness and the perils of ultimate extinction, hath received them into His kingdom of incorruptible glory. Nothing short of His all-encompassing grace, His all-pervading mercy, could have possibly achieved it. How could it, otherwise, have been possible for sheer nothingness to have acquired by itself the worthiness and capacity to emerge from its state of nonexistence into the realm of being?

Having created the world and all that liveth and moveth therein, He, through the direct operation of His unconstrained and sovereign Will, chose to confer upon man the unique distinction and capacity to know Him and to love Him—a capacity that must needs be regarded as the generating impulse and the primary purpose underlying the whole of creation. . . . Upon the inmost reality of each and every created thing He hath shed the light of one of His names, and made it a recipient of the glory of one of His attributes. Upon the reality of man, however, He hath focused the radiance of all of His names and attributes, and made it a mirror of His own Self. Alone of all created things man hath been singled out for so great a favor, so enduring a bounty.

These energies with which the Daystar of Divine bounty and Source of heavenly guidance hath endowed the reality of man lie, however, latent within him, even as the flame is hidden within the candle and the rays of light are potentially present in the lamp. The radiance of these energies may be obscured by worldly desires even as the light of the sun can be concealed beneath the dust and dross which cover the mirror. Neither the candle nor the lamp can be lighted through their own unaided efforts, nor can it ever be possible for the mirror to free itself from its dross. It is clear and evident that until a fire is kindled the lamp will never be ignited, and unless the dross is blotted out from the face of the mirror it can never represent the image of the sun nor reflect its light and glory.

And since there can be no tie of direct intercourse to bind the one true God with His creation, and no resemblance whatever can exist between the transient and the Eternal, the contingent and the Absolute, He hath ordained that in every age and dispensation a pure and stainless Soul be made manifest in the kingdoms of earth and heaven. Unto this subtle, this mysterious and ethereal Being He hath assigned a twofold nature; the physical, pertaining to the world of matter, and the spiritual, which is born of the substance of God Himself. He hath, moreover, conferred upon Him a double station. The first station, which is related to His innermost reality, representeth Him as One Whose voice is the voice of God Himself. To this testifieth the tradition: "Manifold and mysterious is My relationship with God. I am He, Himself, and He is I, Myself, except that I am that I am, and He is that He is." And in like manner, the words: "Arise, O Muḥammad, for lo, the Lover and the Beloved are joined together and made one in Thee." He similarly saith: "There is no distinction whatsoever between Thee and Them, except that They are Thy Servants." The second station is the human station, exemplified by the following verses: "I am but a man like you." "Say, praise be to my Lord! Am I more than a man, an apostle?" These Essences of Detachment, these resplendent Realities are the channels of God's all-pervasive grace. Led by the light of unfailing guidance, and invested with supreme sovereignty, They are commissioned to use the inspiration of Their words, the effusions of Their infallible grace and the sanctifying breeze of Their Revelation for the cleansing of every longing heart and receptive spirit from the dross and dust of earthly cares and limitations. Then, and only then, will the Trust of God, latent in the reality of man, emerge, as resplendent as the rising Orb of Divine Revelation, from behind the veil of concealment, and implant the ensign of its revealed glory upon the summits of men's hearts.

From the foregoing passages and allusions it hath been made indubitably clear that in the kingdoms of earth and heaven there must needs be manifested a Being, an Essence Who shall act as a Manifestation and Vehicle for the transmission of the grace of the Divinity Itself, the Sovereign Lord of all. Through the Teachings of this Daystar of Truth every man will advance and develop until he attaineth the station at which he can manifest all the potential forces with which his inmost true self hath been endowed. It is for this very purpose that in every age and dispensation the Prophets of God and His chosen Ones have appeared amongst men, and have evinced such power as is born of God and such might as only the Eternal can reveal.

Can one of sane mind ever seriously imagine that, in view of certain words the meaning of which he cannot comprehend, the portal of God's infinite guidance can ever be closed in the face of men? Can he ever conceive for these Divine Luminaries, these resplendent Lights either a beginning or an end? What outpouring flood can compare with the stream of His all-embracing grace, and what blessing can excel the evidences of so great and pervasive a mercy? There can be no doubt whatever that if for one moment the tide of His mercy and grace were to be withheld from the world, it would completely perish.

EPILOGUE

For this reason, from the beginning that hath no beginning the portals of Divine mercy have been flung open to the face of all created things, and the clouds of Truth will continue to the end that hath no end to rain on the soil of human capacity, reality and personality their favors and bounties. Such hath been God's method continued from everlasting to everlasting.

—*Gleanings from the Writings of Bahá'u'lláh*, no. 27

BIBLIOGRAPHY

Works of Bahá'u'lláh

Epistle to the Son of the Wolf. New ed. Translated by Shoghi Effendi. 1st ps ed. Wilmette, IL: Bahá'í Publishing Trust, 1988.

Gems of Divine Mysteries. Haifa, Israel: Bahá'í World Centre, 2002.

Gleanings from the Writings of Bahá'u'lláh. Translated by Shoghi Effendi. Wilmette, IL: Bahá'í Publishing, 2005.

The Hidden Words. Translated by Shoghi Effendi. Wilmette, IL: Bahá'í Publishing, 2002.

The Kitáb-i-Aqdas: The Most Holy Book. 1st ps ed. Wilmette, IL: Bahá'í Publishing Trust, 1993.

The Kitáb-i-Íqán: The Book of Certitude. Translated by Shoghi Effendi. Wilmette, IL: Bahá'í Publishing, 2003.

Prayers and Meditations by Bahá'u'lláh. Translated by Shoghi Effendi. 1st ps ed. Wilmette, IL: Bahá'í Publishing Trust, 1987.

Seven Valleys and the Four Valleys. New ed. Translated by Ali-Kuli Khan and Marzieh Gail. Wilmette, IL: Bahá'í Publishing Trust, 1991.

The Summons of the Lord of Hosts: Tablets of Bahá'u'lláh. Wilmette, IL: Bahá'í Publishing, 2006.

Tablets of Bahá'u'lláh revealed after the Kitáb-i-Aqdas. Compiled by the Research Department of the Universal House of Justice. Translated by Habib Taherzadeh et al. Wilmette, IL: Bahá'í Publishing Trust, 1988.

Works of the Báb

Selections from the Writings of the Báb. Compiled by the Research Department of the Universal House of Justice. Translated by Habib Taherzadeh et al. Wilmette, IL: Bahá'í Publishing Trust, 2006.

Works of 'Abdu'l-Bahá

Foundations of World Unity. Wilmette, IL: Bahá'í Publishing Trust, 1972.

Paris Talks: Addresses Given by 'Abdu'l-Bahá in 1911. Wilmette, IL: Bahá'í Publishing, 2006.

Promulgation of Universal Peace: Talks Delivered by 'Abdu'l-Bahá during His Visit to the United States and Canada in 1912. Compiled by Howard Mac-Nutt. 2nd ed. Wilmette, IL: Bahá'í Publishing Trust, 2007.

Selections from the Writings of 'Abdu'l-Bahá. Compiled by the Research Department of the Universal House of Justice. Translated by a Committee at the Bahá'í World Center and Marzieh Gail. Wilmette, IL: Bahá'í Publishing, 2010.

Some Answered Questions. Compiled and translated by Laura Clifford Barney. 1st pocket-size ed. Wilmette, IL: Bahá'í Publishing Trust, 1984.

Will and Testament of 'Abdu'l-Bahá. Wilmette, IL: Bahá'í Publishing Trust, 1944.

Works of Shoghi Effendi

Advent of Divine Justice. 1st pocket-size ed. Wilmette, IL: Bahá'í Publishing Trust, 1990.

Citadel of Faith: Messages to America, 1947–1957. Wilmette, IL: Bahá'í Publishing Trust, 1965.

God Passes By. New ed. Wilmette, IL: Bahá'í Publishing Trust, 1974.

High Endeavours: Messages to Alaska. [n.p.]: Bahá'í Publishing Trust, 1976.

The Unfolding Destiny of the British Bahá'í Community: The Messages from the Guardian of the Bahá'í Faith to the Bahá'ís of the British Isles. London: Bahá'í Publishing Trust, 1981.

The World Order of Bahá'u'lláh: Selected Letters. 1st pocket-size ed. Wilmette, IL: Bahá'í Publishing Trust, 1991.

Compilations of Bahá'í Writings

Bahá'u'lláh, 'Abdu'l-Bahá, Shoghi Effendi and Universal House of Justice. *The Compilation of Compilations: Prepared by the Universal House of Justice, 1963–1990.* 2 vols. Australia: Bahá'í Publications Australia, 1991.

Bahá'u'lláh, the Báb, and 'Abdu'l-Bahá. *Bahá'í Prayers: A Selection of Prayers Revealed by Bahá'u'lláh, the Báb, and 'Abdu'l-Bahá.* New ed. Wilmette, IL: Bahá'í Publishing Trust, 2002.

Helen Hornby, compiler. *Lights of Guidance*. New ed. New Delhi, India: Bahá'í
   Publishing Trust, 1994.

Other Works

Balyuzi, H. M. *Bahá'u'lláh: The King of Glory*. Oxford: George Ronald, 1980.
———. *The Báb: The Herald of the Day of Days*. Oxford: George Ronald, 1973.
Esselmont, J. *Bahá'u'lláh and the New Era*. Wilmette, IL: Bahá'í Publishing,
   2006.
Nábil-i-A'ẓam [Muḥammad-i-Zarandí]. *The Dawn-Breakers: Nabíl's Narrative
   of the Early Days of the Bahá'í Revelation*. Translated and edited by
   Shoghi Effendi. Wilmette, IL: Bahá'í Publishing Trust, 1932.
Taherzadeh, Adib. *The Revelation of Bahá'u'lláh: Baghdad 1853–63*. Oxford:
   George Ronald, 1974.

Bahá'í
PUBLISHING
AND THE BAHÁ'Í FAITH

Bahá'í Publishing produces books based on the teachings of the Bahá'í Faith. Founded over 160 years ago, the Bahá'í Faith has spread to some 235 nations and territories and is now accepted by more than five million people. The word "Bahá'í" means "follower of Bahá'u'lláh." Bahá'u'lláh, the founder of the Bahá'í Faith, asserted that He is the Messenger of God for all of humanity in this day. The cornerstone of His teachings is the establishment of the spiritual unity of humankind, which will be achieved by personal transformation and the application of clearly identified spiritual principles. Bahá'ís also believe that there is but one religion and that all the Messengers of God—among them Abraham, Zoroaster, Moses, Krishna, Buddha, Jesus, and Muḥammad—have progressively revealed its nature. Together, the world's great religions are expressions of a single, unfolding divine plan. Human beings, not God's Messengers, are the source of religious divisions, prejudices, and hatreds.

The Bahá'í Faith is not a sect or denomination of another religion, nor is it a cult or a social movement. Rather, it is a globally recognized independent world religion founded on new books of scripture revealed by Bahá'u'lláh.

Bahá'í Publishing is an imprint of the National Spiritual Assembly of the Bahá'ís of the United States.

For more information about the Bahá'í Faith,
or to contact Bahá'ís near you,
visit http://www.bahai.us/
or call
1-800-22-unite

OTHER BOOKS AVAILABLE FROM
BAHÁ'Í PUBLISHING

CHILDREN OF THE KINGDOM
A Bahá'í Approach to Spiritual Parenting
Daun E. Miller
$16.00 U.S. / $18.00 CAN
Trade Paper
ISBN 978-1-931847-75-9

Children of the Kingdom conveys a practical approach to educating children in a loving and supportive manner, with spiritual principles, virtues, and character development serving as the foundation for their learning and growth. Using the Bahá'í writings, as well as personal experience, author Daun E. Miller demonstrates that there is an alternative to the chaos and confusion that many parents see engulfing the world and that children can be raised to be guided by moral and spiritual principles. Parents and families often run into difficult questions regarding the best way to raise children, and this book provides spiritually based answers. Written in chronological order so that busy parents can find what they need quickly and easily. It designates each age group as an important stage in a child's life and one that demands specific action on the part of parents. The guidance shared in this book focuses on the nature of the soul and the vital reasons why we should educate our children spiritually.

ILLUMINE MY BEING
Bahá'í Prayers and Meditations for Health
Bahá'u'lláh and 'Abdu'l-Bahá
$14.00 U.S. / $16.00 CAN
Trade Paper
ISBN 978-1-931847-69-8

Illumine My Being is a collection of prayers and meditations from Bahá'í scripture that are intended to provide spiritual healing for the individual during times of crises. Many of these prayers ask God for the healing of the individual as well as the community, the nation, and the world. These extracts from the sacred writings explain how individual healing can be achieved through one's relationship with God, and they also elaborate on the nature of spiritual healing and how the healing of the entire human race can be achieved. Healing has always been an essential component of religion, and these prayers and meditations are meant to provide comfort, hope, and reassurance to anyone during these troubled times.

LONGING
Stories of Racial Healing
Phyllis A. Unterschuetz and Eugene F. Unterschuetz
$15.00 U.S. / $17.00 CAN
Trade Paper
ISBN 978-1-931847-68-1

Longing: Stories of Racial Healing is a collection of true stories from the journey of one white couple toward understanding their hidden fears, prejudices, and ultimate connection to African Americans. It contains matter-of-fact statements about the fear and suspicion that both African Americans and whites still harbor toward one another, and it describes how these barriers can, with the right amount of effort, be overcome. As diversity trainers, the authors have traveled throughout the United States, speaking about racial unity and the oneness of humanity. They describe uncomfortable and embarrassing situations, examine mistakes and unconscious assumptions, and share what they have learned about being white. Their stories contain revelations from black friends and strangers who taught them to see beyond superficial theories and to confront the attitudes that have shaped how Americans think about race. But above all, their stories speak about the longing they discovered everywhere they traveled—a longing to connect and to heal from the racial separation that has so deeply wounded this country.

SELECTIONS FROM THE WRITINGS OF 'ABDU'L-BAHÁ

'Abdu'l-Bahá
$14.00 U.S. / $16.00 CAN
Trade Paper
ISBN 978-1-931847-74-2

Selections from the Writings of 'Abdu'l-Bahá is a compilation of correspondence and written works of one of the central figures of the Bahá'í Faith. 'Abdu'l-Bahá, meaning "Servant of the Glory," is the title assumed by 'Abbás Effendi (1844–1921)—the eldest son and appointed successor of Bahá'u'lláh, the Prophet and Founder of the Bahá'í Faith. After his father's passing in 1892, 'Abdu'l-Bahá assumed leadership of the worldwide Bahá'í community until the time of his own passing in 1921. During that time he corresponded with Bahá'ís all over the world, providing them with an abundance of practical and spiritual guidance. The works collected here cover a wide range of topics including physical and spiritual health, death and the afterlife, the spiritual reality of humankind, the oneness of humanity, and the elimination of prejudice. The wisdom imparted in this volume remains as timeless and relevant today as when it was first committed to paper.